Effective Teaching of Reading: Research and Practice

edited by

James V. Hoffman
The University of Texas at Austin

Published by the

INTERNATIONAL READING ASSOCIATION
800 Barksdale Road, Box 8139
Newark, Delaware 19714-8139

Copyright 1986 by the
International Reading Association, Inc.

Library of Congress Cataloging-in-Publication Data
Main entry under title:

The Effective teaching of reading.

 Bibliography: p.
 1. Reading–Case studies. 2. Reading–Research–Case studies. I. Hoffman, James V. II. International Reading Association. Teacher Effectiveness in Reading Committee
LB1050.E33 1986   428.4'07   85-24229
ISBN 0-87207-739-x

Contents

Foreword

The International Reading Association's Board of Directors is to be commended for establishing the Teacher Effectiveness in Reading Committee and charging this committee with the responsibility of distilling and interpreting past and current research on the effective teaching of reading. *Effective Teaching of Reading: Research and Practice* edited by James V. Hoffman is most timely, following the numerous commission and task force reports on the state of education and teaching in this country. The volume provides an important historical perspective on the development of effective teaching research, offers a clear research paradigm for process-product research, and places teaching effectiveness research in the real context of the classroom.

The astute reader will appreciate the care taken by the authors in the first two sections of the book, as they develop an historical overview of research on teaching and offer critical recommendations for improving our understanding of the complex teaching phenomenon. The detailed descriptions of teacher innovation programs in the next three sections of the collection develop an understanding of the key process variables which influence both teacher change and student achievement. The final chapter of the text offers an outstanding and insightful critique of the previous chapters and presents directions for future investigations. The volume serves to inform the graduate student, as well as the practicing professional, of critical teacher research, of important factors in the design and study of approaches to increase teacher effectiveness, and of the value of examining teaching effectiveness within the context of the classroom.

This volume attests to the high priority which the International Reading Association places on effective teaching in reading instruction. Of critical importance at this time is the development of an interdisciplinary derived theory to assist in explaining the complex multiple interactions which take place during a single reading lesson. Such a theory must account for teacher competencies and decisions, student perceptions and attitudes, and classroom and school reading environments. It should enable us to predict and explain learning outcomes, given varied pedagogical arrangements, which have the teacher, child, and reader environment at the center. The development of such a theory is a challenge which remains for the profession, and specifically for the Teaching Effectiveness in Reading Committee. This volume takes an important step toward meeting that challenge.

Robert B. Ruddell
University of California at Berkeley

Preface

Research on effective teaching has established an identity over the past fifteen years both in terms of a research movement and a set of findings related to practice. Some view this literature as a positive force on schooling in general and the teaching of reading in particular, while others regard its direction, focus and value more skeptically. Both groups, however, acknowledge that the findings from this line of work are shaping classroom practices to a degree unparalleled in educational research.

Four years ago the Board of Directors of the International Reading Association established the Teacher Effectiveness in Reading Committee. The Committee was charged with reviewing, analyzing and interpreting the research on effective teaching as it related to reading instruction, and educating IRA's membership in this important area of research activity. This monograph represents the fruits of four years of labor on the part of the Committee.

We have conceptualized, organized and written this monograph with the community of reading educators as our intended audience, be they classroom practitioners, reading supervisors, teacher educators, or researchers. We view the fact that the literature on teacher effectiveness has developed without significant participation or even attention by reading educators as cause for concern. We hope that the thoughts presented and projects described in this monograph will generate a constructive dialogue about the effective teaching of reading among reading educators. Our goal is to stimulate the community of reading educators—those who have first hand knowledge and a long history of involvement with children in classrooms learning to read—to participate actively in this research movement.

At least two themes have guided the organization of the manuscript itself. The first is the notion of research into practice.

Throughout the book the reader will find descriptions of efforts to take the findings from effectiveness research back to the classroom level through various staff development efforts. The second theme of the book is that of the evolution of research on effective teaching in terms of methodologies and perspectives. We have made an effort to reflect how research on effective teaching has changed over its short but active history and included a look toward the future.

The team of authors is drawn from experts in reading education, educational psychology, and general curriculum theory. They address the themes just described through reviews of literature, reports of basic research, case study analyses of program improvement efforts, and speculative argument. Together they weave a story that is as comprehensive as it is complex regarding research on the effective teaching of reading.

JVH

Part One
The Historical Context

No sooner does someone announce something *new* in education than someone else discovers that the new is really quite old. Research on teacher effectiveness is no exception. In their chapter on Research in Effective Teaching, Rupley, Wise, and Logan offer a penetrating historical account of the development of research in effective teaching.

William H. Rupley
Beth S. Wise
John W. Logan

1

Research in Effective Teaching:
An Overview of Its Development

E ffective teaching has always been a major goal of education. It has been investigated in numerous ways and from various perspectives during the twentieth century. Researchers have explored a host of teacher and instructional variables in terms of their effects on students' achievement. Teachers, administrators, teacher trainers, and both advocates and critics of teaching also have voiced opinions about what constitutes effective teaching. Collectively, the research findings and individuals' opinions have often been contradictory, and up until about 1975 very little meaningful information was available for improving the quality of teaching. One general conclusion that seems to be pervasive throughout this century is that the most important factor contributing to students' achievement is the teacher.

The term *teacher effectiveness* has been explored and defined across several dimensions. Early attempts to specify effective teaching often dealt with supervisors' ratings and evaluations in areas such as discipline, promptness, personality, and techniques of instruction. In the 1960s more attention was given to students' learning as an indicator of effective teaching, but emphasis continued on describing effective teacher characteristics. Greater focus on learning outcomes as a measure of effective teaching received considerable support in the mid 1970s and into the 1980s. Much of this contemporary focus has been deemed process-product research, that is, primary attention is given to instruction (process) and its effect on students' learning (product). Research in teacher effectiveness, conducted in the early 1980s, has been expanded to include not only the process-product paradigm but, also, teachers' intentions, goals, judgments, and decision making strategies.

Even though much of the information on teacher effectiveness offers minimal guidance for those concerned with enhancing the quality of teaching and many areas still need further exploration, the literature does provide insights about the complexities associated with teacher effectiveness. Past research inquiries and other pertinent literature on teacher effectiveness follow. This information is organized chronologically and deals with both effective teaching in general and effective teaching of reading.

Teacher Effectiveness Research
Late 1800s to 1940s

As early as the turn of the century, J.M. Rice (a pediatrician who toured the country as a critical journalist) denounced the competency of teachers and called for better teacher preparation in the normal schools of America. Teacher preparation courses during this time included some professional courses designed to expand teachers' basic knowledge and skills. Rice argued, however, that requiring teachers to take more professional courses in their preparation programs would remediate all incompetencies, and enable teachers to gain the culture, scholarship, knowledge, and skills necessary to advance American education (Cremin, 1964).

Early research efforts to observe and examine classroom teacher behaviors were conducted in 1915 by A.E. Boyce and in 1925 by Leroy King. Boyce surveyed public school systems in 350 major cities to gather information on the methods used to determine and record the efficacy of teachers. The results of his investigation indicated that approximately 60 percent of the school systems surveyed used some form of teacher rating form or formal evaluation to assess teacher effectiveness. In compiling similar information on the rating forms, Boyce found that the most often listed areas were discipline, instructional skills, and cooperation. King reported similar findings in a followup of the Boyce investigation. The three predominant variables in the rating system reviewed by King paralleled those that Boyce noted: technique of instruction, teacher personality, and classroom management. The school systems using such rating forms must have greatly valued these characteristics as being indicators of effective teaching.

Other teacher effectiveness related studies in the 1920s and 1930s focused on teacher personality and educational characteristics. For example, Lowth (1933), a normal school principal, listed fourteen factors essential to effective teaching, including good health, loyalty, a positive personality, and good citizenship. Hardesty (1935) investigated the relationship between inservice teachers' command of content, methods, and management and discipline with their grade in student teaching, grades in professional courses, and grades in general college work. Little relation between grades in school and ratings in classroom teaching was found.

The first major study that attempted to discriminate ineffective and effective teaching behaviors was conducted by Barr (1929). Although Barr did include ratings from supervisors as one data source, he also gathered information from general observations about materials and equipment available in classrooms, teacher and pupil behaviors, and time distribution. The results of the inquiry were of limited value since the major criterion for judging effective teaching behavior was based on supervisory judgment, a subjective criterion. As yet no better way to evaluate teachers had evolved.

Several years later, Reavis and Cooper (1945) analyzed over 1,500 items noted in 85 scales of teacher rating forms and reported major weaknesses such as lack of definitions of terms and ambiguous terminology. On the basis of their review they concluded that:

> Ratings appear to be invalid, then, as comprehensive measures of either general or specific teaching ability. There still remains for them, however, the sphere of personal opinion....It is apparent that ratings are valid measures of the rater's opinion of the teacher.

Individuals concerned with research in effective teaching were not totally oblivious to the problems associated with determining the effective teacher through the use of supervisory ratings. Several alternative strategies were being proposed during the 1930s for research in effective teaching. Monroe (1934) recommended experimental research to evaluate teaching methods. He suggested a "controlled experiment" in which two equivalent groups of students would be subjected to educational influences that only differed with respect to the target methodology. He recommended that the difference between the mean gains in achievement of the two groups be calculated as an index of the relative effectiveness of the two methods of instruction.

In February 1935, Barr read a paper before a joint session of the American Educational Research Association and the National Society of the College Teachers of Education in which he assessed the present state of the measurement of teaching ability. After describing a recent experimental study of teacher behavior in the classroom, he emphasized that there were still gaps in effectively measuring this teacher behavior. He posited that the next frontier in research would be the investigation and development of functional tests for measuring the teacher in action.

The challenge from Barr was enjoined by Shannon (1936), who trained observers to use three different instruments, referred to by Shannon as: attention scores; score card scores; and general, informal estimates. He sent the observers forth to observe in actual classroom situations. Although not wholly conclusive, the results did suggest the efficacy of using observation to evaluate teaching.

In the latter half of the 1930s, several individuals published articles concerned with measuring classroom teaching. Olander (1937) supported observation in the classroom; to judge the quality of instruction he had a classroom observer answer questions regarding such variables as attitudes and activities of pupils, knowledge and skills being learned, and sensitivity of teacher to student needs and interests. Gray (1940) reported a study in Texas using a similar checklist as an administrative rating device. Broening (1939) reported on the state of research on the general methods of teaching. She found little scientific research on teaching. Enthusiastic teachers reporting their own introspective perceptions of effective teaching were the most prolific writers.

Summary of Research—Late 1800s-1940s

The early history of teacher effectiveness yielded some interesting information and some surprising insights. The most striking impression from the entire period is the deep concern of researchers and educators regarding teacher ability and accountability. Around the turn of the century and in the early 1900s, concern centered on the preparation of the teacher and on impressions of teaching ability.

In the 1920s and 1930s these concerns continued, and teachers' personal traits, habits, and attitudes became part of the criteria for judging teacher effectiveness. From the vantage point of the 1980s, these criteria appear arbitrary, perhaps even discriminatory; yet the criteria for judging teacher effectiveness in some areas today may be subjective evaluation of the teacher's personal traits, habits, and attitudes.

Rating scales and checklists entered the scene in the 1930s, but the objectivity of their end result was questionable. Supervisors or principals rated teachers on impressions more often than on behaviors; if behaviors were objectively recorded, then subjective judgments were often based on the objective findings recorded previously. The feeling was that teachers who were able to function smoothly in a classroom situation and who had good rapport with children surely had to be "good" teachers. Therefore, they were effective teachers. An occasional researcher (e.g., Jayne, 1945) might suggest that an expert's ratings of teacher instructional behavior could have low reliability and validity, but the large majority of teacher raters ignored these findings.

Teacher Effectiveness Research
1950-1969

In 1953, the American Research Education Association Committee on the Criteria of Teacher Effectiveness reported that the impact of teacher effectiveness research conducted throughout the twentieth century was meager and unstable.

The simple fact of the matter is that after forty years of research on teacher effectiveness during which a vast number of studies have been carried out, one can point to a few outcomes that a superintendent of schools can safely employ in hiring a teacher and granting him tenure, that an agency can employ in certifying teachers, or that a teacher education faculty can employ in planning or improving teacher education programs. (p. 88)

Concern for investigating effective teaching in a manner that went beyond the subjective rating of teachers by supervisors emerged in the late 1940s and early 1950s. This concern was partially addressed in the late 1950s. Research emphasis shifted from a focus on personal characteristics to examining teacher behavior and performance in actual classroom situations (Lanier, 1982). Medley and Mitzel (1958) and Flanders (1960) developed systems for use in the classroom to record observed behaviors. This breakthrough for studying classroom teaching made possible the collection of objective data. Rosenshine (1976) posited that the modern era of research in teaching began in 1957, with the works of Flanders and Medley and Mitzel.

One of the first outcomes of research studies using the Observation Schedule and Record, developed by Medley and Mitzel (1958), corroborated the findings of Anderson (1954), who had found no significant relationship between teacher rating criteria and student attainment criteria. In a study of the teaching of reading, Medley and Mitzel (1959) found that supervisory ratings and students' reactions to their teachers appeared to reflect teacher ability to get along with children, rather than teacher ability to bring about student growth in reading. Teachers, on the other hand, were found to be fair judges of their own effectiveness in teaching children to read.

Medley and Mitzel (1963) published an extensive report encouraging the use of direct observation in the classroom in research on teaching. They decried the fact that observations of classroom behavior were seldom included in the studies they reviewed. They further pointed out that studies in classrooms visited by observers who knew what to look for, how to record what they found, and how to interpret what they recorded, resulted in significant findings about classroom behavior. They emphasized that direct observation should play a key role in unraveling the mystery surrounding teaching behaviors, since the classroom itself is where these behaviors occur. Medley and Mitzel predicted the line of research on which the present teacher effectiveness is based:

> [I]t may also become possible to measure teacher effectiveness in process by direct observation of the teacher. This is not yet possible. Attempts to validate process criteria by correlating them with measured pupil growth have been, on the whole, unsuccessful....The identification of patterns of behavior which differentiate effective and ineffective teachers is still a worthwhile goal for research employing direct observation of classroom behavior. (p. 249)

A lengthy treatise on the analysis and investigation of teaching methods was also published by Wallen and Travers (1963). They found little research on teacher behavior, particularly research that showed that teaching methods made any difference to outcomes. They felt this was because teaching methods had not been based on learning models stemming from psychological research. They hypothesized that these problems would be resolved by a teaching method or methods based on a wide range of learning principles. They felt theory should precede practice for the research of teacher effectiveness to go forward.

This call of Wallen and Travis went unanswered. In the early 1960s research efforts focused on finding a relationship among student personality traits, teacher personality traits, and student growth, by way of direct observation. Researchers assaulted the classroom with surveys, questionnaires, observation instruments, and rating scales. Amidon and Flanders (1961); Amidon and Simon (1965); Christensen (1960); Cogan (1963); Ryans (1961); Solomon, Rosenberg, and Bezdek (1964); and Wodtke and Wallen (1965) were among these. Cogan perhaps summarized their findings best:

Most of the data amounts to superficial, rootless verbalisms....The truth is that these data are so...remote from the sights, sounds, the smell, the feel, and the sense of the classroom that the reality escapes us....The simple truth is that we do not have adequate data for the analysis of the behavior of the teacher. (p. 243)

In the early 1960s Getzels and Jackson (1963) conducted an extensive review on inquiry in teachers' personalities and characteristics. They examined the extensive studies made following the publication of previous reviews, which used the Minnesota Teacher Attitude Inventory, as well as other studies using instruments such as the Allport-Vernon-Lindsey Study of Values, the Kuder Preference Record, and the Strong Vocational Interest Blank. Many studies had used the Minnesota Multiphasic Personality Inventory to try to isolate teacher personality characteristic criteria which could predict teacher success. Getzels and Jackson concluded:

Despite the critical importance of the problem and a half-century of prodigious research effort, very little is known for certain about the nature and measurement of teacher personality, or about the relation between teacher personality and teaching effectiveness. (p. 574)

During the late 1960s and into the 1970s researchers began to examine teachers' instructional behaviors in the classroom. Biddle (1967) set the stage with his critical review of the methods of data collection, and of the widely varying conceptual postures of researchers. Several studies investigated relationships between different types of instructional behaviors and pupil learning. Tallmadge (1968), for example, found no significant interactions in his study on enlisted Navy men, but Baker (1969) found positive relationships between student achievement and teacher use of prescribed learning principles in a study conducted with Peace Corps trainees. Hiller, Fisher, and Kaess (1969) found that "vagueness" (teacher could not remember or never really knew) was the overriding teacher lecturing behavior in a study on experienced social studies teachers of high school seniors. In a study of fifth and sixth grade mathematics teachers comparing the "discovery" with the "expository" method of teaching, Worthen (1968) found that the discovery method resulted in significantly higher student performance.

Several important studies conducted in the 1960s received considerable notoriety. Coleman and colleagues (1966) examined a large number of school characteristics and their relationships to student success, including students' test achievement. They found that most of the variance associated with students' achievement was accounted for by factors other than school variables. They interpreted these findings to mean that teachers made little, if any, difference in students' learning. Although later reanalysis of these data indicated that such an interpretation was invalid, it did stimulate researchers to conceptualize teacher effectiveness research efforts more precisely.

Another major study that focused later attention on teachers' instructional expectations, judgments, and decision making was conducted by Rosenthal and Jackson (1968). In the Oak School Experiment, they studied students' achievement after teachers were told that, based on the results of an examination, certain students were potentially high achievers. The students, however, had been selected on a random basis. As a result of the findings, greater concern developed for the effects of teacher expectations on students' achievement.

A third major inquiry effort of the 1960s was undertaken in 27 separate studies in the Cooperative Research Program in First Grade Reading Instruction (Bond & Dykstra, 1967). The 27 studies were aimed at determining if a particular reading approach (linguistic, basal, language experience and Initial Reading Alphabet) would produce greater reading achievement at the end of first grade. No one method or set of materials resulted in greater student achievement. The researchers concluded that no one approach works best in all situations and no one approach should be used at the exclusion of others; "to improve reading instruction, it is necessary to train better teachers of reading rather than to expect a panacea in the form of material" (p. 123).

Two researchers involved in the Cooperative Research Program, Chall and Feldman (1966), compared different teachers' implementation of a single method (eclectic basal reader approach) in teaching beginning readers. They collected data by direct observation, using an instrument designed for detecting differences in approach, as well as questionnaires and pre and posttests. Several teacher characteristics were significantly associated with reading achievement; a thinking approach to learning, a sound-symbol emphasis in reading, and using the appropriate level of lessons. Realizing the many limitations of the study, Chall and Feldman suggested that other, untested factors might also be significant for first grade reading.

Summary of Research—1950-1969

Although we have mentioned only a few of the many studies conducted during the period, they are representative and should give the reader a feel for the thrust of the investigations in the area of teacher effectiveness during this time.

Research efforts still concentrated on the teacher as the crucial variable in student learning. The development of instruments for measuring teacher and student behaviors through direct classroom observation opened the door to new possibilities in research, but few researchers took advantage of this tool. Many were content to rely on ratings given by principals, rather than to expend time, money, and effort examining classroom behaviors firsthand.

Little theoretical rationale was provided for these studies. The closest thing to a logical basis for most of the studies was the purpose: to provide criteria for the selection, training, employment, or promotion of teachers.

The focus of research during the early part of this period was still primarily on the qualities of the teacher, seeking to isolate characteristics of the "good" teacher across grade levels. Findings were inconclusive. Investigators later began to use classroom observation instruments, and the interactions of teachers and students came into focus. As this happened, teacher behaviors that were significantly correlated with student learning began to surface, albeit only occasionally.

However, observer ratings of classroom interactions were not infallible. Ratings were limited to the behaviors that were a part of the instrument used, as well as the skill of the observer in focusing on the single behavior to be encoded. During this period, one person most often observed a classroom, so that establishing reliability was not possible.

Most research appeared to have been done without regard for the investigations of other researchers. No one had pieced together significant findings with nonsignificant findings to form a pattern to give focus to further research; different conceptual systems of researchers made this an impossible task. Thus, collective research efforts of this period can be characterized as a hodge podge of investigations stemming from a conglomeration of conceptual foundations and producing an occasional significant result.

Teacher Effectiveness Research
1970-Present

Since 1970 considerable advances have been made in the study of teacher effectiveness. Because of the lack of significant findings in past inquiries, researchers began to reevaluate these past efforts in effective teaching research.

Shulman (1970) suggested that even though past research in teacher effectiveness often appeared unsuccessful and clumsy, promising strategies and approaches had emerged. Further, he felt the future should include a radical change in training educational researchers, as well as modification to create the necessary conditions for research.

One major advance during this period was an increased interest in using observation to study teaching in actual classroom settings. Researchers began to focus more on the process of instruction and its effect on students' learning. Duffy (1981) described process-product research as:

> Process-product studies employ observation tools which trained observers use when visiting classrooms to record how often a particular phenomenon noted on the observation form occurs in actual practices. The combined obser-

vations are analyzed, with the individual teacher as the unit of analysis, to determine the correlation between particularly coded items and achievement growth as determined by standardized achievement tests and/or by less formal attitude measures. Influenced by the behavioristic tradition the focus has been the overt acts of teachers and the relation between the frequency of these acts and various measurable outcomes. (p. 116)

The process-product paradigm signaled a major advancement in the study of teaching. Although this approach was criticized for reasons such as weakness in reliability and validity of observation instruments and in design and analysis associated with correlational studies, several clusters of effective teaching strategies did begin to emerge during the 1970s. A major reason for this progress was that investigators were evaluating the use of a process-product research methodology.

Research Conducted in Early 1970s

Using the process-product paradigm, Brophy (1973) studied the stability of teacher effectiveness over time, using second and third grade teachers from a city school system, over three successive years. The findings indicated that, in grades two and three at least, teachers could be identified who were consistent in their overall relative effectiveness. Brophy suggested that observational studies of these consistent teachers, done in the naturalistic setting as they carried out normal activities, should yield greater payoff than the kinds of teacher effectiveness research done in the past, since process measures of their behavior should be both valid and reliable. Brophy also pointed out that, since teacher effectiveness shows great individual differences and only moderate stability from year to year, it would be premature, unfair, and inappropriate to invoke the indiscriminate use of student gain on general achievement tests for assessing teacher ability.

About the same time as Brophy's study, an extensive treatise by McNeil and Popham (1973) was published concerning the assessment of teacher competence. McNeil and Popham posited:

[T]he single most important deficiency in research on teacher effectiveness is the failure to use outcome measures as a criterion, and, instead, to rely upon a priori measures of a teacher's personal attributes, such as his personality or education, his background, or the measures of instructional processes such as his instructional strategies or his verbal behavior in the classroom. When one considers the idiosyncratic backgrounds of teachers and pupils, the great range of typical instructional objectives, and the immense variation in the environments where teaching occurs, it is unlikely that any processes or personal attributes on the part of teachers will invariably produce pupil growth. (p. 220)

According to McNeil and Popham, one problem associated with past research in teacher effectiveness has been that researchers studied teacher behaviors and assumed that these were related to student growth. McNeil and Popham suggested that researchers should use specific direct observation systems designed to obtain accurate accounts of what takes place in the classroom. They believed that these instruments are legitimate tools for the assessment of classroom behavior and should have implications for improving instruction. They also felt that contract plans and performance tests are promising tools for gathering information about teacher effectiveness, and that research on these tools was needed.

At about the same time, Rosenshine and Furst (1973) published a comprehensive study on the use of direct observation to study teaching. Their purpose was to introduce the many and varied instruments available for classroom observations; to encourage researchers to develop procedures for describing teaching in a quantitative manner; to encourage correlational studies in which the descriptive variables are related to measures of student growth; and to encourage experimental studies in which the significant variables obtained in the correlational studies are tested in a more controlled situation.

Four types of uses for observational systems were examined and described at great length: to describe current classroom practice, to train teachers, to monitor instructional systems, and to investigate relationships between classroom activities and student growth. Rosenshine and Furst were concerned over the lack of experimentation in which these instruments were used to the advantage for which they were designed. The tools were there, but tools alone could not accomplish the job. The implementation of these tools in research was the next step.

An entire book on the study of teaching was published by Dunkin and Biddle (1974). Their outlook on the current scene was very optimistic — one of the first optimistic notes in the entire history of the study of teacher effectiveness. Dunkin and Biddle felt that progress had been made in the past twenty years in the study of teacher effectiveness. Whereas early research focused primarily on the study of teacher qualities or training, the focus had shifted to the processes of teaching. Teachers and students in interaction were the focus of research at the time of their study.

Summary of Research Conducted in Early 1970s

The comprehensive and perceptive studies of Saadeh (1970), Shulman (1970), and Snow (1974) which focused on educational research models; of Brophy (1973) which focused on teacher stability over time; and of McNeil and Popham (1973), Rosenshine and Furst (1973), and Dunkin and Biddle (1974) which reviewed past research and suggested a refocused direction for the future, together brought cohesiveness and direction to the area of teacher effectiveness.

A multitude of investigations resulted from their combined challenge, the vast majority of which were concerned with teacher-student interaction in some form. These studies were limited to small or fairly small samples, probably for economic reasons. Patterns of coordination between researchers began to develop, as researchers with common conceptual foundations cooperated with one another to advance research in their particular area of interest. Some of these areas of focus were verbal behaviors of teachers, questioning techniques of teachers, the effect of classroom settings on instruction, instructional pace, and instructional patterns (team teaching, open classroom). Following this mode of research, effective patterns of teaching behaviors began to emerge.

Correlation Studies in Teacher Effectiveness—1972-1978

During the 1970s the National Institute of Education (NIE) poured large sums of money into teacher effectiveness research. The NIE funding enabled researchers to conduct research on a scale large enough to effect reliable outcomes. It also encouraged continued and increased communication among researchers, which resulted in coordinated research in the field of teacher effectiveness.

Following the infusion of money from NIE, expensive teacher effectiveness studies were forthcoming, and important improvements in research design began to appear. Among these were rational, as opposed to convenient, sampling of teachers; including enough teachers in samples to allow for meaningful statistical analysis; collection of many hours of classroom data; the development of more sophisticated classroom coding instruments; and concentration on the individual teacher and class as the unit of analysis. All of these funded studies focused on instruction in basic skills in primary grade classrooms, using standardized achievement tests as the measure of pupil learning (Brophy, 1979a).

The first of the studies funded by NIE was that of Soar and Soar (1972). The NIE studies were funded to learn how to educate disadvantaged children more effectively. The purpose of this particular study was to describe program differences in relatively behavioral terms, and to test the hypothesis that the behavioral dimensions identified relate to pupil growth and add to understanding of effective teaching for disadvantaged pupils. The study was done in classrooms that were a part of the Follow Through Program established by Congress in 1967 under the Office of Economic Opportunity. Twenty-two Follow Through programs were begun when it became apparent that a program was needed in the early grades of public school to reinforce and extend gains made by economically disadvantaged children enrolled in Head Start or similar preschool programs. Seven of the Follow Through programs were still in operation.

The evidence was strong that programs were successful in creating differences in classroom behavior. Certain factors were also found to be related significantly to measures of student growth.

The factors which discriminated programs seemed to represent relatively gross behaviors, such as the extent to which the teacher "structured" the environment, managing, directing, and reinforcing. The factors which related to pupil growth seemed to be less obvious; lower intellectual (rote memory) levels of activities correlated positively with abstract subject matter growth; higher levels of cognitive activity correlated negatively with pupil abstract growth.

Another major study funded by the NIE was the Texas Teacher Effectiveness Study (Brophy & Everston, 1974). This study was designed to follow up on Rosenshine's data (1970) that teacher effectiveness might not be a stable trait, even in experienced teachers.

The Texas Teacher Effectiveness Study yielded three important observations. 1) Teachers who obtained the greatest gains in low SES schools did so by being warm and encouraging and by "overteaching"—as compared with teachers in high SES schools. 2) Skillful classroom management was important to learning in both high and low SES schools. Findings strongly supported the conclusions of Kounin (1970) concerning the use of classroom management techniques that keep children actively engaged in productive work, minimize wasted time and dead spots, and generally avoid letting problems get started in the first place. 3) Teachers who obtained the greatest gains in high SES schools were those primarily concerned with student learning; they pressured students to achieve.

The Beginning Teacher Evaluation Study headed by Berliner (1975) was an NIE study done by the Far West Laboratory for Research and Development to try to isolate effective teacher behaviors in order to insure that beginning teachers receive training in effective teaching behaviors.

In 1975, the study focused on five major tasks. Three of these were: 1) investigating whether ethnographic approaches to the study of teaching could yield new insights into the teaching/learning process; 2) investigating whether the planning and decision making teachers do is different for effective and ineffective teachers; and 3) studying whether the perceptions of effective and ineffective teachers vary when viewing the teaching/learning situation would yield information about which aspects of classroom interaction were important to students. The other two tasks dealt with methodological procedures in the area of time allocation in classroom situations. All of this work was to provide information that could be combined in order to design a large field study examining teacher effectiveness.

Results suggested that high achievement teachers presented students with a clear focus of what was to be learned, provided developmental feedback when needed, structured a common seatwork assignment for the class, and responded to individual students' need for help. High achievement teachers communicated higher performance expectations to students; they demanded more work and achievement from students. They assigned homework more frequently and moved through the curriculum considerably faster than did low teachers.

Another pattern of effectiveness was the students' opportunity for immediate, nonevaluative, and task relevant feedback. Students in effective teachers' rooms felt free to approach the teacher when they wanted or needed information; they asked more questions, called out more answers, and were asked more questions. High teachers praised less than low teachers and criticized less; they were basically nonevaluative. High teachers also had fewer management problems than did low teachers.

A major study also done during this period was not funded by the NIE, but was a part of the Follow Through program (Stallings & Kaskowitz, 1974). This particular program was a project for the University of Arizona. A sample of four first grade and four third grade classrooms was selected in 36 cities and towns representing all geographic regions, urban and rural areas, and several racial and ethnic groups. This sample included a total of 136 first grade and 137 third grade classrooms. Test scores were available on 105 first grade and 58 third grade classes, so only these classes were used.

Results showed that in reading, 118 out of 340 correlations were significant. Of these, the length of the school day and the average time a pupil spent engaged in a reading activity were related to higher reading scores in both first and third grades. Higher reading scores were also found in classrooms with more reading or discussions of reading between adults and children. Higher reading scores were found where systematic instructional patterns were used (i.e., the teacher provides information and asks a question about the information; the pupil responds and receives immediate feedback. If wrong, the pupil is guided to the correct answer; if correct, the pupil receives praise, a token, or some form of acknowledgement).

Small groups were the most effective for teaching first grade reading, while groups of nine or more were productive in third grade. In classrooms where children worked independently and were task oriented, reading scores were higher. In classrooms using textbooks and programed workbooks, higher reading scores resulted.

Summary of Correlational Studies—1972-1978

Findings from these representative major studies indicated that time spent in reading and mathematics activities, and a high rate of drill, practice, and praise, contributed to higher reading and math scores.

These correlational studies, most of which were funded by NIE, covered a variety of grade levels and socioeconomic groups, but were restricted to the teaching of basic skills in mathematics or reading. These studies had little theoretical rationale. They were aimed toward broadening the data base for understanding teaching. Some of the work was experimental, but most of the research was observational and descriptive. Their purposes were to develop coding systems for describing and measuring the processes that take place in the classroom; to generate informational data in order to produce hypotheses; and to develop hypotheses about the relationships among variables (Brophy, 1979a, 1979b).

Taken as a group, these major studies varied in the types of teachers and pupils included, the kinds of variables addressed, and the methods used, but there was replication of findings even though some were more poorly designed than others. This replication of findings does provide a fairly dependable base of knowledge about the relationships between teaching, particularly direct instruction, and pupil learning of basic skills in the elementary grades.

Reviews of Major Process-Product Research—Late 1970s

Toward the latter part of the 1970s several individuals conducted major reviews of process-product studies. Medley (1977) reviewed the literature to find out how research defined good teaching. From this, he defined an effective teacher as one whose students showed significant gains on reading and mathematics achievement tests. Based on a review of 289 studies dealing with the question of how behavior differed in effective and ineffective teachers, Medley focused on fourteen of the studies, most of which were done in grades one to three with children from low socioeconomic status homes.

Medley discovered an important general finding: Children could make maximum achievement gains, yet not dislike school. This finding held across content areas and across socioeconomic classes. He also found that effective teachers devoted more class time to task related activities, structured activities for most of the day, kept instruction at a low level of complexity, and asked simple answer or multiple-choice questions, rather than asking students to analyze, synthesize, or evaluate.

He also found that effective teachers ran more orderly classrooms; they individualized assignments, and spent more time in small group work, with little time in whole class instruction. By contrast, the less effective teachers allowed children to work independently or in small groups without the teacher present.

Medley reported that teaching techniques effective with low SES students were less effective with high SES groups. For example, the effective teacher in high SES groups was likely either to call on a student and then ask a question or ask a question and then call on a student who wanted to answer it. In contrast, the effective teacher in a low SES classroom asked the question and then called on a pupil who had not indicated a desire to answer.

Rosenshine (1978) discussed the findings of recent research on teacher effectiveness. He focused on what he called academic engaged time (student time spent in seatwork and discussion), content covered (student opportunity to learn, attention to relevant academic activities), and direct instruction (activities directly related to making progress in math and reading).

Rosenshine cautioned the investigator to be aware of the limitations of the research findings. The research which Rosenshine reviewed had been limited to a logically and sequentially oriented content. Another caution concerned the overall quality of these studies—many contained methodological flaws. With 500 variables in a single study, many significant correlations were obtained by chance. Consistency across studies did help lend credibility to the findings, however. He argued against the implementation of these initial findings into teacher training programs before validity had been established. Many of the first researchers have become engaged in experimental studies to validate and expand their own findings.

Good (1979) also reviewed the findings of teacher effectiveness studies. Like Rosenshine, he concluded that recent research had found that elementary school teachers did have an effect on student achievement; that classroom management skills were extremely important; and that a pattern of teaching behavior called "direct instruction" positively influenced student achievement in skill oriented subjects. Good indicated that the lack of consistency in recent findings in process-product studies was due to differences in focus and felt that reviewers were not looking at the same variables or looking for the same outcomes. He suggested that outcomes from experimental classroom study would never be predictable, since several teacher behaviors could create the same effect, and identical teacher behaviors could have different impacts on different students. In other words, the number of variables involved in the instructional situation in the classroom makes predicting difficult.

Good noted that support for whole class as opposed to small group instruction (except in early grades) should renew educators' faith in this type of instruction. Group instruction had been criticized as ignoring the level of the individual; research findings, he thought, should change this negative perception. He suggested that whole class instruction was easier to plan and manage, provided more correct modeling for slower students, and avoided labeling that can result from ability grouping.

Good also noted that direct instruction appeared to be an effective technique for teaching basic skills. He felt research showed that some structure was needed for most educational activities, and that more structure was needed in the early grades and for low ability, anxious, or dependent students.

According to Brophy (1979a, 1979b) the correlational studies funded by NIE and reviewed here provided strong support for these generalizations: 1) Teachers make a difference; 2) no specific teaching behavior is appropriate in all contexts, but clusters or patterns of behavior emerge that are consistently related to learning gains; 3) one of these clusters includes teacher expectations and role definitions; 4) another includes classroom management skills, student engagement/time on task, and student opportunity to learn material; 5) another includes the various elements of direct instruction.

Brophy felt that, although these large scale correlational studies had identified clusters of effective teaching behaviors, the time for this type of study had passed: Researchers should move in the direction of the experimental classroom study, wherein they can systematically test the causal hypotheses implied through these process-outcome studies. Brophy noted, however, that for variables such as those relating to classroom management, not enough knowledge exists to design a classic experiment that holds everything else constant while a single variable is manipulated.

Many of the researchers who reviewed the findings of the large correlational studies from the mid-seventies pointed out methodological flaws, but appeared willing to sacrifice "the classical experiment" for the patterns of effective teacher behaviors these studies were revealing. Although some contradictory findings were apparent, most findings were related and reinforced one another. After 80 years of research with few significant results, researchers were able to isolate teacher behaviors that may correlate consistently and significantly with students' learning growth.

Experimental Studies of Teacher Effectiveness — Late 1970s

Another event of paramount importance occurred during the late 1970s. Classroom based experimental studies of teacher effectiveness were designed to test the validity of the results of the large scale correlational studies. In these studies, teachers were trained to incorporate in their teaching the specific behaviors that had been associated with students' learning growth. Data were collected on teacher behaviors and on student gain. This type of study was called for by McNeil and Popham (1973), Rosenshine and Furst (1973), and Brophy (1979b).

There is a paucity of experimental studies where researchers randomly selected an experimental group from a population of teachers, equipped members of the group with
specific performance competencies and then measured the
extent to which these teachers (as opposed to their controls)
both a) performed differently in their classrooms, and b) enhanced the cognitive growth of students. (McNeil and Popham, 1973, p. 224)

Given the large number of workshops and inservice
training programs which have been held to train teachers to
modify their behavior in a variety of ways, and given the
resources available to many regional educational laborato-
ries which have conducted some of these workshops, it is
unfortunate that the training has not been followed by experimental studies on student growth measures of interest in
which the trained teachers served as the experimental
group. Hopefully such studies will appear in the future.
(Rosenshine and Furst, 1973, p. 158).

Programatic research that tests hypotheses derived
from correlational work, identifies causal relationships, and
builds upon these in developing teacher education approaches is needed if teaching is to become the applied science that it can and should be. (Brophy, 1979b, p. 1)

The Missouri Mathematics Effectiveness project was an experimental research study done by Good (1978). He designed an
instructional model for use by fourth grade teachers in conducting
mathematics lessons, based on the findings of an earlier correlational study by Good and Grouws (1977). Outcomes from this study
were combined with findings from other recent research on mathematics teaching to formulate the lesson model that served as treatment in the study. The model consisted of instruction that focused
on pupil comprehension of concepts, presentations and explanations
by the teacher, supervised practice, homework, and scheduled review. Lessons were to be taught to the whole class, as opposed to
small groups, and teachers were to maintain a fast pace through the
material and hold students accountable for seatwork and homework.
Specific suggestions were given for carrying out each step.

The sample included 40 fourth grade mathematics teachers from 27 predominantly lower SES schools in an urban district. Treatment teachers attended a training session and were given copies of a 45 page manual containing definitions, rationale, and detailed descriptions of the lesson components. Two weeks after the treatment began, the researchers met with the treatment teachers for a 90 minute period of question answering. There was no further training.

Teachers in the control group were aware of the purpose of the study. Researchers urged the control teachers to teach as they normally did, telling them that they would be observed, that their students' achievement would be evaluated, and that at the completion of this phase of the project, they would be given feedback regarding their own instructional behaviors, as well as be trained in the techniques of the instructional model. The experimenters hoped to create a strong Hawthorne effect in both groups through encouragement and attention.

Performance of students of treatment teachers exceeded performance of students of control teachers on all measures. The control teachers' students made better than expected gains, suggesting that the encouragement and attention given to them had beneficial effects; these students did not gain as much, however, as did those of treatment teachers.

Significant positive relationships were found between achievement and use of review, assignment of homework providing practice in mental computations, and requiring accountability for seatwork. The researchers concluded that significant increases in pupil achievement in mathematics were related to instructional strategies that were apparently influenced by the treatment given to teachers.

The Stanford Program on Teaching Effectiveness (Crawford et al., 1978) was an experimental research study done by a number of researchers. The treatment in this study was based on variables derived from four correlational studies of teaching effectiveness: Brophy and Everston (1974), McDonald and Elias (1976), Soar and Soar (1972), and Stallings and Kaskowitz (1974). Each of these studies focused on teacher and student behaviors in elementary reading classrooms and included variables that correlated significantly with reading achievement at the second and/or third grade levels. These variables were incorporated into 22 recommendations in three broad categories: behavior management and classroom discipline, instructional methods, and questioning and feedback strategies. Behavior management included the "withitness" recommended by Kounin (1970); a system of procedures for taking care of students' personal needs; and moving around the room to monitor student behavior. Instructional methods included minimizing time spent giving directions, organizing for instruction, and instructing small groups and individuals, in order to maximize the time spent in direct instruction and supervision of all students. Questioning and feedback strategies included patterns of feedback and responding to correct and incorrect answers, as well as adjusting the difficulty level of questions for students of different cognitive abilities.

Maximum treatment teachers received one manual a week for five weeks describing the treatment and attended a two hour inservice meeting each week to discuss the topic. Minimum treatment teachers received the weekly manual through the mail, with no opportunity to discuss the materials. The control group received no training. Each week, all treatment teachers completed tests and questionnaires after reading the materials. A refresher course was given to all treatment teachers in the spring following the established pattern: Minimum treatment teachers received their refresher materials through the mail; maximum treatment teachers were videotaped and given personal feedback.

Students' achievement scores revealed that treatment groups had higher adjusted achievement scores on reading tests; minimum treatment teachers' students scored higher than maximum treatment teachers' pupils. Classes receiving teacher effectiveness training and the parent-assisted program outscored all other groups.

The researchers concluded that teachers in the treatment groups used the suggested behaviors more than did teachers in control groups; student achievement scores also favored the treatment groups. The relationships between the content processes and the outcomes, however, did not strongly support the conclusion that the content of the treatment was most responsible for changes in behavior and outcomes. The researchers suggested the possibility that the increased attention to reading and simply participating in a treatment program could have been responsible for the increased pupil achievement.

The First Grade Reading Group Study was an experimental study done by Anderson, Everston, and Brophy (1978). The study also was designed to test the outcomes from a correlational study by Brophy and Everston (1974).

The treatment in this study used an instructional model based on the process-outcome relationships from Brophy and Everston's study; other sources were Kounin (1970), as well as two studies done at the kindergarten level. The treatment consisted of instruction on 22 principles of small group instruction related to management of the entire group with emphasis on maintaining student attention, sequencing information clearly for students, and providing information about the relevant aspects of a question or answer.

Seventeen teachers received treatment; only ten of these were observed. Each teacher in the treatment group received a short manual describing teacher behaviors. The researchers met with treatment teachers to explain the study and leave the booklet; they returned in about a week to discuss the treatment and answer questions. Control teachers received no materials, and did not meet with the experimenters. Treatment was applied in October. Observations of teachers began in November and continued through May.

Many of the process-outcome relationships were those expected on the basis of earlier research. Consequently, many of the principles in the instructional model were substantiated. In general, the processes associated with reading achievement were those for which differences in implementation were revealed. This suggested that the treatment content was at least partly responsible for greater pupil growth in treatment groups.

In all three of these experimental studies, changes in teacher behaviors and in student growth followed treatment. The purposes of these studies were to reinforce the findings of the earlier correlational studies, and to determine if treatment interventions are effective in changing teacher behaviors. Actual teacher classroom behaviors reflected implementation of treatment behaviors in all three studies; however, in no case were all of the suggested treatment behaviors implemented. Student growth provided evidence that treatment behaviors were implemented by the teachers in their classroom instruction.

Current Research in Teacher Decision Making in Effective Teaching

The process-product paradigm of the late 1970s changed the direction of research. Teacher effectiveness is now perceived as a complex concept that Duffy (1981) describes as "reciprocal interactions between teacher and context with effectiveness being a multifaceted function of this interaction" (p. 118).

Shulman (1980) supports this conclusion, arguing that the teacher's multiple role of instructor, curriculum planner, organizational member, and tutor needs to be recognized. He stated that teachers need to work effectively within each grade level while negotiating across grade levels. Shulman believes that the concept of teacher effectiveness differs depending upon how researchers define and assess effectiveness.

Recently, researchers have recognized that teaching is not a unidimensional phenomenon. This recognition has led to the emergence of research in effective teaching that focuses on teachers' judgments and decision making. (A more detailed discussion of this topic can be found in Chapter 8).

Lanier (1982) reports that contemporary teacher training programs emphasize practical know how. Heavy emphasis on practical technique conveys to teachers that someone "higher up" in the system usually makes important decisions. In addition, she notes that teachers receive little training in learning to analyze and "make difficult decisions of uncertainty, such as selecting from and deciding upon various means of monitoring student progress, so that effective feedback and subsequent decisions regarding new or revised learning tasks can be appropriately related" (p. 22).

Shavelson and Stern (1981) have identified two fundamental assumptions about the thought processes of teachers in a recent review of literature. The first assumption is that teachers are rational professionals who make judgments and carry out decisions in an uncertain, complex environment. Shavelson and Stern contend that this assumption refers to teachers' intentions for their judgments and decisions rather than to their behavior for two reasons: 1) Some teaching situations call for immediate rather than reflective responses that may preclude rational processing of information to make an informal judgment or decision, and 2) the capacity of the human mind for formulating and solving complex problems like those presented in teaching is small compared to the enormity of some "ideal" model of rationality. They explain that, in order to deal with problems at hand, an individual will construct a simplified model of a real situation. The teacher, then, exhibits behaviors with respect to this simplified model of reality. Generally, teachers behave "reasonably" in making judgments and decisions in an uncertain, complex educational environment. They caution that "while teachers may act reasonably, this does not necessarily mean that their decisions are optimal with respect to the teacher's goal or someone else's goal" (p. 457).

The second assumption is that a teacher's behaviors are guided by thoughts, judgments, and decisions. Yet, research in this area is difficult because we must first understand how thoughts transfer into action.

Nisbett and Ross (1980) pointed out the question of the relationship between thought and action in teaching:

> We also say little about precisely how people's judgments affect their behavior. This is neither an oversight nor a deliberate choice. We simply acknowledge that we share... psychology's inability to bridge the gap between cognition and behavior, a gap that in our opinion is the most serious failing of modern psychology. (p. 11)

Recent Studies on Teacher Decision Making for Reading Instruction

Several studies concerning teacher decision making strategies about reading instruction have been conducted in recent years. In an experimental laboratory study, Russo (1978) examined the effects of pupil characteristics, teachers' educational beliefs, and the nature of the instructional task on teachers' decisions about grouping students and planning reading instruction. In this study, thirty-one second grade teachers were asked to complete an educational attitudes measure. They received descriptions of thirty two hypothetical students who varied in reading and math achievement, sex, class participation, and problematic behavior. The teachers were asked to use this information to determine the likelihood that each student would master second grade skills. Then, the teachers were to group the students into four groups of eight pupils for reading instruction. Three descriptions of instructional lessons were also provided so that teachers could make preinstructional decisions concerning appropriate strategies for teaching each lesson to each group. Two of the lessons were based on cognitive objectives (initial consonant blends and sequencing of events in a story) and the third lesson dealt with an affective objective (reading for fun).

Russo reported that in grouping for reading instruction, teachers focused on students' reading ability, sex, participation in class, and problematic behavior. The major factor that teachers considered was information regarding the pupils' reading achievement. Approximately half of the thirty two teachers relied solely on reading ability in making grouping decisions.

Barr (1975) examined the bases for teachers' decisions about grouping students and pacing reading instruction. First grade teachers and their students in twelve classrooms from four schools participated in the investigation. Two of the schools (one predominantly Black, the other predominantly Hispanic) were located in urban lower to lower middle class neighborhoods. The other two schools were located in a nearby middle to upper middle class Caucasian neighborhood. Interviews at the beginning of the school year determined the composition of reading groups within the classrooms and the pace at which each child was reading (defined as number of stories read). Again at the end of the year, teachers provided information about grouping and pacing of the pupils. Teachers also described their methods of instruction, their training in reading instruction and years' experience teaching at the first grade level, and the classroom behaviors and reading strengths and weaknesses in their classes. In addition, two independent judges rated the teachers' attitudes toward students and knowledge of the teaching of reading.

This information and such data as standardized scores and anecdotal records were examined in terms of their potential influence in grouping and pacing decisions.

Barr reported that teachers used information regarding students' reading ability in planning reading instruction. The teachers greatly relied on direct observation of students' performance and reading work. They also valued readiness test scores and anecdotal records from kindergarten teachers. Cumulatively, this information formed a comprehensive picture of students' reading abilities.

While most of the teachers grouped students on the basis of reading ability, their purposes for grouping differed. For example, some teachers grouped students for basal reading, but used whole class instruction to teach phonics and structural analysis. Other teachers grouped students at the beginning of the year for phonics instruction, but used the basal reader with the whole class. Grouping for basal reader instruction did not happen until after the third month of school. A third group of teachers grouped for basal reading and phonics from the beginning of the school year.

The diverse grouping practices of the teachers were attributed to two major factors: school environment and teachers' concepts of reading. School environment played an important role in this study in that suburban teachers, who had phonics workbooks available, tended to group students for phonics instruction, while teachers in urban schools without workbooks mainly used whole group instruction. Barr speculated that teachers without workbooks did not have enough time to "prepare and sequence phonics instruction for several different groups" (p. 487). In addition, teachers with large classes or with classes with great ranges in student ability grouped students to a greater extent than did teachers who worked with small or homogeneous groups. Availability of resources, class size and composition are all important features of how the school environment can influence teachers' decision making policies for reading instruction.

In discussing the second consideration, teachers' concepts of reading, Barr stated:

> Teachers who only grouped children for basal reading mentioned (as important in reading) word lists, interesting sto-

ries, listening centers, and student-written stories. Those who grouped for phonics instruction and for basal instruction, at least some time during the year, described the most effective activities as those designed for learning "sounds" and word building in addition to those mentioned by (the other) teachers. (p. 487)

Overall, teachers tended to group children only for the kind of reading instruction that, according to their beliefs, will have the greatest impact on reading achievement.

In an ethnographic study, Stern and Shavelson (1980) investigated how teachers assimilate information in order to form small group reading instruction. Twice a week for six months they observed two teachers and twenty students during their forty-five minute small group reading instruction. Each teacher had taught for at least five years. The students were six boys and four girls in the high reading group, and six boys and four girls in the low reading group. Of the latter group, eight had been determined to be either learning, emotionally, or physically handicapped.

From detailed accounts of each classroom observation, Stern and Shavelson reported that teachers gathered information from these sources: 1) anecdotal reports from other teachers; 2) notes written by parents; 3) interviews with parents; 4) school records; 5) students' classroom assignments; 6) students' verbal reports; 7) teachers' observations; and 8) classroom and standardized test scores. They suggested that teachers have a wide range of information on which to base decisions regarding grouping for classroom reading instruction.

Summary of Research in Teacher Decision Making

The above recent research investigations dealt with teacher thoughts, judgments, and decisions during reading instruction. With the increased interest in cognitive psychology and cognitive information processing, many teacher effectiveness researchers are looking beyond direct instruction, management, and psychological conditions to determine goals, intentions, judgments, decisions, and information processing. Teacher effectiveness researchers have begun to examine the nature of teacher rationales. Duffy (1982) stated that teachers' behaviors are guided by what they think and that studies in reading have hypothesized that theories or models of reading influence teachers' instruction. In addition, clinical and remedial decision making in reading reflects a rational model, and teachers can apply diagnostic-prescriptive techniques in teaching reading. The research dealing with teachers' intentions, goals, judgments, and decisions has only recently been deemed credible and studies are currently being conducted to substantiate these efforts further (Borko, Shavelson & Stern, 1981).

Summary

For almost one hundred years, teacher effectiveness has been a primary concern of educational research. Inquiry efforts have focused on variables ranging from teachers' personality to teachers' decision making. Data have been gathered through supervisors' opinions, questionnaires, checklists, observations, and simulations. As noted in the introduction, the results did little to enhance the quality of teaching across all grade levels and content areas.

Since the mid 1970s, however, several promising findings have emerged about the effects of selected process variables on students' achievement in the basic skill areas of reading and math. Researchers have realized that the complexities of classroom life cannot be ignored in terms of their effects on competent teaching. Such results in teacher effectiveness research may seem meager, but in the context of where such research has been and the directions in which it is headed, they represent tremendous progress in identifying effective teaching.

References

American Education Research Association, Committee on the Criteria of Teacher Effectiveness, 1953. Second Report of the *Journal of Educational Research*, 1953, *46*, 641-658.
Amidon, E., and Flanders, N.A. The effects of direct and indirect teacher influence on dependent-prone students learning geometry. *Journal of Educational Psychology*, 1961, *52*, 286-291.

Amidon, E., and Simon, A. Teacher-pupil interaction. *Review of Educational Research,* 1965, *35,* 130-139.

Anderson, H.M. A study of certain criteria of teaching effectiveness. *Journal of Experimental Education,* 1954, *23,* 66-71.

Anderson, L.M., Everston, C.M., and Brophy, J.E. *The first grade reading group study: Technical report of experimental effects and process-outcome relationships,* Report No. 4071. Austin: Research and Development Center for Teacher Education, University of Texas, 1978.

Baker, E.L. Relationship between learner achievement and instructional principles stressed during teacher preparation. *Journal of Educational Research,* 1969, *63,* 99-102.

Barr, A.S. *Characteristic differences in the teaching performance of good and poor teachers of the social studies.* Bloomington, IL: Public School Publishing, 1929.

Barr, A.S. The measurement of teaching ability. *Journal of Educational Research,* 1953, *28,* 561-569.

Barr, R. Instructional pace differences and their effect on reading acquisition. *Reading Research Quarterly,* 1975, *9,* 526-554.

Berliner, D.C. *The beginning teacher evaluation study: Overview and selected findings, 1974-1975.* Paper presented at the National Invitational Conference on Teacher Effects: An Examination by Decision-Makers and Researchers, Austin, TX, November 1975. (ED 128 339)

Biddle, B.J. Methods and concepts in classroom research. *Review of Educational Research,* 1967, *37,* 337-357.

Bond, G.L., and Dykstra, R. The cooperative research program in first grade reading instruction. *Reading Research Quarterly,* 1967, *2,* 5-141.

Borko, H., Shavelson, R.J., and Stern, P. Teachers' decisions in the planning of reading instruction. *Reading Research Quarterly,* 1981, *3,* 449-466.

Boyce, A.C. Methods of measuring teachers' efficiency. *Fourteenth Yearbook of NSSE, Part II.* Bloomington, IL: Public School Publishing, 1915.

Broening, A. General methods of teaching. *Review of Educational Research,* 1939, *9,* 295-302.

Brophy, J.E. *Advances in teacher effectiveness research.* Paper presented at the annual meeting of the American Association of Colleges for Teacher Education, Chicago, March 1979a. (ED 170 281)

Brophy, J.E. *Advances in teacher effectiveness research, Occasional Paper No. 18.* Washington, DC: National Institute of Education, April 1979b. (ED 173 340)

Brophy, J.E. Stability of teacher effectiveness. *American Educational Research Journal,* 1973, *10,* 245-252.

Brophy, J.E., and Everston, C.M. *Process-product correlations in the Texas Effectiveness Study, final report,* Report No. 74-4. Austin: Research and Development Center for Teacher Education, University of Texas, 1974.

Chall, J., and Feldman, S. First grade reading: An analysis of the interactions of professed methods, teacher implementation, and child background. *Reading Teacher,* 1966, *19,* 569-575.

Christensen, C.M. Relationships between pupil achievement, pupil affect-need, teacher warmth, and teacher permissiveness. *Journal of Educational Psychology,* 1960, *51,* 169-174.

Cogan, M.L. Research on the behavior of teachers: A new phase. *Journal of Teacher Education,* 1963, *14,* 238-243.

Coleman, J.S., Campbell, E.Q., Hobson, C.J., McPartland, J., Mood, A.M., Weinfeld, F.D., and York, R.L. *Equality of educational opportunity.* Washington, DC: U.S. Government Printing Office, 1966.

Crawford, J., Gage, N., Corno, L., Stayrook, N., Mitman, A., Schunk, D., Stallings, J., Baskin, E., Hanvey, P., Austin, D., and Newman, R. *An experiment on teacher effectiveness and parent assisted instruction in the third grade.* Stanford, CA: Center for Educational Research at Stanford, Stanford University, 1978.

Cremin, L.A. *The transformation of the school.* New York: Vintage Books, 1964.

Dunkin, M.J., and Biddle, B.J. *The study of teaching.* New York: Holt, Rinehart and Winston, 1974.

Duffy, G. Fighting off the alligators: What research in real classrooms has to say about reading instruction. *Journal of Reading Behavior,* 1982, *14,* 357-372.

Duffy, G. Teacher effectiveness research: Implications for the reading profession. In M.L. Kamil (Ed.), *Thirtieth Yearbook of the National Reading Conference.* Chicago: National Reading Conference, 1981, 113-136.

Flanders, N.A. *Teacher influence, pupil attitudes, and achievement.* Minneapolis: University of Minnesota (U.S. Office of Education Cooperative Research Project No. 397), 1960. (ED 002 865)

Gage, N.L., and Giaconia, R. Teaching practices and student achievement: Causal connections. *New York University Education Quarterly,* Spring 1981, 2-9.

Getzels, J.W., and Jackson, P.W. The teacher's personality and characteristics. In N.L. Gage (Ed.), *Handbook of research on teaching.* Chicago: Rand McNally, 1963, 506-582.

Good, T.L. Teacher effectiveness in the elementary school. *Journal of Teacher Education,* 1979, *30,* 52-64.

Good, T.L. *The Missouri mathematics effectiveness project: A program of naturalistic and experimental research.* Paper presented at the annual meeting of the American Educational Research Association. Toronto, March 1978. (ED 159 056)

Good, T.L., and Grouws, D.A. Teaching effects: Process-product study fourth grade mathematics classrooms. *Journal of Teacher Education,* 1977, *28,* 49-54.

Gray, H. Improvement of classroom instruction. *Texas Outlook,* 1940, *24,* 52+.

Hardesty, C.D. Can teaching success be rated? *The Nation's Schools,* 1935, *15,* 27-28.

Hiller, J.H., Fisher, G.A., and Kaess, W. A computer investigation of verbal characteristics of effective classroom lecturing. *American Educational Research Journal,* 1969, *6,* 661-675.

Jayne, C.D. A study of the relationship between teaching procedures and educational outcomes. *Journal of Experimental Education,* 1945, *14,* 101-134.

King, L.A. The present status of teacher rating. *American School Board Journal,* 1925, *70,* 44-56.

Kounin, J. *Discipline and group management in classrooms.* New York: Holt, Rinehart and Winston, 1970.

Lanier, J.E. Teacher education: Needed research and practice for the preparation of teaching professionals. In D.C. Corrigan, D.J. Palmer, and P.A. Alexander (Eds.), *The future of teacher education: Needed research and practice.* College Station, TX: Deans Grant, College of Education, 1982, 13-36.

Lowth, F.J. What makes a successful teacher? *Journal of Education,* 1933, *116,* 392-393, 420-421.

McDonald, F.J., and Elias, P. *Beginning teacher evaluation study, phase II, Executive summary report.* Princeton, NJ: Educational Testing Service, 1976. (ED 142 592)

McNeil, J.D., and Popham, W.J. The assessment of teacher competence. In R.M.W. Travers (Ed.), *Second handbook of research on teaching.* Chicago: Rand McNally, 1973, 281-344.

Medley, D.M. *Teacher competency and teacher effectiveness: A review of process-product research.* Washington, DC: American Association of Colleges for Teacher Education, 1977.

Medley, D.M., and Mitzel, H.E. A technique for measuring classroom behavior. *Journal of Educational Psychology,* 1958, *49,* 86-93.

Medley, D.M., and Mitzel, H.E. Measuring classroom behavior by systematic observation. In N.L. Gage (Ed.), *Handbook of research on teaching.* Chicago: Rand McNally, 1963, 247-328.

Medley, D.M., and Mitzel, H.E. Some behavioral correlates of teacher effectiveness. *Journal of Educational Psychology,* 1959, *50,* 239-247.

Monroe, W.S. Controlled experimentation as a means of evaluating methods of teaching. *Review of Educational Research,* 1934, *4,* 36-42.

Nisbett, R.E., and Ross, L. *Human inferences: Strategies and shortcomings of social judg-ment*. Englewood Cliffs, NJ: Prentice-Hall, 1980.

Olander, H.T. How to measure classroom teaching. *The School Executive*, 1937, *56*, 470-471.

Reavis, W.C., and Cooper, D.H. Evaluation of teacher merit in city school systems. *Supple-mentary educational monographs*, No. 59. Chicago: University of Chicago, 1945.

Rice, J.M. *The public school system of the United States*. New York: Century Company, 1983.

Rosenshine, B.V. *Instructional principles in direct instruction*. Paper presented at the annual meeting of the American Educational Research Association, Toronto, March 1978. (ED 155 152)

Rosenshine, B.V. Recent research on teaching behaviors and student achievement. *Journal of Teacher Education*, 1976, *27*, 61-64.

Rosenshine, B.V. The stability of teacher effects upon student achievement. *Review of Educa-tional Research*, 1970, *40*, 647-662.

Rosenshine, B.V., and Furst, N. The use of direct observation to study teaching. In R.M.W. Travers (Ed.), *Second handbook of research on teaching*. Chicago: Rand McNally, 1973, 122-183.

Rosenthal, R., and Jacobson, L. *Pygmalion in the classroom*. New York: Holt, Rinehart and Winston, 1968.

Russo, N. *The effects of student characteristics, educational beliefs and instructional task on teachers' preinstructional discussion in reading and math*. Unpublished doctoral dis-sertation, University of California at Los Angeles, 1978.

Ryans, D.G. Inventory estimated teacher characteristics as covariants of observer assessed pupil behavior. *Journal of Educational Psychology*, 1961, *52*, 91-97.

Saadeh, I.Q. Teacher effectiveness or classroom efficiency: A new direction in the evaluation of teaching. *Journal of Teacher Education*, 1970, *21*, 73-91.

Shannon, J.R. A comparison of three means for measuring efficiency in teaching. *Journal of Educational Research*, 1936, *29*, 501-508.

Shavelson, R.J., and Stern, P. Research on teachers' pedagogical thoughts, judgments, deci-sions, and behavior. *Review of Educational Research*, 1981, *51*, 455-498.

Shulman, L.S. Reconstruction of educational research. *Review of Educational Research*, 1970, *40*, 371-397.

Shulman, L.S. Reflections on individual differences in the study of teaching. Unpublished manuscript, Michigan State University, 1980.

Snow, R.E. Representative and quasirepresentative designs for research on teaching. *Review of Educational Research*, 1974, *44*, 265-291.

Soar, R.S., and Soar, R.M. An empirical analysis of selected Follow Through programs: An example of a process approach to evaluation. In I. Gordon (Ed.), *Early childhood education*. Chicago: National Society for the Study of Education, 1972, 229-261.

Solomon, D., Rosenberg, L., and Bezdek, W.E. Teacher behavior and student learning. *Journal of Education Psychology*, 1964, *55*, 23-30.

Stallings, J.A., and Kaskowitz, D. *Follow Through classroom observation evaluation, 1972-1973*. Menlo Park, CA: Stanford Research Institute, 1974. (ED 104 969)

Stern, P.R., and Shavelson, R.J. *The relation between teachers' grouping decisions and in-structional behaviors: An ethnographic study of reading instruction*. Unpublished manuscript, University of California at Los Angeles, 1980.

Tallmadge, G.K. Relationships between training methods and learner characteristics. *Journal of Educational Psychology*, 1968, *59*, 32-36.

Wallen, N.E., and Travers, R.M.W. Analysis and investigation of teaching methods. In N.L. Gage (Ed.) *Handbook of research on teaching*. Chicago: Rand McNally, 1963, 448-505.

Wodtke, K.H., and Wallen, N.E. The effects of teacher control in the classroom on pupils' creativity test gains. *American Educational Research Journal*, 1965, *2*, 75-82.

Worthen, B.R. A study of discovery and expository presentation: Implications for teaching. *Journal of Teacher Education*, 1968, *19*, 223-242.

Part Two
Process-Product Research

T he three chapters in Part Two introduce process-product research for studying teacher effectiveness. The attention given to this paradigm is not intended to place a value on its use over other paradigms for research on teaching, but rather to reflect the fact that during the 1970s and early 1980s it emerged as the dominant method for analyzing the characteristics of effective teaching. In Chapter 2, Hoffman develops a conceptual framework for process-product research drawing on the work of Dunkin and Biddle. This "primer" poses a series of questions for evaluating process-product type studies. The subsequent chapters by Brophy and Stallings contain actual reports of process-product studies. The two projects discussed in these chapters are clearly among the most cited studies of basic research into effective teaching.

James V. Hoffman

2

Process-Product Research on Effective Teaching: A Primer for a Paradigm

T his chapter discusses process-product research on effective teaching from a methodological perspective. The goal is to provide a conceptual framework to help the reader understand and interpret the studies in this book and, in addition, to provide some guidelines for analyzing other research studies using this paradigm.

Research on Teaching

A good starting point for this discussion is to consider how teaching effectiveness research fits into the larger world of research on teaching. Dunkin and Biddle (1974) have proposed categorizing our knowledge of teaching into six classes. Studies of teaching can have as their goal the advancement of the knowledge base in any one or combination of these classes.

The first class of knowledge relates to *conceptualizing the processes of teaching. Processes* refers to the actual activity of teaching in classrooms. At this level of research the basic activities associated with teaching are defined and described in concrete terms. Examples of this would be efforts to categorize the questions the teacher asks and to identify the characteristics of the feedback the teacher provides to pupils who make errors. An understanding of teaching processes can be refined through intensive study of the component parts of the instructional process. This intense scrutiny may also enhance the researchers' powers of observation and exploration.

The second class of knowledge relates to *discovering the rate at which the conceptualized processes occur* in the typical classroom. That is, having identified the aspect of the instructional process one wishes to study, one could study the degree of frequency with which the phenomenon occurs. How often are certain kinds of questions asked? How often does the teacher use certain types of feedback to pupil learning errors? Within this class of knowledge, the rate of occurrence is often examined in terms of degree as well as quantity. For example, how often are students praised strongly for a correct response? Praised moderately? Not praised?

The third class of knowledge of teaching is in *identifying the relationships between the context for instruction and the process of instruction. Context* refers to those features of the instructional environment about which the teacher can do little. Many pupil characteristics (sometimes referred to as status variables) such as sex and ethnicity represent one type of context variable. Examples of research questions in this class of knowledge include: What is the relationship between the socioeconomic status of pupils and teacher questioning behavior? How does the sex of the pupil relate to teacher verbal feedback patterns? Context variables are not limited to pupil status but may also include such areas as school and community characteristics.

A fourth class of knowledge relates to an *understanding of "presage" factors*. Dunkin and Biddle describe presage factors as variables related to the influence of general teacher characteristics or experience on their instructional processes. For example, how does their preservice training relate to what teachers do during reading instruction? How do teachers' beliefs about reading relate to the kind of verbal feedback they offer to student miscues?

The fifth class of knowledge refers to *understanding the relationships among processes*. Research in this area investigates how processes interact with one another, such as the way in which teachers affect pupil behavior and vice versa. An investigation of how teachers' expectations for success affect pupil performance and how pupil performance affects teachers' expectations for success is an example.

The final area or class of knowledge concerns *process-product relationships*. The term *product* is used to refer to learning outcomes. In reading, the outcomes could be anything from growth in decoding skills to shifts in attitude toward reading. Studies which investigate this class of knowledge attempt to explore the ways in which and the degree to which certain processes associated with teaching activity contribute to change in learning outcomes (products). Researchers interested in process-product relationship might be interested in such questions as the degree to which higher order questioning relates to or predicts pupil growth in reading comprehension skills. Within this class of process-product knowledge, the recent body of teacher effectiveness research fits into the world of research on teaching.

The Process-Product Paradigm:
From Research Design to Data Analysis

A study using the process-product paradigm might be designed as follows: The researcher first identifies the learning outcomes (products) he or she wishes to investigate. The researcher then selects a suitable measure (usually a test) for this outcome (i.e., the product or the dependent variable) and gives it to the students involved in the study both before the study begins (pretest) and after it has ended (posttest). During the intervening period, the researcher observes and monitors predetermined aspects of the teaching activity. The processes (i.e., independent variables) to be monitored are usually determined before the study begins based on existing research literature or some conceptual argument for an expected relationship. For example, if growth in reading comprehension is an expected outcome, the researcher may select levels of teacher questioning behavior as the primary process variable to scrutinize. If the level of the outcome variable changes from pre to posttesting, the researcher can analyze the relationships between the instructional variables observed and the concomitant change in outcome. In this example, the researcher could attempt to discover the degree to which the incidence or frequency of certain kinds of teacher questioning behaviors contributes, or at least relates, to growth in reading comprehension ability.

This scenario, of course, oversimplifies the paradigm and there are many variations on the theme. In some studies, a number of process and outcome variables are measured and related using a "shotgun" approach. The significant relationships between process and product measures which are uncovered are then explained after the fact.

In other studies, researchers have set out to identify teachers who are consistently effective in producing growth in students for the outcome measures under study. They then compare the teaching behaviors of this "highly effective" group with the behaviors of a control group consisting of "typical" teachers. Such a study might suggest that highly effective teachers of reading comprehension rely significantly more on certain kinds of questions than do less effective teachers.

The techniques for data gathering and analysis used in research on teaching vary depending on 1) the class of knowledge under investigation and 2) the design of a given study. For example, researchers interested in class one knowledge (conceptualization) often employ descriptive research methods such as case study reports or ethnography to identify and isolate potentially important variables. Often, such studies generate hypotheses and provide the framework for subsequent, more quantitative investigations.

Researchers interested in class two type knowledge typically use quantitative methods to describe the frequencies or rates of occurrence of the conceptualized teaching variables. They often report data in raw frequencies (i.e., the number of times something was observed) or in proportional terms. Such proportions may be expressed as a percentage of a total (e.g., the percent of all questions at the literal level) or as a rate (e.g., the number of inferential questions per hour or per 100 words of text read).

Beginning with class three knowledge, which concerns context effects on processes, we move further into the area of inferential statistics where researchers make generalizable statements about differences in the rates of occurrence of certain process variables as a function of the context. For example, a researcher might investigate how teacher feedback to miscues varies with the achievement level of the student.

With presage-process (class four) and process-process (class five) areas of investigation, we find continued use of inferential statistics. Most of these studies employ simple correlational or more complex forms of statistical regression analyses. They focus on discovering the patterns and strength of relationships among variables. For example, in a process-process study we might find a correlation of .60 between the teacher's use of verbal reinforcement and student ontask academic behavior. These data suggest that a relationship exists between the two variables but is not necessarily causal in either direction. That is, one can't say whether the ontask behavior causes the verbal reinforcement. All one can say is that the two processes co-occur.

Most process-product (class six) studies employ similar analyses. Some researchers regard them as being one step closer to yielding causal inferences, since process variables are most often used to predict gain in the outcome variable. For example, a study of teacher questioning might reveal a negative correlation between the incidence of literal level questions and gain in reading achievement. This does not mean that the literal level of questioning retards growth in achievement. These are still correlational data, and any inference toward causal relationships rests on thin ice. The level of questioning may be correlated only incidentally to another variable that is causally related to achievement. Simply changing the level of questioning may not necessarily lead to achievement growth.

To make causal inferences one must resort to experimental studies. In these studies, the hypothesized variables (i.e., the ones suspected of having causal relationships to the outcome variable) are manipulated and the effects of the manipulation on the outcome variable studied. A small but growing number of teacher effectiveness studies use such an experimental approach. Studies of this type are, in fact, reported in the next two chapters. In such instances, a group of teachers is trained in a process, the implementation of the process is monitored, and the associated effects measured.

For example, teachers randomly assigned to an experimental group are trained to use higher level questioning strategies while the control group is not. Both groups' use of these questioning strategies is monitored during the treatment period. Student comprehension performance within the experimental and control groups is compared at the end of the study. The researcher who uses this type of experimental design and finds differences has a basis for making causal inferences.

From this level of research classroom practice is informed. This is not to suggest that research of other types or into other classes of knowledge is unimportant. In fact, a firm grounding in the other classes of knowledge is a prerequisite for such experimental investigations.

Evaluating Research Using the Process-Product Paradigm

While teaching effectiveness research has only recently begun to explore process-product relationships, it has quickly become voluminous in quantity. The neophyte approaching this literature from a reading background should keep three thoughts in mind.

First, the genesis and major thrust for this line of research came from individuals interested in discovering general principles of effective teaching in schools. They were and by in large are not particularly interested in the teaching of reading. Reading has served as the focal point for many studies because of 1) its recognized importance in schooling, and 2) the many measures available to assess outcomes.

Second, with two or three notable exceptions, the researchers most active in this area are not reading educators. Thus, the terminology and concepts in this literature may be somewhat unfamiliar to the reader.

Third, research on effective teaching is one of the few areas of research where the reviews of research may outnumber the actual studies. The limited number of studies is attributable in part to the fact that the area is relatively new and in part to the costs (both in time and money) of conducting studies which involve field based methods. The need for so many reviews of research is in deference to the fact that in a single study many process variables may be observed that cut across a large number of conceptual areas (e.g., questioning, feedback, sex differences in achievement, and so on). Reviews of research in teaching are often attempts to take pieces of studies and synthesize them into coherent statements about a particular area of concern. While these reviews are invaluable, the reader of this literature should keep in mind that such reviews are no stronger than the studies on which they are based.

What follows then is a series of questions for the reader of teacher effectiveness studies to keep in mind in judging their quality and importance. While perhaps not all questions will apply to all studies, most should be relevant. The comments after each question are offered as explanations of the point. The reader may want to create a checklist using these questions, rating the studies as strong or weak with respect to the point being addressed.

1. *Are the process variables under study clearly described and classified appropriately?* The problem in this area relates most often to the conceptualization of teaching processes. Once researchers identify instructional (or process) variables to study, they often observe in classrooms for instances of those teaching behaviors, and then record their presence or absence (usually onto a predetermined coding system). The consumer of research involving observation should carefully examine the original coding system to determine how the researcher conceptualized those variables. For example, if a teacher reading a book aloud to a class is coded on a given instrument as an instance of a "nonacademic social interaction," it is because the researcher viewed it as such. The findings of such studies, when reported in the literature, often reflect only the statistical analyses performed on the descriptive categories — not the specific behaviors observed. Thus, the reader should examine the researcher's assumptions about processes closely before accepting or judging the findings.

2. *Are the processes conceptually tied to the products or outcome variables?* The distinction or categorization of more or less effective teachers is often made solely in terms of student achievement. Sometimes, however, the processes of teaching being observed include ratings on more affective variables such as teacher

warmth or use of praise. To discover that such processes are not different between more and less effective teachers or that the processes show no relationship to the outcome measures should not be interpreted as meaning that they are insignificant — merely that they may be unrelated in clear ways to the product (i.e., achievement) measured. One should look for various outcome measures in studies which relate theoretically to the processes observed. For example, how does the use of praise relate to growth in self-esteem or self-concept? How do teachers who are effective in developing positive student attitudes toward reading differ in classroom organization patterns from less effective teachers?

A promising trend in teacher effectiveness research is the move away from multiple process/single product studies toward studies which focus on one (or just a few) process variable(s) and then measure the effects on multiple outcome variables. Such an approach saves us from throwing out the baby with the bath water every time we find a teaching practice that is unrelated to pupil achievement on standardized tests.

3. *Is effective teaching of basic skills being equated with effective teaching of reading?* Few would deny the importance of students developing good decoding skills, but other legitimate goals in a reading program relate to such areas as critical reading, appreciation of literature, and so on. The consumer of teacher effectiveness research should carefully examine the outcome measures used in studies to discover which levels of reading proficiency are being addressed. Doyle (1982) has recently suggested that some of the findings from teacher effectiveness research regarding the teaching of basic skills (e.g., the benefits of "Direct Instruction") may apply only to the basic skill areas and then only in reference to beginning learners or those experiencing difficulty. He argues that unless these effective approaches are combined with instruction in higher order decision processes, few long term consequences for student achievement can be expected.

4. *Are the pupil characteristics clearly specified or controlled?* In teacher effectiveness research one should look for a consideration of pupil status variables which have been shown to be related to achievement (or whatever other outcome variable is under

consideration). This would include the specification of the grade or age level of the students, sex and ethnicity of students, and so on. Brophy (1981), for example, reports that the effects of certain types of verbal praise on students vary dramatically as a function of grade and ability level. Not all studies need to make multiple comparisons of pupil status variables and their relationship to outcomes, but at a minimum they should clearly describe the pupils under study so that the reader can judge how representative or generalizable the findings are.

5. *Is there sufficient observation time of the teaching processes across specified task conditions?* One of the most important changes that took place in research on teaching since the mid-1960s has been the increased reliance on direct observation. Before this period, studies of teacher effectiveness had used interviews, questionnaires, and other self-report techniques as the primary source of process data. The consumer of teacher effectiveness research should examine carefully the actual amount of observation time of teaching processes within a given study. Is it enough to be representative of a teacher's behavior?

Beyond this quantitative concern, the consumer must consider the degree of focus for the observation. The teaching processes one observes are in large part dependent on what task is being observed (Doyle, 1979). Studies of teacher questioning yield quite different results if one observes a teacher guiding an oral reading session as opposed to observing a teacher guiding book sharing even though both activities might have occurred during reading time. This is because the task relates to quite different educational goals. To observe teacher questioning from 9:00-11:30 A.M. five days a week is not a sufficient control for differences across tasks. The observation of teaching processes must be tied to a specific task if the results are to be interpreted meaningfully. Thus, a study might look at feedback to learning errors during sight word drill or feedback to miscues during guided oral reading as being examples of processes tied to specific tasks.

6. *Are the school context variables clearly specified?* A good deal of evidence suggests that significant patterns in teacher behavior are tied to the nature of the curriculum in a particular school or

district. Studies which are conducted entirely within a school system or a single school need to describe its reading program clearly. One recent study in a junior high school setting showed a negative correlation between gain in reading achievement and the amount of time spent in silent reading. This seems incomprehensible until one realizes that the school where the study was conducted mandated a one hour per week uninterrupted sustained silent reading program for all classes.

7. *Are "real" data given?* The researcher should provide the reader, to the degree possible, the basic data which were collected and analyzed. At a minimum, real means (expressed in frequencies) and standard deviations for the variables under study should be reported. Correlation matrices with accompanying tests of statistical significance may be of value, but they cannot be interpreted directly in terms of the actual processes observed.

8. *Are correlational findings being interpreted causally?* Field based research is very complicated and presents enormous methodological and data analysis problems. To deal with these problems we see increasing use of multivariate statistical procedures such as path analysis and canonical correlation. These are useful procedures in that they help us understand how many variables can simultaneously relate to one another. While they help us clarify relationships, they are still correlational. They cannot tell us that one process variable causes change in another process or outcome variable. Only in the context of an experimental or quasi experimental design can such inferences be made.

9. *Is nonstatistical significance interpreted as unimportant?* A given study might report that a process variable was not significantly related to a change in outcome measures. For example, a researcher might report that the use of contextually oriented prompts to student miscues is not correlated in a statistically significant way to growth in reading skills. This may be an accurate statement. To interpret that contextual prompts are unimportant, however, goes quite a bit beyond the findings of the study. Perhaps the instances of contextual prompts were too few to reveal a powerful statistical relationship with the outcome variable. The two variables may be in fact very closely related. A treatment study in which teachers are trained

in the use of contextual prompts might reveal strong relationships to outcomes.

9. *Is statistical significance interpreted as important?* On occasion, researchers may attempt to interpret statistical significance as meaning that a process variable is related in important ways to the criterion or product variable. The level of statistical significance (often reported in terms of a probability value) has to do with the likelihood that the relationship between the two variables is a function of chance. Whether a relationship is statistically significant depends in part on the strength of the relationship and in part on the number of observations. This means that process variables that bear only a slight relationship to outcome variables may show a statistically significant relationship to one another if observed often enough. What is important in correlational or regression analyses is the strength of the relationship which is reflected in the magnitude of the correlation coefficient. In multivariate analyses using regression models the statistics are a bit different, but there is still the basic distinction between statistical significance (i.e., the likelihood that the relationship can be explained by chance) and the explanation of variance (i.e., the magnitude of relationship between the predictor variable(s) and the criterion). In judging the relative importance of a relationship between process and a product, the reader should concentrate on the data related to variance explained.

10. *Is the status of teaching presented as the standard?* Teacher effectiveness studies often compare how subgroups of teachers use certain process variables. Often, the designation of a more effective or less effective teacher is determined by splitting the teacher group in half based on student outcome levels. Even if the more or less effective teachers are appropriately classified in a given study, it is well beyond the data to infer that these are "high effective" or "low effective" teachers relative to the world of teachers outside the sample or the world of *what could be*. For example, to find that more effective teachers are spending more time than less effective teachers on decoding skills is to compare those teachers with what else *is* going on in that school or district—not what else *might* be going on. To describe or hold up the "best" of what there is as the ideal or standard is a dangerous step.

11. *Does the researcher place the research into the context of ongoing classroom research?* Our understanding of teacher effectiveness is destined to grow gradually over many years and many studies. The consumer of research should look to see where the piece of work under consideration fits into or has evolved from a continuous line of research. Much research has evolved in such a manner including areas such as teacher expectations (Cooper, 1979), teacher praise (Brophy, 1981), and teacher decision making (Shavelson & Stern, 1981). In these and other areas we are beginning to see patterns of replication in the findings that go beyond one shot statistical analysis.

12. *Are the implications drawn appropriate to the class of knowledge about teaching being investigated?* It has become almost a tradition in educational research that findings from studies must inform practice. This is an erroneous notion. Studies of teaching can inform any one of the classes of knowledge of teaching outlined earlier. However, only those studies addressing the process-product class of knowledge are designed to inform practice directly and then only to the degree that causal relationships are established.

Concluding Remarks

Anyone who ventures into the arena of research on teaching realizes quickly that the classical experimental designs discussed in every research methods class are next to impossible to implement in real classroom settings. The process-product paradigm offers researchers, at a minimum, one way to begin to engage in the scientific study of reading and learning to read in classrooms. The reader of research in effective teaching which uses this paradigm should be critical and demanding in terms of the questions just raised but at the same time considerate of the difficulties in conducting such research.

References

Brophy, J. On praising effectively. *Elementary School Journal*, 1981, *81*, 269-278.
Brophy, J. Teacher behavior and student learning. *Educational Leadership*, 1979, *37*, 33-38.
Cooper, H. Pygmalion grows up: A model for teacher expectation communication and performance influence. *Review of Educational Research*, 1979, *49*, 389-410.

Doyle, W. Academic work. Austin: Research and Development Center for Teacher Education, University of Texas at Austin, 1982.

Doyle, W. *The tasks of teaching and learning in classrooms*, Report No. 4103. Austin: Research and Development Center for Teacher Education, University of Texas at Austin, 1979.

Duffy, G.D. Teacher effectiveness research: Implications for the reading profession. In M.L. Kamil (Ed.), *Directions in reading research and instruction*, Thirtieth yearbook of the National Reading Conference. Washington, DC: National Reading Conference, 1981.

Dunkin, M.J., and Biddle, B.J. *The study of teaching*. New York: Holt, Rinehart and Winston, 1974.

Good, T. *Research on teaching*. Address presented at the annual convention of the American Educational Research Association, Boston, 1980.

Shavelson, R.J., and Stern, P. Research on teachers' thoughts, judgments, decisions, and behavior. *Review of Educational Research*. 1981, *51*, 455-498.

3   Jere Brophy

Principles for Conducting First Grade Reading Group Instruction*

I n reviewing research that included direct observation in classrooms, Rosenshine and Furst (1973) noted the need for more
research that followed a "descriptive-correlational-experimental
loop." Such work would begin with detailed observation and description of classroom events, leading to the conceptualization of
important teacher or student behaviors and development of ways to
measure these behaviors (classroom process variables) validly and
reliably.

At this point, the stage would be set for correlational process-
product work. Here, selected classrooms would be visited periodically for using coding systems, rating scales, and related
instruments to develop systematic records of classroom processes,
and classroom process scores developed from these observational
data would be correlated with measures of student achievement, attitudes, or other outcomes ("products") of instruction. Significant
process-product correlations linking teacher behaviors to student

*This work is sponsored in part by the Institute for Research on Teaching, Michigan State
University. The Institute for Research on Teaching is funded primarily by the National Institute of Education, United States Department of Education. The opinions expressed in this
publication do not necessarily reflect the position, policy, or endorsement of the National
Institute of Education. (Contract No. 400-81-0014)

outcomes would provide promising leads to identification of causal linkages, especially when postscores on the product measures were adjusted to control for any systematic differences on the prescores.

Still, such data would remain correlational, and causal connections between teacher behavior and student outcome could not be demonstrated convincingly until the researchers manipulated teacher behavior systematically and monitored the effects of these manipulations on student outcomes. While conducting such programmatic work, investigators ordinarily would develop additional insights about relevant classroom processes, leading to new conceptualization, measurement, and research—hence, the description of such work as a "loop" rather than as a linear process that stops following experimentation.

Even as late as 1973 when their chapter was published, Rosenshine and Furst's descriptive-correlational-experimental loop was describing an ideal more than reality. Remarkably little process-product research had been conducted, and the little available was confined mostly to one shot studies, except for the more programmatic work of Flanders (1970) in the United States and of Nuthall and Church (1973) in New Zealand. A great deal of process-product research was done in the next decade, however, spurred by Rosenshine and Furst's chapter, Dunkin and Biddle's *The Study of Teaching* (1974), and the reports of a national conference on research on teaching convened by the National Institute of Education (1974).

This flurry of research activity produced significant increases in the quantity and quality of process-product data, focusing in particular on the relationships between teacher behavior and student learning of basic academic skills. Several teams of investigators in different parts of the country found that achievement gain correlated with such teacher characteristics as: emphasis on actively instructing students in the academic curriculum; expectations that the students can and will master the curriculum; use of effective classroom management techniques to insure that time allocated to academic activities is actually spent on those activities; and pacing which is brisk or demanding in that the teacher expects students to progress through the curriculum, but which is nevertheless matched to students' present levels of achievement (see Brophy, 1979; Good, 1979; and Rosenshine & Stevens, 1984).

Some of this process-product research involved programmatic work that was carried through to the point of experimentation, and some of these experiments focused specifically on reading instruction. The latter work includes the studies done by Stallings and her colleagues (see next chapter) and the study described in this chapter called the "first grade reading group study." (Readers are referred to Anderson, Evertson, & Brophy, 1978, 1979, for details of instrumentation, procedures, and findings not included here about the latter study.)

The primary research base for the first grade reading group study was the Texas Teacher Effectiveness Study, a two year, correlational, process-product study of teacher behavior and student learning in second and third grade classrooms (Brophy & Evertson, 1976). That study had developed findings concerning such teacher behavior (process) variables as classroom organization and group management skills; appropriate level of difficulty of questions and assignments; active teaching with frequent recitation activities and response opportunities, and methods of distributing those response opportunities among the individual students; and responding to students following their reading performance in reading groups or their answers to teacher questions. Teacher-student interaction in this study had been analyzed separately according to whether it occurred during whole class or small group (largely reading group) activities, so some of the findings were specific to the small group instructional setting. We decided to concentrate on these principles for small group instruction in designing our first experimental test of principles developed from correlational process-product findings for several reasons.

First, we wanted to develop and test a "package" of principles that fit together into a systematic approach to instruction, rather than attempting to study only one principle dealing with only one specific teacher behavior. This meant that we would be conducting a quasiexperiment rather than a true experiment in which only one factor is varied and everything else is held constant. We were willing to accept this loss of precision, however, because we wanted our treatment to be powerful enough to affect students' end-of-year standardized achievement test scores in basic skills, in the sense that students taught by teachers trained in the treatment principles would outperform students taught by control teachers using their usual methods. Because so many factors affect students' end-of-year achievement test scores, manipulation of any single teacher behavior is unlikely to have a significant effect on these scores by itself. A more comprehensive treatment involving a package of teacher behaviors organized into a systematic approach to teaching, however, might be expected to have significant effects.

We were also attracted to reading groups as the setting for our study. First, they occur in small group settings, and teacher-student interaction in small groups is generally easier to observe and record systematically than teacher-student interaction in whole class settings. Second, reading groups are virtually universal in the early grades, particularly first grade. Furthermore, they address similar content and skills and involve similar teacher and student activities even when materials from different publishers are used (except for DISTAR and other highly circumscribed special programs). Thus, by working with first grade reading groups, we could apply our treatment principles to a setting that occurs naturally in most classrooms, could concentrate on a particular subject matter (beginning reading), and could be reasonably confident that even though we were working within naturalistic classroom settings, any significant differences between groups that we might document would be due to differences in how the teachers taught (whether they systematically used our treatment principles) rather than in how much they taught or what they taught (the nature of the curriculum and the time spent in reading groups would be similar across the groups of teachers).

Our initial interest was in testing principles for conducting small group academic lessons in the primary grades, with emphasis on organizing the group to use the time efficiently and maximize attention and task engagement, and on controlling the timing and nature of students' public response opportunities. No curriculum development or preparation of special instructional materials was involved; the treatment was designed to be used in connection with any of the commercially published reading programs (other than those like DISTAR, that specify in detail the instructional procedures to be used with the materials). Once we identified first grade reading groups as the setting for the research, we supplemented the principles developed from the Brophy and Evertson (1976) correlational work with other principles we believed appropriate for small group instruction of young children. We drew these mostly from the work of Blank (1973) on teaching young children through questioning and from principles of small group instruction developed for use in the preschool and primary grade programs of the Southwest Educational Development Laboratory (1973).

The Treatment Principles

The 22 principles composing the experimental treatment are shown in Figure 1. The first two principles concern management of attention. Students facing the teacher with their backs toward the rest of the room should be less distracted and predictable structure in the form of a standard "let's get started" signal should condition the children to pay full attention when the teacher is ready to begin. Principles 3-6 elaborate the concept that once the students are paying attention, the teacher should provide advance organizers and build a "mental set" for learning the material in the day's lesson. At minimum, this would involve an overview statement about what will occur during the lesson, but it may also involve demonstrations, presentations of new words, and other activities.

Figure 1. The 22 principles in the instructional model.

1. The teacher should use a standard signal to get the children's attention.
2. Once in the group, children should sit with their backs to the rest of the class; the teacher should face the class.
3. The introduction to the lesson should give an overview of what is to come in order to prepare the students for the presentation.
4. New words and sounds should be presented to the children at the beginning of a lesson so they can use the words and sounds later when they are reading or answering questions.
5. The teacher should have the children repeat new words or sounds until they say them satisfactorily.
6. After moving into the lesson, but before asking the children to use the new material or undertake new tasks, the teacher should present a demonstration or an explanation of any new activity.
7. The teacher should work with one individual at a time in having the children practice the new skill and apply the new concept, making sure that everyone is checked and receives feedback during the lesson.
8. The teacher should use a pattern (such as going from one end of the group to the other) to select children to take turns reading in the group or answering questions (rather than calling on children randomly and unpredictably).

9. To keep each member of the group alert and accountable at all times, between turns the teacher should occasionally question a child about a previous response from another child.

10. Calling on volunteers should be restricted chiefly to parts of the lesson in which children are contributing personal experiences or opinions.

11. When a child calls out an answer, the teacher should remind the child that everyone will get a turn and must wait to answer in turn.

12. The teacher should avoid leading questions or rhetorical questions. Also, avoid answering one's own questions and repeating questions.

13. At some point during the lesson, the teacher must make a fundamental decision about whether the group as a whole can or cannot meet the objectives of a lesson.

14. If the teacher decides that the group as a whole cannot reach the objectives at the same time, because of large individual differences in comprehension of the material, he or she should teach the more able students through to the end of the lesson, dismiss them, and keep in the group those few who need extra help.

15. Sometimes the teacher may wish to use one or more children who have mastered the objectives to serve as models for the others.

16. If one or more children still do not meet the objectives within the time available for the lesson, tutorial assistance should be provided.

17. After asking a question, the teacher should wait for the child to respond and make sure that other children do not call out answers. If the child does not respond within a reasonable time, the teacher should indicate that some response is expected and then simplify according to Principle 19.

18. When the child is incorrect, the teacher should indicate that the answer is wrong and then simplify according to Principle 19.

19. The appropriate simplification procedure is determined by the type of question: If the question deals with factual knowledge that cannot be reasoned out, the teacher should give the child the answer and then move on. If the question is one that the child could reason out with help, the teacher should provide clues or simplify the question. If the clues still do not help the child, the teacher should supply the answer. The teacher should never ask another child to supply the answer.

20. If the student answers correctly, the teacher should acknowledge the correctness and make sure that everyone else heard and understood the answer.

21. Praise should be used in moderation. The teacher should praise thinking and effort more than just getting the answer. Praise should be as specific and individual as possible.

22. Criticism should be as specific as possible and should include specification of desirable or correct alternatives.

Principles 5 and 7 derived from the notion that children in the primary grades do not learn efficiently from merely watching and listening, but need to practice new skills, with corrective feedback as necessary. Thus, Principle 5 calls for having the students repeat new words or sounds aloud, and Principle 7 calls for the teacher to be sure to see that each individual practices skills and receives feedback. This principle implies that students will be questioned individually rather than as a group. It was based on data from Brophy and Evertson (1976) indicating that choral responses were negatively correlated with student learning gain. Note that the DISTAR program uses choral responses successfully, but only after training the teachers to listen carefully for each student's response, and also to train students to speak loudly and clearly and to follow the teacher's hand signals concerning when to respond. The Brophy and Evertson findings suggest that teachers who did not have this special training and were not using the hand signals and related specialized DISTAR techniques were not using choral responses effectively, and that teachers who avoided choral responses and concentrated on questioning students individually were getting better results. Hence Principle 7.

Principles 8-12 were designed to help students know when to respond and when to stay quiet (but attentive) during lessons. Principle 8, concerning the use of patterned turns, was taken directly from the Brophy and Evertson findings. In both years of that study, the data indicated that teachers who used the patterned turns method got better results than teachers who called on students randomly. These data were surprising, because most sources of advice to teachers suggest that random questioning keeps students more alert and accountable, and Kounin (1970) recommended random questioning as a group alertness and accountability technique. Nevertheless, our process-product data were clear in supporting patterned turns.

In combination, principles 8-11 structure the interaction so that the teacher controls public response opportunities (essentially by using the patterned turns method). Students are discouraged from volunteering to respond or calling out answers, but are assured that each will get a fair share of turns. Principle 12 was included to enhance the clarity of teachers' questions and to condition the students to realize that each teacher question calls for an answer.

Principles 13-16 concern the problem of what to do when some group members have mastered the objectives but others need intensive reteaching. We based these principles on techniques developed in the Southwest Educational Development Laboratory's preschool programs (1973), and called for dismissing the students who had mastered the objectives in order to concentrate on those who needed additional instruction.

Finally, Principles 17-22 concern methods of questioning and responding to students. These principles were developed from the Brophy and Evertson findings, supplemented by ideas taken from Blank (1973). The teacher trains students to respond to each question asked, gives feedback about the correctness of the response, and works for improvement of an unsatisfactory response. The guidelines called for emphasis on giving feedback following each response to indicate correctness, but discouraged more intensive or personalized praise or criticism. Earlier work (Brophy & Evertson, 1976) had indicated that personal criticism for incorrect responses to academic questions is usually inappropriate (except when the problem stems from persistent inattention or other inappropriate behavior), and also that praise should be used in moderation. These findings suggested that occasional high quality praise supported learning progress, but that overly frequent praise is distracting or intrusive, and inappropriate praise is confusing (for a more recent and detailed discussion of findings on praise, see Brophy, 1981).

These 22 principles, taken together and used systematically, constituted the treatment package. A 45 page manual listed these principles, described the underlying rationales, and suggested guidelines for their implementation.

Procedures

The experiment involved training first grade teachers to use the instructional model, observing in their classrooms to monitor implementation of the model, and assessing student achievement gain.

The Teachers

The study was conducted in twenty-seven first grade classrooms in nine schools serving predominantly middle class, Anglo students in Austin, Texas. The nine schools were grouped into three sets of three schools each, which were then randomly assigned to an experimental condition. Thus, all of the first grade teachers in any particular school were in the same experimental condition. The experimental conditions included two treatment groups and a control group. The ten teachers in the treatment-observed group were trained to use the instructional model and then observed periodically during the school year. The seven teachers in the treatment-unobserved group were trained to use the model, but were not observed. Finally, the ten teachers in the control group were not trained to use the model (they were asked to teach their reading groups as they normally did), but were observed periodically. Achievement testing was done in all twenty-seven classrooms.

Thus, the design allowed for replication of process-product relationships as well as for assessment of implementation and treatment effects. The observations in the treatment-observed group allowed us to monitor the degree to which these teachers followed through on their training by implementing the 22 principles; the observations of the control group allowed us to determine the degree to which these untrained teachers employed the principles in their reading instruction (although they had not been trained in the systematic use of our instructional model, most used at least some of the 22 principles due to prior training or experience). No implementation data were available on the treatment-unobserved group, but the student achievement data from these classrooms provided information about the effectiveness of the treatment in classrooms where no observers were present to provide subtle pressure on the teachers to follow the recommended guidelines.

Teacher Training

Because most of the principles included in the model were already in use in at least some classrooms, and because most involved concepts and behaviors already familiar to teachers, we believed that the teachers would learn the principles rapidly and implement them without much difficulty. Furthermore, we wished to minimize the time and expense involved in teacher training, and to maximize the potential exportability of the model. Consequently, the treatment was minimal in time and cost.

Researchers met with the seventeen treatment teachers in October to describe the purpose of the study, explain the principles in the model, and leave a copy of the manual with the teacher. They met again with each teacher a week or two later, administered a brief mastery test to insure that the teachers had read and understood the manual, and responded to any questions or addressed any concerns that the teachers expressed. As expected, the teachers found most of the principles familiar, face valid, and feasible for use in their reading groups. A few teachers expressed reservations about the "patterned turns" principle, but agreed to use the method after hearing an explanation of the data supporting this recommendation and the reasons why it seems appropriate for primary grade small group instruction. No additional training occurred after this second meeting with each teacher, and we made no attempts during the year to boost the treatment in any way.

Classroom Observation

The 10 treatment-observed and 10 control classes were observed about once a week from November through April, using a complex, primarily low inference coding system keyed to the teacher behaviors specified in the 22 principles. In addition to this information directly related to implementation of the treatment model, the observers recorded information about the basal readers and other materials being used, the time spent in each group, and the types of questions asked and content covered.

Student Achievement Data

The Metropolitan Readiness Tests had been administered at the beginning of the school year in each class. The Total Readiness scores from these tests were used to adjust end-of-year achievement scores. The latter scores were acquired by administering the reading subtests of the Metropolitan Achievement Tests, Level I in May in each of the 27 classes. The Total Reading Scores from these tests, adjusted for Total Readiness Scores on the readiness tests, provided the measures of student learning gain described in this chapter. (See Anderson, Evertson, and Brophy, 1978, for additional findings concerning the Word Knowledge and Reading subtests of the Metropolitan Achievement Tests, Level I, which are similar to the data reported here for the Total Reading scores.)

Findings

The findings include information on student learning gain, treatment implementation, and process-product relationships.

Effects on Student Learning

A series of regression models was tested for evidence of interactions between readiness levels and response to the treatment (none was observed) and for main effects of treatment. The latter analyses indicated no significant differences in adjusted reading achievement between the two treatment groups, but both treatment groups significantly outperformed the control group. Thus, training teachers to implement our treatment model resulted in significantly higher student achievement, and these treatment effects were not moderated by the presence of observers in the treatment-observed group.

Treatment Implementation

The observation yielded over 500 variables, although many of these overlapped or lacked sufficient variance to allow analysis. From this total, we selected the 55 variables that relate most directly to the treatment model or that measure other aspects of beginning reading instruction considered important to practitioners. Data concerning implementation and process-product relationships for these 55 variables are given in Table 1 (data on the remaining variables are given in Anderson, Evertson & Brophy, 1978).

Assessment of degree of implementation of the 22 principles requires attention both to the absolute scores of the treatment teachers (i.e., the ten teachers in the treatment-observed group) and to the comparison between these scores and the scores of the control teachers. Sometimes the treatment group scores were high and the control group scores were low, indicating both good implementation by the treatment group and a significant difference between the groups. However, sometimes these scores were very high for both groups, so that there was no significant group difference. This score pattern indicates that both the treatment teachers and the control teachers were implementing the principle consistently (i.e., the treatment teachers probably had been employing this principle even

Table 1

RESULTS OF ANALYSES OF CLASSROOM PROCESS VARIABLES

Classroom Process Variable	Treatment Implementation Data*						Process-Product Data†				
	Mean Score	Standard Deviation	Mean Score	Standard Deviation	F	p	Mean Score	Standard Deviation	Difference in R^2	Beta	p
Getting and maintaining the students' attention											
1. Percent of transitions begun with a signal	88	9	80	20	1.16	ns	84	15	.02	-.14	ns
2. Percent of lessons begun with a signal	7	9	5	5	.27	ns	6	7	.02	.16	ns
3. Percent of lesson time spent in transitions	9	2	13	4	6.79	.02	11	4	.13	-.36	.04
4. Average time (in minutes) spent in getting lesson started once all persons were present	.99	.24	1.46	.86	2.71	ns	1.23	.64	.09	-.29	.09
5. Rating of appropriateness of teacher seating (5-point scale; 5 = most appropriate)	3.63	.47	3.30	.98	.94	ns	3.46	.74	.15	.41	.02
6. Rating of appropriateness of student seating (5-point scale; 5 = most appropriate)	2.72	.44	2.17	.88	3.12	.09	2.45	.72	.02	.15	ns
Introducing the lesson and the material to the students											
7. Percent of lessons with no overview of any kind	51	20	66	19	2.83	ns	58	20	.09	-.32	.08
8. Percent of new words given at the beginning of the lesson instead of during the lesson	73	26	72	29	.01	ns	73	26	.00	-.07	ns
9. Percent of new words given to the students with no clues about how to read them	31	19	48	32	2.02	ns	40	27	.11	-.34	.05
10. Percent of new words repeated by the students	27	30	47	32	2.16	ns	37	31	.04	-.20	ns
11. Rating of sufficiency of demonstration (5-point scale; 5 = most sufficient)	2.68	.60	2.66	.54	.00	ns	2.67	.54	.00	.04	ns
Calling on individual students in the group											
12. Number of academic interactions per minute with individual students in reading turns and for questions that were not in reading turns	2.20	.42	1.86	.39	3.62	.07	2.03	.42	.09	.30	.08
13. Number of academic interactions per minute with individual students for questions that were not in reading turns	1.64	.36	1.20	.40	6.63	.02	1.42	.42	.21	.47	.01
14. Number of oral reading turns per minute given to individual students	.36	.10	.40	.14	.53	ns	.38	.12	.04	-.20	ns

15. Number of academic interactions per minute with individual students in oral reading turns	.56	.19	.65	.22	.93	ns	.61	.20	.10	-.34	.07
16. Number of choral responses per minute	.10	.09	.17	.10	2.86	.10	.14	.10	.11	-.34	.05
17. Number of group call outs per minute	.13	.09	.27	.16	5.43	.03	.20	.14	1‡	–	.04‡
18. Percent of all academic interactions that were selected by ordered turns	72	14	24	19	39.48	< .01	48	29	.12	.37	.04
19. Percent of all academic interactions that were given to nonvolunteers who were not selected systematically	11	5	31	11	26.98	< .01	21	13	.16	-.41	.02
20. Percent of all academic interactions that were given to volunteers	8	9	19	7	8.17	.01	13	10	.06	-.28	ns
21. Percent of all academic interactions that were taken by call outs	5	3	11	6	10.05	.01	13	11	.12	-.34	.04
Responding to individual differences in the group setting											
22. Percent of lessons in which the group was broken up because of different rates of learning the objectives	3	4	1	3	1.50	ns	2	3	.02	.15	ns
23. Percent of lessons in which one student was used as a model for others	0	0	0	0	–	ns	0	0	0	–	ns
Giving feedback to incorrect answers and failures to respond											
24. Percent of incorrect answers that received terminal feedback rather than sustaining feedback	44	8	62	12	15.22	< .01	53	13	.18	-.45	.01
25. Percent of incorrect answers not occurring in reading turns that received terminal feedback rather than sustaining feedback	36	11	52	8	13.59	< .01	44	12	.10	-.33	.06
26. Percent of incorrect answers in oral reading turns that received terminal feedback rather than sustaining feedback	57	18	66	18	1.25	ns	61	18	.04	-.20	ns
27. Percent of incorrect answers that were followed by the teacher asking another student	8	4	15	9	4.98	.04	11	7	.00	-.05	ns
28. Percent of incorrect answers that were improved through the use of successful sustaining feedback	39	7	27	9	10.98	.01	12.	10	.10	.33	.06

Table 1 (continued)
RESULTS OF ANALYSES OF CLASSROOM PROCESS VARIABLES

Classroom Process Variable	Treatment Implementation Data*						Process-Product Data†				
	Mean Score	Standard Deviation	Mean Score	Standard Deviation	F	p	Mean Score	Standard Deviation	Difference in R^2	Beta	p
29. Percent of failures to respond that were improved (i.e., the student made some response) through the use of successful sustaining feedback	40	9	21	8	25.54	.01	31	12	.17	.41	.01
30. Percent of use of sustaining feedback that was successful (i.e., led to an improved response by the student)	73	5	68	8	2.39	ns	70	7	.00	.01	ns
31. Percent of incorrect answers followed by process feedback (an explanation of *how* the answer was obtained)	3	2	3	3	.34	ns	3	2	.17	.43	.01
Giving feedback to correct answers											
32. Percent of correct answers that were followed by repetition of the answer	31	12	40	12	2.98	.10	36	12	.04	-.19	ns
33. Percent of correct answers that were not given any acknowledgement or feedback by the teacher	10	10	4	3	2.97	.10	7	8	.09	.31	.09
34. Percent of correct answers followed by process feedback (an explanation of *how* the answer was obtained)	2	2	2	2	.01	ns	2	2	C§	—	.02§
35. Percent of correct answers followed by a new question	20	5	17	7	.89	ns	18	6	.18	.43	.01
Using praise and criticism											
36. Percent of academic interactions that included teacher praise	7	4	14	7	6.99	.02	10	6	.12	-.35	.04
37. Percent of academic praise that specified what was being praised	6	5	3	2	4.08	.06	4	4	.13	.37	.04
38. Percent of academic interactions that included teacher criticism	1	<1	1	1	.01	ns	1	1	.07	.26	ns
39. Percent of all criticism (academic plus behavioral) that specified desired alternatives	7	4	6	4	.24	ns	6	4	.11	.33	.06

Types of questions											
40. Percent of questions focusing on word attack skills	10	6	10	6	.00	ns	10	6	.16	.55	.02
41. Eight other categories of questions	—	—	—	—	—	ns	—	—	—	—	ns
Error rates											
42. Percent of all academic interactions that included correct answers	73	5	66	8	4.56	.04	69	7	.24	.49	< .01
43. Percent of all academic interactions that included student failure to respond to the question	10	2	14	6	3.86	.06	17	10	.12	-.35	.05
44. Average number of errors made during an oral reading turn	.60	.18	.79	.36	2.35	ns	.69	.29	.13	-.37	.03
45. Percent of oral reading turns that were completed without error	68	8	60	12	2.70	ns	.64	.11	.11	.34	.05
Corrections for misbehavior											
46. Percent of all teacher-student interactions that were corrections of misbehavior within the reading group	6	3	9	4	2.91	.10	8	4	.11	-.33	.05
47. Percent of all teacher-student interactions that were with students out of the reading group	7	4	9	5	1.06	ns	8	4	.18	-.42	.01
48. Percent of all corrections for misbehavior that were moderately severe with evident irritation	17	6	21	8	1.54	ns	26	14	.29	-.54	< .01
Use of time											
49. Average time in minutes spent in reading group lessons	24.02	3.51	22.53	6.46	.41	ns	23.28	4.99	.24	.58	< .01
50. Average time in minutes spent in teacher questions to individual students, with no use of workbooks or the basal reader	6.26	3.05	5.83	5.00	.05	ns	6.04	3.94	.24	.57	< .01
51. Percent of time spent in teacher questions to students, with no use of workbooks or the basal reader	25	11	24	19	.01	ns	25	14	.18	.48	< .01

Table 1 (continued)

RESULTS OF ANALYSES OF CLASSROOM PROCESS VARIABLES

Classroom Process Variable	Treatment Implementation Data*						Process-Product Data†				
	Mean Score	Standard Deviation	Mean Score	Standard Deviation	F	p	Mean Score	Standard Deviation	Difference in R^2	Beta	p
Content covered and curriculum used											
52. Percent of reading groups that used the Economy series as principal basals	63	49	24	44	12.38	< .01	43	50	‖	–	.02‖
53. Percent of reading groups that used the Harcourt Brace Jovanovich series as principal basals	8	27	30	47	6.29	.01	18	39	.00	.01	ns
54. Percent of reading groups that used the Houghton Mifflin series as principal basals	24	43	45	51	3.84	.05	35	48	.01	-.10	ns
55. Number of basals completed by each reading group	5.11	1.06	4.52	1.58	3.48	.06	4.77	1.32	#	–	< .01#

*N=10 classes for each group except for Variables 52-55, where N=38 reading groups for the treatment group and 34 reading groups for the control group.

†N=20 classes except for Variables 52-55, where N=66 reading groups.

‡There was a significant *interaction* with entering readiness. For classes that were higher in entering readiness, the slope was negative. For classes that were lower in entering readiness, the slope was positive.

§The relationship with achievement was *curvilinear*, such that moderate amounts of the behavior were related to higher achievement.

‖There was a significant *interaction* with entering readiness. For classes that were higher in entering readiness, the slope was positive. For classes that were lower in entering readiness, the slope was negative.

#There was a significant *interaction* with entering readiness. Although both higher and lower groups showed a positive slope (and the test for the total group revealed that it was significantly different than zero), classes with higher entering readiness had a steeper slope than classes with lower entering readiness.

This table is adapted from Table 3 in L. Anderson, C. Everton, and J. Brophy, An experimental study of effective teaching in first grade reading groups. *Elementary School Journal* (1979), *79*, 193-223. Copyright 1979 by University of Chicago Press.

before being exposed to the treatment). For other principles, the scores of the treatment teachers were significantly higher than those of the control teachers, but were not high in an absolute sense. Such data indicate that the treatment succeeded in increasing the frequency of certain teacher behavior, but not in bringing that behavior to a high frequency or consistency. Finally, the data for some principles reveal low scores for both groups, indicating that the treatment failed to induce the teachers to follow the principles.

The first 6 variables in the table concern getting the lesson organized and started (Principles 1 and 2). These data indicate that the treatment teachers were more successful in that they spent only about 9 percent of their lesson time in transitions, compared to 13 percent for the control group. The data on teacher and student seating marginally favor the treatment group, but the scores are moderate rather than high, indicating room for improvement. Both groups of teachers tended to begin the transition with a signal, and neither group tended to begin the lesson with a signal. Thus, although the group differences were all in the right direction and the treatment teachers spent less time in transitions than did the control teachers, implementation of Principles 1 and 2 was only moderate except for beginning transitions with a signal. The very low implementation scores for beginning lessons with a signal suggest that this procedure (recommended on the theory that young children need a lot of structure) may be unnecessary or somehow inappropriate by the time children begin first grade.

Implementation of Principles 3-6 is reflected in the scores for introducing the lesson and the material to the students. There was no significant group difference on any of these variables and the absolute scores suggested a small degree of implementation. Treatment teachers began only about half of their lessons with an overview (compared to almost two-thirds for the control group). They did present most new words at the beginning of the lesson and usually gave clues about how to read these words, but they usually did not have the students repeat new words aloud (here again, perhaps this suggestion is important for preschoolers but unnecessary for first graders). Finally, the demonstrations of the treatment teachers were rated as only fair and no better than those of the control teachers.

Principles 7-11 call for the teacher to control response opportunities by using the patterned turns method and occasionally calling on nonvolunteers. Data relevant to these principles appear as variables 12-21 in the table. These data indicate that the treatment teachers provided about the same number of reading turns to their students as did the control teachers, but that the treatment teachers asked more questions. Most of this difference was accounted for by questions asked before or after rather than during reading turns, suggesting that the treatment teachers did more group instruction and recitation in their reading groups than the control teachers did.

The remaining data in this section of the table indicate that the treatment teachers generally followed the patterned turns recommendation, and minimized volunteering, call outs, and choral responses. Taken together, the data in this section indicate good implementation of Principles 7-11, with the treatment teachers' scores usually differing significantly from those of the control teachers.

No data in the table relate directly to Principles 9 or 12. Principle 9 suggests that teachers occasionally question students about previous responses by other students, as a way to keep everyone alert and accountable during their peers' reading turns. Neither group of teachers did this often enough to generate reliable data, so that principle clearly was not implemented. Perhaps such alerting and accountability behaviors are not necessary in small group activities in which the students are seated in close proximity to the teacher. In any case, none of the teachers had serious classroom management problems.

Principle 12 suggests that teachers avoid leading questions or rhetorical questions, and that they avoid answering their own questions or repeating them before students respond. The data indicated that these undesirable questions did not appear often enough to generate reliable scores. This can be taken as evidence of high implementation by the treatment group, although the equally good scores for the control group indicate that first grade teachers typically do not ask these types of questions in reading groups.

Principles 13-16 call for dismissing students who have mastered objectives in order to concentrate on those who need extra help. The data indicate that teachers only rarely subdivided their reading groups for these purposes, with no significant difference between the treatment and control groups. The data do not reveal whether teachers did not implement these suggestions because they were unnecessary (teachers try to keep the groups, usually organized by achievement level, together so gross disparities may be rare), or whether the teachers should have used these techniques but failed to do so.

Principles 17-20 call for the teacher to wait for a response to each question (and to make sure the other children wait also rather than calling out answers), and to give feedback about the correctness of the response. If the response is incomplete or incorrect, teachers are to give the answer, but to simplify the question and seek an improved response when possible. Judging the degree of implementation of these principles is difficult, because of the even more basic need to maintain lesson momentum and student involvement. Thus, ideal percentages for some of these variables are not clear. In any case, data indicated that the treatment teachers more often stayed with students and attempted to improve their response (i.e., provided "sustaining" feedback), instead of giving the answer or calling on someone else (i.e., providing "terminal" feedback). Teachers gave sustaining feedback more frequently when a student could not answer a question, than when a student read incorrectly during reading turns (when teachers more typically supplied the word). In any case, the treatment teachers not only sought to improve student answers more often than the control teachers did, but were more successful in doing so.

Both groups of teachers gave process feedback (explaining how an answer is derived rather than just giving the answer itself) following only 3 percent of students' incorrect answers. Although the importance of providing explanations when children are confused was not included among the treatment principles (in retrospect, we realize that it should have been), we were surprised at how seldom teachers offered these explanations following inadequate student responses. Given that these are basic skills lessons involving a great deal of rote learning, simply providing the correct answer may often be the best (or at least an adequate) form of feedback. This is unlikely to be true 97 percent of the time, however.

Both groups of teachers gave feedback following virtually all incorrect answers (no data on this appear in the table because there was not enough variance to analyze). Feedback following correct answers was also very high, although the mean for the control group was unexpectedly higher than the mean for the treatment group (96 percent versus 90 percent). Control teachers also repeated correct answers somewhat more often than the treatment teachers (40 percent versus 31 percent). Each group asked a follow up question after eliciting an original correct response about 20 percent of the time, and provided process feedback (explanations) following correct answers only about 2 percent of the time (explanations would not ordinarily be expected following correct answers, so these low percentages are not as surprising as the low percentages of process explanations following incorrect answers).

Principles 21 and 22 called for teachers to praise moderately and criticize infrequently, always specifying what they were praising or criticizing. The data indicated treatment effects in that the treatment teachers praised half as often as the control teachers and were twice as likely to specify what they were praising. The treatment teachers rarely criticized their students' academic responses (this was true of the control teachers as well); when they did, they were slightly more likely to specify desired alternative behavior (this difference was not significant). These comparisons of the treatment with the control teachers suggest good implementation, but the absolute percentages tell a different story. Even in the treatment group, only 6 percent of praise statements specified what was being praised; only 7 percent of criticisms specified desirable alternative behaviors.

What the ideal percentages here should be is not clear, because the reason for praise or criticism is often understood in context so that specific elaboration is not necessary. Even so, such elaboration probably is appropriate one-third or one-half of the time, and not less than 10 percent of the time, as observed here.

Variables 40-55 on the table present information on reading group processes that were not directly mentioned in the treatment. These data indicate no group differences in the kinds of questions asked the students, in performance during oral reading, in frequency of severe misbehavior, or in the average time spent in reading group lessons or recitation activities. The treatment teachers less often failed to obtain any response at all when they asked questions, and they more often obtained correct answers from their students. Some of this difference may be attributed to the simplification procedures and the general emphasis on obtaining correct answers which were included in the treatment. Perhaps the treatment also had indirect effects by making teachers more aware of their questioning strategies and of "programing for success" in their students' reading group experiences.

Although neither group of teachers had serious management problems, the treatment teachers had to correct misbehavior within the reading group less often (6 percent of their interactions with students were for this purpose, compared to 9 percent for the control teachers). Some of this difference may be attributed specifically to the difference in student seating (Variable 6 on the table) noted earlier, although some improvement in smooth functioning of reading groups could be expected from implementation of the treatment as a whole.

Finally, information on content covered and curriculum used identified two important differences between the groups. First, the treatment teachers covered more basals during the year (an average of 5.11 compared to 4.52 for the control teachers), so that the differences in achievement may be due in part to differences in content covered (which in turn would be due in part to the effects of some of the treatment principles, especially those dealing with management and time use). Second, the teachers used different curricula. The treatment teachers used the Economy series with 63 percent of their groups, the Harcourt Brace Jovanovich series with 8 percent, and the Houghton Mifflin series with 24 percent. In contrast, the control group used the Economy series with only 24 percent of their groups, the Harcourt Brace Jovanovich series with 30 percent, and the Houghton Mifflin series with 45 percent.

Process-Product Relationships

The data from the 20 classrooms observed (10 treatment and 10 control) were combined into a single sample of 20 classrooms for purposes of assessing the relationships between classroom process variables and adjusted student achievement scores. These analyses involved comparisons of linear regression models testing possible relationships between classroom behavior and achievement: curvilinear, linear and interactive, linear and noninteractive, or no relationship. The results of these analyses are shown in the table. The R^2 difference column indicates the increase in predictive power achieved by including the classroom process variable in equations along with the initial reading readiness scores. The p-values given in the last column of the table indicate the level of statistical significance associated with the increase in R^2 produced by the process variable (and thus the likelihood that the observed relationship between variance in the process variable and variance in adjusted achievement is due to chance). Low p-values suggest statistically significant process-product relationships.

The results of most regression analyses indicated simple, noninteractive linear relationships between the process variable and adjusted achievement. In these cases, beta weights are given to indicate the direction and relative size of the relationship. Where results indicated nonlinear or interactive relationships, beta weights are omitted and an explanation is given at the bottom of the table.

There were no significant relationships for beginning transitions or lessons with signals. The data on seating, however, supported the notion that the teacher should be able to monitor both the reading group and the rest of the class, and the data on transitions indicated that minimizing time spent in transitions and beginning lessons promptly were associated with achievement gain.

Data on introducing the lesson and the material to the students showed no significant relationships for introducing new words specifically at the beginning of the lesson, or for having the students repeat new words. However, expected positive relationships were observed for beginning lessons with overviews of the content and objectives, and for cueing recognizable features or giving other word attack information in the process of presenting new words to the students. Surprisingly, the ratings for sufficiency of demonstrations showed no relationship with learning gain.

The data on calling on individual students to read or answer questions indicated that higher achievement was associated with longer, more error free reading turns and with inclusion of frequent questions about the reading in addition to opportunities to read. Variable 15 (number of academic interactions per minute during reading turns) has a negative relationship to achievement gain. These interactions occur because the student makes mistakes and needs help or correction from the teacher. Thus, students of the more successful teachers not only did better on end-of-year achievement tests but read more successfully in everyday lessons, possibly because their teachers more often began lessons with overviews, taught word attack skills when introducing new words, and concerned themselves with reading comprehension in addition to the mechanics of oral reading.

As expected, the "patterned turns" method of calling on students to read was positively associated with learning gain, and choral responses and call-outs were correlated negatively (although occasionally allowing the group to call out answers was positively associated with learning gain in low ability groups). In general, the data support the notion that the teacher should control public response opportunities by using the patterned turns method, training the students to wait their turns and respect the turns of their peers, and discouraging calling out answers or handwaving.

We believe that this approach is effective for two reasons. First, it insures roughly equal participation by all group members. Theoretically, calling on students randomly should produce the same effect, but research on teacher-student interaction (reviewed in Brophy and Good, 1974) indicates that the brighter and more assertive students garner many more public response opportunities than slower or more reticent students, even when teachers believe they are distributing response opportunities randomly and equally. Second, the patterned turns method imposes structure and predictability on group interaction. Slower or more anxious students probably are reassured by such structure, and brighter and more assertive students are discouraged from attempting to get the teacher to call on them.

The interaction of group call-out effects with readiness scores was similar to earlier findings of Brophy and Evertson (1976) indicating interaction between call-out effects and student socioeconomic status. The general implication of such data seems to be that teachers must retain tight control over public response opportunities in classes where many of the students are high achieving and eager to respond (so that everyone will get equal opportunities and attention will focus on the academic content rather than on the "contest" to see on whom the teacher will call). In contrast, in classrooms where most students are low achievers, and especially where many students are anxious or alienated during academic activities, the teacher may need to concentrate on getting acceptable academic responses (or in some cases, any responses at all). Here, occasional call outs may be acceptable or even productive.

No significant relationships were observed for behaviors relevant to Principles 13-16, probably because these behaviors were very rarely observed. As noted earlier, the problem of gross discrepancy in mastery of lesson objectives by subgroups within reading groups may not occur often in homogeneous reading groups, so that these principles may not be relevant.

The data on responding to incorrect answers and response failures showed the expected positive relationships for attempting to improve responses by paraphrasing or simplifying questions rather than merely giving the student the answer. These relationships were stronger for teacher reactions to incorrect answers to questions than for teacher reactions to incorrect reading during reading turns, and stronger for reactions to failures to respond than for reactions to incorrect responses. Thus, it was especially important for teachers to get some kind of response from the student, and to work for an improved response when there was no danger of losing lesson momentum and the question was amenable to rephrasing or simplification.

These teachers used sustaining feedback (stayed with the student to attempt to improve the response) 47 percent of the time, and terminal feedback (giving the answer or calling on someone else) 53 percent of the time (Variable 24). They were successful in improving the response about 70 percent of the time that they attempted to do so (Variable 30). There was no significant relationship with learning for the percentage of the time that teachers used sustaining feedback successfully rather than unsuccessfully (most teachers had high scores on this measure in any case), but the frequency of use of sustaining feedback was positively associated with learning gain. Thus, most attempts to improve student response were successful, and higher frequencies of such attempts were associated with greater learning gain.

It had been expected that, when terminal feedback was necessary, it would be better for the teacher to supply the answer rather than to call on another student. However, this variable did not yield a significant relationship with learning gain (Variable 27).

The data on teacher reactions to correct answers contained some surprises. First, repetition of correct answers was not associated significantly with learning gain (and the nonsignificant trend was negative). Thus, there was no support for the value of this teacher behavior. Contrary to expectation, failure to give feedback following correct answers was *positively* associated with learning gain. Note, however, that this behavior occurred only 7 percent of the time. That is, the teachers did affirm the correctness of 93 percent of the students' correct answers. Thus, data for Variable 33 do not suggest that feedback following correct answers is unimportant. Instead, they suggest that such feedback can be omitted occasionally when it does not seem to be necessary (most probably during fast paced reviews or drills in which most answers are correct and students understand that the teacher will simply move on following a correct response).

The percentage of correct answers that were followed by a new question was positively associated with learning gain, providing more support for the value of sustaining rather than terminal feedback reactions to student responses. The relationship of process feedback following correct answers to learning gain was curvilinear, indicating that an optimal amount was preferable to either too much or too little. However, this finding was based on a behavior that occurred only 2 percent of the time, so it probably is not stable.

The data on academic praise confirmed expectations in that the frequency of such praise was negatively associated with learning gain, but the specificity of such praise was positively associated. These data support the notion that the quality of academic praise is more important than its frequency.

Academic criticism showed no significant relationship to learning gain, possibly in part because it was rare; despite its rarity, the specificity of such criticism did correlate positively with learning gain, as expected. The larger implication from these praise and criticism data is that teachers' feedback to students' academic responses should stress substantive information about their responses, rather than intensive praise or criticism, which may be intrusive or distracting.

Data on teacher behaviors not included in the instructional model indicated that the more successful teachers asked more word attack questions, were more successful in eliciting correct answers to the questions they asked, were more likely to elicit a substantive response (even if incorrect) than to accept student failure to make any response at all, were less likely to correct their students for misbehavior, spent more time teaching reading group lessons, and spent more time questioning their students. Their students made fewer errors during reading turns and completed more basal readers during the year. Use of the Economy reading series was associated with greater learning gain in high ability groups but lesser learning gain in low ability groups. Use of the Harcourt Brace Jovanovich and Houghton Mifflin series was unrelated to learning gain. Thus, although the treatment and control teachers differed in their degree of use of the three basal series, these differences cannot explain the differential effects of the groups of teachers on student reading achievement. Presumably these effects were due to instructional methods rather than curricula and materials.

Discussion

Our experiment was successful in obtaining its predicted effects in at least two ways. First, the two treatment groups outperformed the control group, indicating that the treatment led to better student achievement, and that this effect did not depend on the presence of classroom observers. Second, many of the principles included in the model were both well implemented by the treatment teachers and significantly associated with student achievement gain: frequent individualized opportunity to read and answer questions, minimal choral responses, patterned turns and teacher control of active participation in lessons, working for improved responses when initial responses were inadequate (sustaining feedback), moderate use of praise, and efficient group organization and time management. To an extent, we can say that the experiment produced the expected results for the expected reasons.

There are complications, however. Some principles were not well implemented, even though the process-product data again verified their relationship to student learning gain (appropriate teacher seating, beginning lessons with overviews, being specific when praising or criticizing). Other principles were implemented but did not have the expected relationships with learning gain (minimizing response opportunities obtained by volunteering, providing affirmative feedback following each correct answer). Other principles were not implemented at all (beginning lessons with a signal, breaking the group into subgroups in order to concentrate on those who needed extra instruction), or were implemented to some degree but did not have the expected relationship to learning gain (beginning transitions with a signal, seating the students as directed, giving new words at the beginning of the lesson, having the students repeat new words, giving demonstrations rated as sufficient). Finally, the process-product data showed that several teaching variables not addressed by the treatment model nevertheless were associated with student learning gain. There were treatment versus control group differences on some of these variables (content covered, student success rate, rate of corrections for misconduct) but not others (including word attack clues when presenting new words, time spent in lessons, time spent in question/answer format, frequency of word attack questions).

Taken together the data provide a degree of support for the model and indicate a need for revising and extending it. Many of the elements most consistently supported in the data are the same ones that receive consistent support in process-product research (Brophy, 1979; Good, 1979): allocation of adequate time for instruction (allocated time); an academic emphasis and use of efficient classroom organization and management skills to insure that most of the time allocated to academic activities is actually spent engaged in those activities (engaged time); selection of appropriate academic activities, backed by effective instruction, to enable students to make continuous progress but in small steps with high rates of success

(success rate); frequent lessons involving presentation of information, recitation, drill, or supervised practice (active teaching, in which the teacher carries the content to the students personally rather than expecting them to learn largely on their own in independent activities). In addition, there was support for elements of instruction specific to primary grade reading groups: the patterned turns method for regulating overt participation, questioning the students about the reading in addition to having them read and giving word attack information and asking word attack questions in addition to presenting new words and supervising reading practice.

Other instructional principles were not supported by the data and may need to be dropped or revised (their distributions showed good variance, and yet they were not associated with achievement gain in the expected ways). The data are ambiguous about still other variables (their distributions did not show enough variance to allow a reliable test of their relationship to achievement gain). These subtleties, as well as interpretive complications such as interactional or curvilinear relationships, must be taken into account in drawing instructional implications from the data.

For example, the data simply do not support the notion that it is important to have the students repeat new words after they are presented, so it is probably best to drop this principle from the model. Other principles were rarely implemented, either because they are unnecessary or irrelevant in the first grade reading group context or because they were too unfamiliar or difficult for the teachers to acquire from the minimal treatment used in this experiment. Some of these principles probably are unnecessary and can be eliminated or minimized in importance (using a standard signal to begin each lesson; using particular students as language models for other students). Other principles that were rarely implemented nevertheless appear to be valid and deserving of remaining in the model. Some of these are supported by the process-product data (beginning lessons with overviews, being specific when praising or criticizing, giving process explanations following incorrect answers). Others remain essentially untested, but might show the expected relationships with achievement gain if teachers could be induced to implement them sufficiently (breaking up the group to concentrate remedial instruction on those who need it most). Still other principles should be retained largely intact but elaborated or qualified to take into account exceptions or special cases (giving affirmative feedback following correct answers, minimizing volunteer and call-out response opportunities, giving process explanations following correct answers).

Conclusion

Guided by the data obtained in this experiment, we have revised our treatment model by eliminating some principles, adding others, and qualifying or elaborating most of the rest. In addition, we have reorganized the model to highlight the basic ideas and to structure and sequence its content more logically. The revised model appears in Figure 2. It should be adaptable to most small group instruction in beginning reading.

Figure 2. Anderson, Evertson, and Brophy's revised principles for small group instruction in beginning reading (1982).

General Principles

1. Reading groups should be organized for efficient, sustained focus on the content.
2. All students should not be merely attentive but actively involved in the lesson.
3. The difficulty level of questions and tasks should be easy enough to allow the lesson to move along at a brisk pace and the students to experience consistent success.
4. Students should receive frequent opportunities to read and respond to questions, and should get clear feedback about the correctness of their performance.
5. Skills should be mastered to overlearning, with new ones gradually phased in while old ones are being mastered.
6. Although instruction takes place in the group setting, monitor each individual and provide whatever instruction, feedback, or opportunities to practice are required.

Specific Principles

Programming for Continuous Progress

1. *Time.* Across the year, reading groups should average 25-30 minutes each. The length will depend on student attention level, which varies with time of year, student ability level, and the skills being taught.
2. *Academic focus.* Successful reading instruction includes not only organization and management of the reading group itself, but effective management of the students who are working independently. Provide these students with: appropriate assignments; rules and routines to follow when they need help or information (to minimize their need to interrupt you as you work with your reading group); and activity options available when they finish their work (so they have something else to do).
3. *Pace.* Both progress though the curriculum and pacing within specific activities should be brisk, producing continuous progress achieved with relative ease (small steps, high success rate).

4. *Error rate.* Expect to get correct answers to about 80 percent of your questions in reading groups. More errors can be expected when students are working on new skills (perhaps 20-30 percent). Continue with practice and review until smooth, rapid, correct performance is achieved. Review responses should be almost completely (perhaps 95 percent) correct.

Organizing the Group

5. *Seating.* Arrange seating so that you can work with the reading group and monitor the rest of the class at the same time.
6. *Transitions.* Teach the students to respond immediately to a signal to move into the reading group (bringing their books or other materials), and to make quick, orderly transitions between activities.
7. *Getting started.* Start lessons quickly once the students are in the group (have your materials prepared beforehand).

Introducing Lessons and Activities

8. *Overviews.* Begin with an overview to provide students with a mental set and help them anticipate what they will be learning.
9. *New words.* When presenting new words, do not merely say the word and move on. Usually, you should show the word and offer phonetic clues to help students learn to decode.
10. *Work assignments.* Be sure that students know what to do and how to do it. Before releasing them to work on activities independently, have them demonstrate how they will accomplish these activities.

Insuring Everyone's Participation

11. *Ask questions.* In addition to having the students read, ask them questions about the words and materials. This helps keep students attentive during classmates' reading turns, and allows you to call their attention to key concepts or meanings.
12. *Ordered turns.* Use a system, such as going in order around the group, to select students for reading or answering questions. This insures that all students have opportunities to participate, and it simplifies group management by eliminating handwaving and other student attempts to get you to call on them.
13. *Minimize call outs.* In general, minimize student call outs and emphasize that students must wait their turns and respect the turns of others. Occasionally, you may want to allow call outs to pick up the pace or encourage interest, especially with low achievers or students who do not normally volunteer. If so, give clear instructions or devise a signal to indicate that you intend to allow call outs at these times.
14. *Monitor individuals.* Be sure that everyone, especially slow students, is checked, receives feedback, and achieves mastery. Ordinarily this will require questioning each individual student, and not relying on choral responses.

Teacher Questions and Student Answers

15. *Academic focus.* Concentrate your questions on the academic content; do not overdo questions about personal experiences. Most questions should be about word recognition or sentence or story comprehension.
16. *Word attack questions.* Include word attack questions that require students to decode words or identify sounds within words.
17. *Wait for answers.* In general, wait for an answer if the student is still thinking about the question and may be able to respond. However, do not continue waiting if the student seems lost or is becoming embarrassed, or if you are losing the other students' attention.
18. *Give needed help.* If you think the student cannot respond without help but may be able to reason out the correct answer if you do help, provide help by simplifying the question, rephrasing the question, or giving clues.

19. *Giving the answer when necessary.* When the student is unable to respond, give the answer or call on someone else. In general, focus the attention of the group on the answer, and not on the failure to respond.
20. *Explain the answer when necessary.* If the question requires one to develop a response by applying a chain of reasoning or step-by-step problem solving, explain the steps one goes through to arrive at the answer in addition to giving the answer itself.

When the Student Responds Correctly
21. *Acknowledging correctness (unless it is obvious).* Briefly acknowledge the correctness of the response (nod positively, repeat the answer, say "right," etc.), unless it is obvious to the students that their answers are correct (such as during fast paced drills reviewing old material).
22. *Explain the answer when necessary.* Even after correct answers, feedback that emphasizes the methods used to get answers will often be appropriate. Onlookers may need this information to understand why the answer is correct.
23. *Follow up questions.* Occasionally, you may want to address one or more follow up questions to the same student. Such series of related questions can help the student to integrate relevant information. Or, you may want to extend a line of questioning to its logical conclusion.

Praise and Criticism
24. *Praise in moderation.* Praise only occasionally (no more than perhaps 10 percent of correct responses). Frequent praise, especially if nonspecific, is probably less useful than more informative feedback.
25. *Specify what is praised.* When you do praise, specify what is being praised, if this is not obvious to the student and the onlookers.
26. *Correction, not criticism.* Routinely inform students whenever they respond incorrectly, but in ways that focus on the academic content and include corrective feedback. When it is necessary to criticize (typically only about 1 percent of the time when students fail to respond correctly), be specific about what is being criticized and about desired alternative behaviors.

References

Anderson, L., Evertson, C., and Brophy, J. An experimental study of effective teaching in first grade reading groups. *Elementary School Journal,* 1979, *79,* 193-223.

Anderson, L., Evertson, C., and Brophy, J. *The first grade reading group study: Technical report of experimental effects and process-outcome relationships.* Report No. 4070. Austin, TX: Research and Development Center for Teacher Education, University of Texas at Austin, 1978.

Anderson, L., Evertson, C., and Brophy, J. *Principles of small group instruction in elementary reading.* Occasional Paper No. 58. East Lansing, MI: Institute for Research on Teaching, Michigan State University, 1982.

Blank, M. *Teaching learning in the preschool: A dialogue approach.* Columbus, OH: Charles Merrill, 1973.

Brophy, J. Teacher behavior and its effects. *Journal of Educational Psychology,* 1979, *71,* 733-750.

Brophy, J. Teacher praise: A functional analysis. *Review of Educational Research,* 1981, *51,* 5-32.

Brophy, J., and Evertson, C. *Learning from teaching: A developmental perspective.* Boston: Allyn and Bacon, 1976.

Brophy, J., and Good, T. *Teacher-student relationships: Causes and consequences.* New York: Holt, Rinehart and Winston, 1974.

Dunkin, M., and Biddle, B. *The study of teaching.* New York: Holt, Rinehart and Winston, 1974.

Flanders, N. *Analyzing teacher behavior.* Reading, MA: Addison-Wesley, 1970.

Good, T. Teacher effectiveness in the elementary school: What we know about it now. *Journal of Teacher Education,* 1979, *30,* 52-64.

Kounin, J. *Discipline and group management in classrooms.* New York: Holt, Rinehart and Winston, 1970.

National Institute of Education. Panel reports from the National Conference on Studies in Teaching (10 reports). Washington, DC: U.S. Department of Health, Education, and Welfare, National Institute of Education, 1974.

Nuthall, G., and Church, J. Experimental studies of teaching behaviour. In G. Chanon (Ed.), *Toward a science of teaching.* London: National Foundation for Educational Research, 1973.

Rosenshine, B., and Furst, N. The use of direct observation to study teaching. In M.W. Travers (Ed.), *Second handbook of research on teaching.* Chicago: Rand McNally, 1973.

Rosenshine, B., and Stevens, R. Classroom instruction in reading. In P.D. Pearson (Ed.), *Handbook of reading research.* New York: Longman, 1984.

Southwest Educational Development Laboratory. *Bilingual kindergarten program inservice manual, Volume 1.* Austin, TX: National Educational Laboratory Publishers, 1973.

Jane A. Stallings

4

Effective Use of Time in Secondary Reading Programs

This chapter reports the findings of Phase I of a three phase study, Teaching Basic Reading Skills in Secondary Schools. The purpose of this study was to identify effective instructional strategies for teaching secondary students to read competently. The National Institute of Education funded this study as part of its effort to address a growing national concern about those students graduating from high schools who are functionally illiterate. This problem was dramatically illuminated in several malpractice suits filed against school systems by disillusioned parents of graduated students who could not fill out job applications or pass reading exams given by the United States Army (Saretsky, 1973).

Plummeting test scores from 1957-1975 reported by Harnischfeger and Wiley (1975) and confirmed by school districts throughout the country have stimulated many state legislatures and school boards to draw up lists of educational standards that students in high schools should meet at various stages of their education. The movement has spread so rapidly that all but four states now have competency tests for graduation.

Testing students to assess deficiencies in basic skills is useful only if strong remediation measures are taken. In several states, legislation mandates that all students failing the competency test must be provided with school programs that will make it possible for them to gain the skills required to pass the test. The requirement that secondary schools provide remediation for all of these students has had a great impact on school planning. We were particularly interested in how reading was being taught since a poor reader is likely to have difficulty in all subject matter classes. Our hunch was that strategies identified by research as being effective in teaching reading in elementary classrooms would also be effective in teaching reading to secondary students.

Most of the research relating institutional processes to student outcomes has been conducted in elementary schools (e.g., Fisher and Berliner, 1978; Good, 1978; McDonald and Elias, 1976; and Soar, 1973). The process variables most often found to be related to achievement are carefully structured, teacher directed activities and the amount of time students spent on reading tasks. The Brophy and Evertson (1974) study of seventh and eighth grades in Austin, Texas indicated that efficient teaching strategies for reading were related to student on-task behavior and that misbehavior had a negative relationship with achievement. In their study of first and third grade Follow Through classrooms, Stallings and Kaskowitz (1974) found an interaction between classroom process variables, student entering school scores, and student reading achievement scores. Comprehensive reviews of the effective teaching research can be found in the March 1983 *Elementary School Journal* and in Brophy's chapter in *Handbook of Research on Teaching*, third edition (in press).

A Brief Description of the Three Phase Project

This three phase study of Teaching Basic Reading Skills in Secondary Schools is unique among research studies in that it provided participating secondary school districts a process for using research findings in a regenerative way. In Phase I, forty-three secondary reading classrooms were observed and the relationships between teaching processes and students' gain in reading were examined. The results of this study provided some specific guidelines for efficient instructional strategies to use with secondary remedial reading students. Of the teachers in the study, 50 percent had training to teach reading. Of those, only 20 percent had reading credentials. Interestingly, student achievement gain was not found to be greater in the classrooms of teachers with reading credentials (Stallings, et al., 1978).

In Phase II, findings regarding effective lesson design and classroom interactions were translated for use in a teacher training program. This program included a series of six workshops. These were provided to forty-seven teachers in seven school districts. One-half of the teachers in each district were trained and the other half were in a control group that did not receive training until the end of the experiment. The workshops were well attended, and experimental teachers changed behaviors on 26 out of 31 variables in recommended ways. What is more important, their students made more reading gain than did students of teachers in the control group (Stallings, Needels, & Stayrook, 1979). Teachers were enthusiastic about the program and recommended that training be offered to other teachers in their districts.

To accommodate these requests, which were beyond the scope of our staff, we developed the Phase III dissemination program in which we monitored trained teachers as they trained other teachers in their districts. This three phase effort left the districts with a cadre of teacher trainers to carry on the process of training secondary teachers to use effective methods for helping students gain basic reading skills. The dissemination model was subsequently funded by the National Diffusion Network and twenty Certified Trainers are now administering the Effective Use of Time Program in thirteen different states.

Only Phase I of the project which identified effective teaching strategies will be reported here.

Phase I Design

The Phase I design was based on two premises. The first was that teaching processes could be identified that predict test scores and absence rates at the junior and senior high school level. A second premise was that, at the secondary level, the processes related to achievement would be similar to those reported for elementary classrooms in the Follow Through Planned Variation evaluation.

Phase I was designed to test four hypotheses which were based on the empirical findings of the Follow Through Planned Variation study (Stallings & Kaskowitz, 1974):

1. Teacher reinforcement of correct responses and guidance for incorrect responses are positively related to academic achievement. The value of feedback has been well documented in learning theory and in the Follow Through studies.
2. The frequency of reading related verbal interactions is positively related to student achievement in reading.
3. The number of social interactions that occurs during class has a negative relationship with reading achievement.
4. Student absence is related to the positive effect recorded in the classroom, i.e., the more supportive the environment, the lower the absence rate.

These hypotheses were tested by examining the relationships between instructional process variables developed from data recorded with the Secondary Observation Instrument and from Student Rating of Instructor Sales, and student reading achievement and absence rates.

For one class period, forty-three teachers representing six school districts were observed for three days (morning only). Reading scores from April 1976 to 1977 and student absence rates were obtained for as many students as possible in the classes being observed. Partial correlation and multiple regression analyses were conducted to test for relationships between instructional processes and changes on student outcome variables.

Selection of Schools and Teachers

Six San Francisco Bay Area districts were selected to be in the study on the following bases:

1. Each district had to offer remedial compensatory programs in basic skills areas at the junior or senior high school level.
2. Each district had to administer standardized achievement tests each year to all students.

3. A mix of urban, suburban, and rural school districts had to be represented in the sample.
4. Each district had to be located in northern California to minimize travel and other data collection expenses.

Within each participating district, the local Director of Special Projects identified those schools offering remedial or compensatory reading instruction either directly as a special basic skills class or indirectly through a content area course. Teachers offering such instruction were invited to an informational meeting at their schools. At this meeting, the project was described and compared with previous teacher effectiveness research. Teachers were told what demands would be made on their time, what services were required during the course of the study, and what benefits they could expect during Phase II. The research staff promised to provide individual feedback to each participating teacher regarding his or her own classroom behavior based upon the objective observations. At all sites, school administrators emphasized that participation was voluntary and, to the best of our knowledge, no pressure was exerted on teachers to participate. Criteria for acceptance in the study were that the focus of the class be on basic reading skills instruction, that the students enrolled in the class were likely to stay in that class all year, and that all students be tested with standardized achievement tests.

Of the fifty-one teachers who attended the informational meetings in December, forty-seven participated in the study. When we collected data in the spring, four teachers decided not to participate. As a result, the sample initially included forty-three classrooms with 905 students.

The study was designed to have an equal number of classrooms from each district. However, because it was impossible to complete that design, we accepted all teachers who volunteered to be in the study. Representation from the six districts is uneven, so no analysis could be conducted at the district level. Several demographic factors might affect the reading programs being provided, e.g., the amount of money available per student and the number of students with limited English speaking ability (see Table 1). These demographic differences were tested for effects upon reading scores.

Table 1

SAMPLE DISTRICT AND SCHOOL DESCRIPTORS

District / School	1 District Size	2 Per Pupil Expenditure	3 School Size	4 % Low Income	5 % Limited English Speaking	6 Number of Categorical Aid Programs	7 % Program Participants	8 Funding Per Participant
Fresno	54,749	1,331						
School A			612	79	1	3	100	487
School B			2,079	36	0	2	28	528
School C			1,286	43	10	2	92	441
School D			804	55	8	2	68	513
School E			905	20	5	1	57	522
Monterey	15,397	1,400						
School A			950	3	5	0	0	0
School B			787	4	5	0	0	0
Ravenswood	3,406	1,152						
School A			496	43	1	3	100	268
Salinas	15,447	1,475						
School A			1,926	17	15	2	19	461
School B			1,342	15	14	2	55	401
Sequoia	10,535	1,975						
School A			2,125	6	0	0	0	0
School B			2,080	6	0	0	0	0
Tulare	4,427	1,039						
School A			534	37	0	0	0	0
School B			555	16	0	0	0	0

Instruments

To describe classroom processes, we used a low inference classroom observation instrument that we modified for secondary reading classrooms. In addition, students completed a rating scale so we could assess their perceptions of their classroom processes and environment. We assessed student outcomes by means of an achievement test given by the school district, and student absence data.

*Secondary observation instrument (*SOI*).* The Secondary Observation Instrument is based upon previous observation systems developed at SRI International. As a result of workshops conducted with secondary reading teachers, we revised the instrument to permit the recording of events that occur in junior and senior high school reading classrooms.

The SOI objectively and comprehensively records the instructional and social activities of the classroom: types of classroom activities, materials, and the interactions between teachers and students. Three observations of one class are made over a five to seven day period. During each observation, five equally spaced sweeps or snapshots of the classroom are made to record classroom activities, materials used, student groupings, and student off-task rates. Over the course of three observations, fifteen such sweeps or snapshots are made. After each sweep, the observer focuses on the lead teacher and for five minutes records all persons with whom the teacher interacts. The nature of each interaction—that is, whether an interaction is academic, organizational, behavioral, or social and whether it is a question, command, comment, or response—is also recorded. A minimum of 750 interactions are recorded over three observations. The data collected are reported in terms of frequency counts or percents of time.

Reading achievement tests. District achievement scores were obtained for as many students as possible who were in the sample classrooms in the spring of 1977. All school districts used the CTBS (Comprehensive Test of Basic Skills) except for Fresno. Fresno administered the CAT. For the districts with CTBS data, a program was written to convert scores from the various forms and levels (Forms R, S, T and levels 2, 3, 4) to Form S/T standard scores.

Classroom environment scale. We used the Classroom Environment Scale, Form R (Moos and Tricket, 1974) to examine students' perceptions of the instructional process occurring in the classroom. This particular scale was normed on a sample similar to our sample population. It yields nine subscales of four items each and can be completed in approximately ten minutes. The subscale reports student perceptions of 1) involvement in classroom activities, 2) affiliation with others in the class, 3) receiving teacher support, 4) task orientation, 5) competition, 6) order and organization, 7) rule clarity, 8) teacher control, and 9) teacher innovation.

Absence rate form. Student attendance data were obtained from each classroom teacher. A form was developed by the investigators which listed each student by name and an identification number, the student's entry and leaving dates for that class, and total number of days absent categorized by excused absences, unexcused absences, and cuts. The total number of school days was also recorded.

Selecting and training data collectors. Participating school districts selected data gatherers with whom the observed teachers were likely to feel comfortable. All data gatherers were credentialed teachers; some were retired and others were regular substitutes. Training occurred over a seven day period and included coding videotapes and checking interrater agreement. An 85 percent degree of accuracy was required of each coder on a final test coding a criterion tape.

Description of the data collected. Despite efforts to create the best theoretical study plan, the realities of the experimental setting often require modification of that plan, especially in natural classrooms in real schools. During this study, several problems became apparent as the data were logged.

As a criterion for being included in the study, we had asked that classrooms have students who were assigned to that class for the entire year. In four out of forty-three classes, students were reassigned at mid-semester. We also asked that all classes focus upon basic reading skills, expecting that all students would be deficient in reading skills. We found that the grade equivalent scores of students within some classes ranged from Grade 2 to Grade 13. Most classrooms had some students scoring well above the 49th percentile on the CTBS.

We relied upon achievement test data collected at the schools and asked that all classes have fall and spring CTBS data. In Fresno and Monterey, students were tested in the spring only. Since it was our largest site, we could not eliminate Fresno from the sample. Thus, we decided to use Spring 1976 and Spring 1977 test scores for all districts. Then we found that three different levels and four different forms of the CTBS had been used in the districts. In each instance, we converted the total reading raw score (for the CTBS form and level) to the appropriate standard score. While standard scores for Forms Q and R are equivalent, they must be converted for comparison to standard scores for Forms S and T. All test scores were converted into Form S/T standard scores.

One district had either Spring 1976 or Spring 1977 test data for their four classrooms. These could not be used in the analysis. One classroom with an enrollment of eight had pretest and posttest data for only one student. A decision rule was established that classrooms with fewer than one-third of the students with pretest and posttest data would not be included in the analysis. With this criterion, thirty-six of the forty-three classrooms had sufficient test data to be included in the analysis that included classroom process and test score data.

We collected complete observation data for each of the forty-three classrooms. Absentee reports were obtained from thirty-five teachers. Previous arrangements had been made with teachers to report absentee data for their classes, and they were given $10 for reporting these data. The Classroom Environment Scale was completed by 718 students.

Analysis of instructional processes. Since there was little research to guide us in our search for effective instructional processes to teach reading in secondary schools, we elected to use partial correlations (a shotgun approach) to identify significant relationships between the variables of interest. Given that secondary students needing remediation might range in reading level from first grade to sixth grade, classrooms were grouped to see how effective teaching processes might differ for different reading achievement levels.

Correlations. Our purpose was to identify how effective teachers used their available classroom time. To see how time was spent, the data were organized according to time spent in management and organization, interactive instruction, student seatwork, and off task behavior (see Table 2).

TABLE 2
PARTIAL CORRELATIONS OF READING CTBS SCORES
AND PROCESS VARIABLES

Organizing	*v*	*p*
Organizing interactions	-.34	.05
Teacher organizing (alone)	-.24	.05
Teacher offers students choices	-.33	.05
Intrusion/Interruptions	-.25	.05
Interactive on Task Instruction		
Review/discuss homework or seatwork	.40	.001
Teacher instructs/chalkboard	.23	.10
Students reading aloud	.59	.001
Praise and support	.25	.05
Teachers guide to correct solution	.52	.001
Drill and practice	.29	.05
Seatwork		
Student silent reading	-.30	.05
Sustained silent reading	-.20	.10
Written assignments	-.21	.10
Off Task		
Social interactions	-.52	.001
Negative interactions	-.29	.05

The correlations indicate that students of teachers who spent more class time organizing made less gain in reading than did students in classrooms of more efficient teachers. A negative relationship was found between students' reading gain and teachers offering students a number of choices about materials and activities. Intrusions from loudspeakers, tardy students, and pull out programs were also negatively related to reading gain.

In classrooms where teachers were effective organizers and provided more interactive instruction, students made more gain in reading. In this situation, the teacher reviewed and discussed homework or seatwork. Students were acknowledged or praised for correct work and guided to acceptable answers when necessary. When presenting new work, effective teachers used the chalkboard or overhead to structure lessons.

Gains in reading were greater in classrooms where students more often read aloud. The principal investigator went to the classrooms identified as effective and made anecdotal records of how teachers carried out oral reading activities and specifically how time was used. The strategies used in oral reading activities are explained in the following sections.

The indepth study of effective teachers indicated that those who allocated 35 percent or less of class time to seatwork had students who gained more in reading. Those teachers also actively monitored that seatwork. In our sample, the time students spent doing seatwork ranged from 3 percent to 90 percent. Thus, some students seemed to have been spending nearly all of their time in seatwork activities with few teacher interactions. High rates of seatwork were associated with high off task rates and with little reading gain (see Table 2).

Overall, teachers on the average were found to distribute their time as shown in the top graph on Figure 1. Effective teachers distributed their time as shown in the bottom graph on Figure 1. Obviously, seatwork and organization are necessary. However, the benefit to student achievement is in the proportion of time teachers spend in interactive instruction. Teachers on the average spent only 12 percent of their classroom time providing interactive instruction. Teachers of classes experiencing the greatest gains in reading achievement spent more than four times that amount, or 50 percent of their time, on interactive instruction.

Comparison of Achievement Levels

Another objective of the Basic Skills Study was to examine the relationships between classroom processes and achievement by determining those processes most relevant to producing high test score gains. In order to explore these relationships, "gain" must be tempered by the level of the pretest. It was hypothesized that a classroom with a pretest-posttest difference of 50 units and an initial low test level would differ in instructional processes from a classroom with an identical gain but a high pretest level. A scattergram plotting

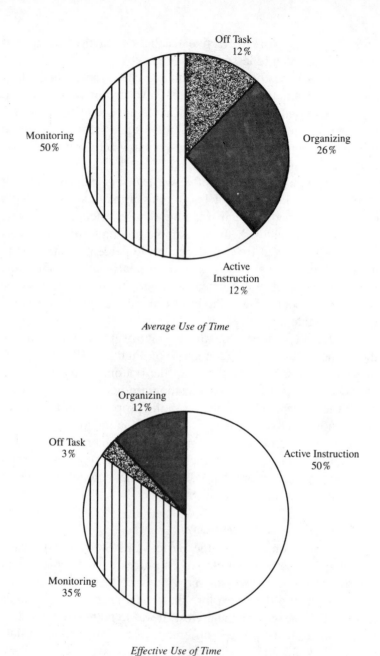

Average Use of Time

Effective Use of Time

Figure 1.   Allocated time for a 50-minute reading period.

posttest score versus pretest scores of the thirty-six classrooms was created to attempt a clustering of classes on the basis of pretest level and amount of test score gain. For ease of interpretation, scores were transformed into grade level equivalencies (see Figure 2).

The determination of achievement groups required several steps. First, a "no gain" line was defined (posttest to pretest equals 0). Second, consistent with other studies of this type (McDonald, 1976), the gain line was set at one-third of the standard deviation of the mean class gain score above the no gain line (see Figure 2). The no gain group became those classrooms with posttest/pretest differences falling below the one-third standard deviation gain line. Twenty classes of thirty-six were identified as no gain classrooms. The remaining sixteen gain classrooms were assigned to three groups on the basis of their pretest scores. Group I initially had students achieving from the first to fifth grade level. In classrooms 2, 10, 13, and 23, on the average students made as much as two years' gain in one year. Seven Group II classrooms had students achieving at the fourth to sixth grade level who made one to two years' gain for the year. Group III had students reading at sixth grade or above and also made impressive gains during the year.

The interesting question is what might those teachers be doing that is similar within groups but different across groups? To confirm the legitimacy of the four a priori groups, a stepwise discriminant function procedure was conducted using an F-to-enter criterion of .10. Based upon prior research findings and the utility of the variables in describing classroom processes, nineteen variables were selected for the analysis. The results showed that eleven process variables and two discriminant functions correctly classified all the classrooms into the appropriate a priori groups. Therefore, the four groups should have differed in classroom processes. This analysis provided a measure of confidence in proceeding with analysis of within-group composition and intergroup differences.

Demographic characteristics of the four achievement groups are presented in Table 3. Between groups comparisons showed that gain score differences could not be explained by class size or days absent.

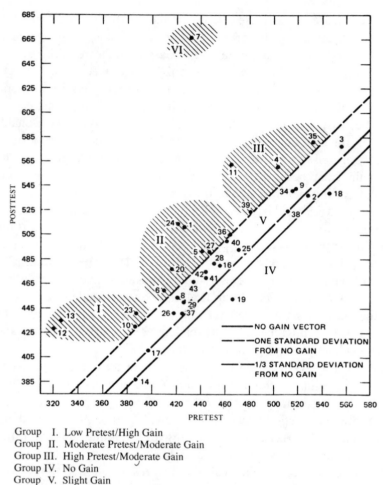

Group I. Low Pretest/High Gain
Group II. Moderate Pretest/Moderate Gain
Group III. High Pretest/Moderate Gain
Group IV. No Gain
Group V. Slight Gain
Group VI. Case Study Classroom

Figure 2. Scattergram of pretest and posttest – CTBS scores.

The principal differences between groups were found in how teachers spent the time available for instruction (see Table 4). Teachers in all gain groups (I, II, and III) were more effective managers of organizing tasks than were the no-gain teachers in Group IV. That is, teachers in the gain groups spent significantly less time completing organizational tasks than the no-gain teachers. The gain group teachers also provided more active instruction. These teachers started the class by reviewing the homework or seatwork, or they gave a quiz checking for understanding during the lesson.

Table 3

DEMOGRAPHIC CHARACTERISTICS OF THE ACHIEVEMENT GROUPS

Group	Number of Classes	Number of Students		Days Absent		Pretest Scores (CTBS)		Posttest Scores (CTBS)		Gain	
		$\overline{X}$	SD	$\overline{X}$	SD	$\overline{X}$	SD	$\overline{X}$	SD	$\overline{X}$	SD
Phase I											
I Low Pretest/ High Gain	4	26.50	2.08	13.77	4.39	354.43	35.65	433.12	5.80	78.69	33.74
II Moderate Pretest/ Moderate Gain	7	23.00	7.37	15.86	4.71	423.25	19.30	492.77	20.00	60.52	21.20
III High Pretest/ Moderate Gain	4	25.50	4.04	8.80	5.67	495.71	29.50	557.91	24.93	62.20	25.46
IV No Gain	7	22.29	4.07	10.19	6.44	465.26	64.83	470.63	63.16	5.37	11.14

Table 4

Distribution of time across activities in
four ability groups in secondary reading classrooms*

	Group 1 ($\overline{X}$ Percent)	Group II ($\overline{X}$ Percent)	Group III ($\overline{X}$ Percent)	Group IV ($\overline{X}$ Percent)
Interactive On Task Activities				
Reading aloud	21	9	1	1
Instruction	16	11	17	10
Discussion/Review	12	5	3	1
Drill and practice	4	4	4	2
Praise/support**	19	16	7	11
Corrective feedback**	20	16	4	12
Noninteractive On Task Activities				
Classroom Management	12	15	17	27
Reading silently	9	16	12	21
Written assignments	4	22	23	28
Off Task Activities				
Social interactions	5	6	3	8
Students uninvolved	6	4	4	9

Notes: Group I.   Low pretest/high gain
　　　Group II.　Moderate pretest/moderate gain
　　　Group III.　High pretest/moderate gain
　　　Group IV.　No gain.
　　　X = Group mean.

*These activities may occur simultaneously; therefore, the sum is greater than 100 percent.
**This variable is reported as frequency of occurrence per 300 interactions.

Teachers in Group I allocated more time than others to interactive activities. These teachers spent 32 percent of their time providing instructions and always structured and linked the new lessons with what was known. Drill and practice (4 percent) occurred only after students understood the concepts and vocabulary. Students in this group were provided oral reading activities 21 percent of the time.

The importance of oral reading has been stressed by several researchers (Chall, 1980; Hoffman, 1981). Hoffman, for example, argues that oral reading with provision for differential feedback is a valuable learning strategy. Chall and Hoffman encourage teachers to employ this teaching technique. Certainly the research presented here underlines the importance of oral reading for secondary reading students.

Given the controversy regarding the effectiveness of oral reading with upper grade students and our findings in Phase I that oral reading was an effective reading skill builder, the project leader made visits to the four high gain (Group I) teachers' classrooms. In three classrooms, oral reading was conducted in small groups while other students did written work or silent reading. The teachers routinely developed vocabulary and concepts before asking students to read aloud. Oral reading activities were structured to develop comprehension, not just to have students say words. After students read a few lines, the teacher would quickly check for understanding. Specific praise or guiding corrections were generously provided. Students had opportunities to listen and speak as well as to read silently and do written assignments. This combination of activities seemed to enable students to integrate what they were learning.

Teachers in Group II provided instruction, review, and drill and practice about 20 percent of the time. Their students operated from approximately the fourth to sixth grade levels. The students participated in oral reading activities (9 percent) as well as written and silent reading activities. These teachers were second highest in providing praise and support and guiding corrective feedback.

Teachers of the more able students in Group III provided a healthy amount of instruction, some review and practice, but very little oral reading. Their students spent more time working independently on written and silent reading assignments than did the other two gain groups. Teachers in these classrooms actively monitored students' seatwork, e.g., checking for understanding and correcting errors.

Group IV teachers spent a greater proportion of time than all the others in classroom management activities and a smaller proportion of time in active instruction. Their students spent more time doing seatwork and were off task more often than students in other groups.

Student Ratings and Student Outcome Data

How do students' ratings of teachers relate to student achievement and absence rates? At the secondary school level, we thought that students may be able to provide useful information regarding classroom process by reporting their experiences in the classroom.

Was the teacher prepared? Were the rules clear? Did the teacher keep control of the class? Partial correlations (holding Spring 1976 CTBS reading scores constant) were computed to examine the relationship between achievement and absences, and the student ratings.

Classroom environment scale. The Classroom Environment Scale has thirty-six items that were read aloud to students with the teacher absent from the room. The thirty-six items represent nine subscales of four items each. Table 5 reports the correlation of each subscale with student reading achievement.

Student involvement, the perception of students of their own involvement in the class, is mostly highly correlated with student achievement ($r = .27$, $p < .05$). The next highest correlations are with teacher Support (.26), Task Orientation (.26), and Order and Organization (.25). These subscales suggest that reading achievement is greater in orderly classrooms where students are involved in their tasks.

Absence rate. The absence rate of students in junior and senior high schools is a national problem. Average absence rates for the thirty-five classrooms reporting absence data ranged from six days per student per year to thirty-five days per student per year. The burden on the teacher and the learner is great when students are absent frequently.

In the Follow Through Classroom Observation Evaluation in 1972-1973, we identified instructional process variables that ac-

Table 5

PARTIAL CORRELATIONS OF THE CLASSROOM ENVIRONMENT SCALE
WITH READING ACHIEVEMENT*
(N = 718 students in 36 classrooms)

Subscales	r	p
Involvement	.27	.05
Affiliation		
Teacher support	.26	.06
Task orientation	.26	.06
Competition		
Order and organization	.25	.06
Rule clarity	.17	.16
Teacher control		
Innovation	.18	.13

*Spring 1976 CTBS reading scores were held constant.

counted for 67 percent of the variance in absence rate in grade three classrooms. In classrooms where the students had more choice of materials, activities, and work groups, and where they could ask questions and talk to one another a little more, they were absent less often. Based upon this prior research, we wanted to see whether similar classroom variables at the junior and senior high level related to student absence rate.

Pearson product moment correlations. Correlations were computed using all of the student rating subscales and selected classroom process variables with absence rate. Out of the 140 correlations, 14 were significant at $p < .05$). Variables found significantly related to student absence rates are shown on Table 6.

The subscale most related to low absence rate is Affiliation. This indicates that students go to class more frequently when they feel that students in that class are friendly. This finding is interesting but not surprising. Most people at any age prefer classes where they know and like the other students. The second subscale most related to low absence rate is Rule Clarity.

In addition, these data suggest that in classrooms where teachers were warm and supportive (Variable 120) and acknowl-

Table 6
CORRELATION OF ABSENCE RATE AND PROCESS VARIABLES
(N = 35 Classrooms)

Variable Number	Description	r	p
A	Affiliation	-.60	.001
RC	Rule clarity	-.34	.05
TEM9	Teacher discusses reading	-.34	.05
TLM9	Teacher manages classroom	-.36	.05
IAM8	Students use leisure reading books	+.34	.05
IGMS5	Students do written assignments in reading kits	-.41	.01
10	Students ask teachers questions about the task	-.32	.05
77	All teacher's acknowledgement given to students' performance	-.32	.05
85	Teacher praises and acknowledges students for reading	-.38	.05
86	Teacher acknowledges student for reading and other tasks	-.33	.05
87	All praise and acknowledgement to students	-.36	.05
90	Guiding corrective feedback	-.35	.05
116	All positive interactions	-.32	.05
120	All warm supportive interactions	-.33	.05

Effective Use of Time in Secondary Reading Programs   103

edged or praised students for achievement in reading of task related work (Variables 77, 86, and 87), the students are absent less often (Variables 77 and 86 are a subset of Variable 87). In classrooms where the teacher spent time managing (Variable TLM9), held discussions (Variable TEM9), and made the rules clear (Variable RC), the students were absent less often.

An unanticipated relationship was found between leisure reading and absence rate. Students came to class less frequently in classrooms where they more frequently engaged in leisure reading. We had expected that students would enjoy leisure reading and be absent less frequently in such classrooms. Perhaps such classrooms lacked rule clarity and more leisure reading may have been the result of less structure. Furthermore, leisure reading may relate to absence differently in subgroups of classrooms depending on reading skills.

The process variables related to absence rate in the Basic Skills Study are somewhat different than those found in the Follow Through Study of elementary classrooms. In the Follow Through Study, elementary students were absent less often when they were in open class structures, that is, when they had more choice about the activities and made more social comments to each other. In the Basic Skills Study, secondary students were absent less often when they felt other students were friendly, when the rules were clear, and when they could ask questions about the reading tasks. However, data from both studies show significant relationships between warm, supportive, orderly classroom environments and low student absenteeism.

Summary of Findings

To summarize, these data from Phase I support our four hypotheses about the relationships between teaching processes and student achievement and absence rates in secondary reading classes. First, our analyses indicate that teacher reinforcement of correct responses and guidance when incorrect responses are given are indeed positively related to reading achievement gains. Second, the frequency of reading related verbal interactions, including interactive instruction and oral reading, positively relates to achievement. Third, we found that the number of social interactions and other off task behaviors that occur during class have a negative relationship to achievement. Finally, our data indicate a relationship between positive effect recorded in the classroom and student absence rates. We found lower student absence rates associated with the more positive and supportive classroom environments. Furthermore, we found greater gains in reading achievement associated with these environments.

Subsequent Analysis

The findings from Phase I were the basis for an experiment where twenty-six teachers were trained in a series of workshops to use the time allocations of strategies identified as effective in Phase I. A control group of teachers was also observed and tested in a pretest and posttest design. The treatment teachers implemented 26 out of 31 variables and the students gained one year, eight months on the CTBS Total Reading Test. Findings from Phase I and II correlations and analysis of variance were remarkably similar. Summarizing the two data sets, we established the criteria shown for Sarah Smith in Figure 3.

Activities per % of Time	R*	Criterion	Criterion Percent	Teacher Baseline Percent	Teacher Postobservation Percent
Preparation					
Making assignments	Less	—X	7	8	
Organizing	Less	—X	5	7	
Teacher working alone	Less	——X	3	15	
Interactive Instruction					
Review/Discussing	More	X—	10	6	
Informing	More	X—	20	14	
Drill and practice	OK	X	2	2	
Oral reading	More	X—	9	2	
*Noninteractive***					
Doing written work	OK	X—	25	20	
Silent reading	Less	—X	9	20	
Off Task					
Students socializing	Less	—X	4	8	
Students uninvolved	Less	—X	5	15	
Teacher disciplining	Less	—X	1	6	

*R = Recommendations
**Students Work Alone

Figure 3. Profile of Sarah Smith.

These criteria then form the basis for our recommendations for teacher change in behavior. The criteria is adjusted according to the achievement level of the students. This program, which has been related to teacher behavior change and student gain in reading, has been approved by the Federal Joint Dissemination Review Panel and is now funded by the National Diffusion Network as a program that works.

References

Brophy, J., and Evertson, C. Process-product correlation in the Texas teacher effectiveness study. Research and Development Center in Teacher Education, University of Texas, June 1974.

Brophy, J. *Handbook of research on teaching*, third edition. New York: Macmillan, in press.

Chall, J. Comments delivered in response to the symposium *Advances on Remedial Reading Instruction* at the annual meeting of the American Educational Research Association, Boston, 1980.

Fisher, C.W., Filby, N.N., Marliave, R.S., Cahern, L.S., Dishaw, M.M., Moore, J.E., and Berliner, D. *Teaching behaviors, academic learning time, and student achievement.* Final report of Phase III-B, Beginning Teacher Evaluation Study. San Francisco, CA: Far West Regional Laboratory, 1978.

Good, T.L. *The Missouri mathematics effectiveness project.* School of Education, University of Missouri at Columbia, 1978.

Harnischfeger, A., and Wiley, D.E. *Achievement test score decline: Do we need to worry?* Chicago: ML Group for Policy Studies in Education, CEMREL, 1975.

Hoffman, J.V. Is there a legitimate place for oral reading instruction in a developmental reading program? *Elementary School Journal*, 1981, *81*.

McDonald, R., and Elias, P. *The effects of teaching performance on pupil learning, beginning teacher evaluation study: Phase II.* Final Report, Vol. 1. Princeton, NJ: Educational Testing Service, 1976.

Moos, R.H., and Trickett, E.J. *Classroom environment scale.* Palo Alto, CA: Consulting Psychologists Press, 1974.

Saretsky, G. The strange case of Peter Dow. *Phi Delta Kappan*, May 1973.

Soar, R. *Follow Through process evaluation, 1970-1971.* Gainesville, FL: Institute for Human Development, University of Florida, June 1973.

Stallings, J., and Kaskowitz, D. *Follow Through classroom observation evaluation, 1972-1973.* Menlo Park, CA: Stanford Research Institute, 1974.

Stallings, J., Needels, M., and Stayrook, N. *How to change the process of teaching basic reading skills in secondary schools.* Final report to the National Institute of Education. Menlo Park, CA: SRI International, 1979.

Stallings, J.A., Cory, R., Fairweather, J., and Needels, M. *A study of basic reading skills taught in secondary schools.* Menlo Park, CA: SRI International, 1978.

Part Three
Research into Practice

P recious few examples in the history of education clearly link research findings to changes in classroom practices. One might consider many reasons for why this might be the case. Researchers studying basic processes in reading, as a group, have not shown a great deal of interest in what has been going on in schools. Method A versus Method B comparison studies, which dominated instructional research in reading for years, reveal a remarkable insensitivity to life in classrooms and the constraints on teachers. Little surprise that practitioners often approach the topic of research with distrust and even disdain.

The same cannot be said for research on effective teaching. This literature, in particular research using the process-product paradigm, has generated enormous response and activity at the level of practice. In most major school systems today, staff development efforts are drawing from this literature. Whether this level of impact is because process-product research was spawned and nurtured in real classroom settings or because of heightened public attention to the need for improvement in schools cannot be determined. Whatever the reason, rapid change is underway and the focal point is research on effective teaching. The chapters in this section report on the efforts of three school districts to effect change in classroom practices related to the effective teaching of reading. There are clear differences in the modes of implementation and the success realized across the three sites. The reader is encouraged to explore the reports for clues to understanding successful implementation.

Mark W.F. Condon
Marilyn B. Kapel

5

Case Study of a Changing Reading Program and the Role of Teacher Effectiveness Research

I n the past ten years, research on reading programs has shifted its focus from the effectiveness of lesson formats to the effectiveness of teachers and to the effectiveness of schools. This transition to larger and larger units of analysis for effectiveness by researchers has been echoed by the changing focus of public school districts attempting to improve the effects of their reading programs for children.

Jefferson County, Kentucky, a large urban school district, was analyzed in its thrust over the past few years to improve teacher effectiveness in reading instruction. This analysis was accomplished by chronicling the changes of the district's program focus from the model of diagnostic/prescriptive instruction to the implementation of a program based on the findings of research into teacher effectiveness and, since 1983, to the concerns of instructional leadership in the schools. This chapter describes one program that was designed from the findings of teacher effectiveness research as perceived by the administrators and supervisors, as documented by school board and administration records and inhouse publications, and as understood (and implemented) by the teachers in the district.[1]

While teacher effectiveness research was an integral concern in the district's planning process for the new program, actual implementation of new ideas was effected by a gradual shift in emphasis. The shift has been from a district level concern for effective instructional behaviors by the teacher to a clear emphasis on the management system and the curricular materials necessary to the program. The nature of the shift and its results will be discussed in detail.

Merger of City and County Schools Necessitated Change

Currently the school system serves approximately 95,000 students, K-12, from Jefferson County, including the city of Louisville, population 290,000. Jefferson County School District is the twenty-second largest in the United States, comprising eighty-six elementary schools (grades 1-5), twenty-three middle schools (grades 6-8), twenty high schools (grades 9-12), and six vocational schools. Court ordered racial desegregation has been accomplished via cross-county busing since 1976.

In addition to the regular curriculum, the county offers several optional programs. Families can elect to send their children to "traditional" schools. These schools are offered from kindergarten through grade 12. They emphasize basic education and strict discipline in a highly structured environment. An "alternative" school provides open, informal student-centered education in cross-age grouping for grades 3 to 12. The "advance program," a subgrouping within many schools, is available to the academically gifted who meet established criteria. Youth Performing Arts School accepts talented high school students, and a select number of middle school youngsters though audition. A magnet high school emphasizing an academic specialty is projected for 1984-1985.

Before 1975, city and county school districts were separate entities. Financial problems resulted in a county absorption of city schools in that year. County school leadership and curriculum predominated. As a result of the merger, four basal reading series were used in the primary grades (1-3), and five basals were used in grades 4 to 6. Clearly, the number of basals created educational and logistical problems for the merged district.

To compound this problem, a Continuous Progress Program (CPP) had been adopted by the original Jefferson County elementary schools in 1959. In this program, a student progressed through 19 continuous levels. Skills were written in behavioral terms with criterion referenced testing at the end of each level. The list of skills was long; although CPP was accepted by the merged new system, in 1978 it was decided to revise the continuum to focus on the basic skills that require sequential instruction. This decision was supported by a Board of Education commitment to the priority of teaching basic skills. As a result, on February 12, 1979, the Board of Education authorized the administration to seek out an instructional management system based on a revised skills continuum.[2] The eventual outcome, which will be developed further in the next section, became known as Specific Expectations in Reading, or SER.

As part of the development of the new basic skills program, research attending to teacher impact upon student behavior and learning was surveyed. An SER development team researched the then current literature, including the works of Becker (1977), Berliner and Tikunoff (1976), Brophy (1976), Cruikshank (1976), Durkin (1978), Rosenshine (1978), and Stallings (1976). The team attempted to isolate, from this long list of research findings on effective teacher behaviors, key factors that led to reading achievement.

Development of the SER reading program was based on teacher effectiveness research. The findings were collected into what the program developers called the Direct Instruction Model (DIM). "Regardless of the circumstances, the teacher behavior was to include directed oral activity; a high rate of student response; and immediate, accurate teacher feedback to the student" (Jefferson County Public Schools, 1979a, pp. iii-2). Jefferson County chose to supplement the basal-based Direct Instruction Model with trade books, vocabulary building activities and other language development activities (e.g., Young Authors). The decision to employ direct instruction in teaching basic reading developed from the conviction that the model captured the essence of the current literature on teacher effectiveness: increased time on task, increased student mastery of content, and active teacher-student interaction.

[We have conducted a review of the research in teacher effectiveness available in the late 1970s. Our findings concur to a large extent with those of the Jefferson County reading committee. Like Brophy (1982), we felt that research of the period indicated rather specifically which teacher behaviors affect student learning.]

The Direct Instruction Model specifies high levels of student engagement within teacher directed classrooms and carefully sequenced and structured materials. In direct instruction, the teacher controls instructional goals, chooses material appropriate to the student's ability level, and paces the instructional episode. Interaction is characterized as structured, but not authoritarian; learning takes place in a convivial academic atmosphere.

Specific strategies directed to be used with the SER program include:

1. Claim each child's attention before beginning a lesson.
2. Inform the students of the goals for the lesson.
3. Present small chunks of new learning in a single lesson—student response should be 70-90 percent correct; students with less ability should have the highest percentage of accurate answers.
4. Control practice of new learning via modeling, pacing, prompting, and frequency of response.
5. Use a variety of questioning techniques.
6. Match seatwork to ability level.
7. Provide immediate feedback (Jefferson County Public Schools, 1979a).

The Direct Instruction Model of Teaching was the major component of the new program, SER (see Figure 1). Specifically, SER involved a strong academic focus with more time on task (150 minutes per day) dedicated to language arts (Jefferson County Public Schools, 1980a). Time on task activity was to be teacher directed. Independent learning activities, while part of the language arts program, were to be explored in time periods other than the established block of time. (Subsequent events did not permit implementation of this directive.) Direct instruction was to be conducted in both small and large group interaction (Figure 2, Jefferson County Public Schools, 1979b). Regardless of which type of organization was employed for instruction, close teacher supervision remained a constant.

SER

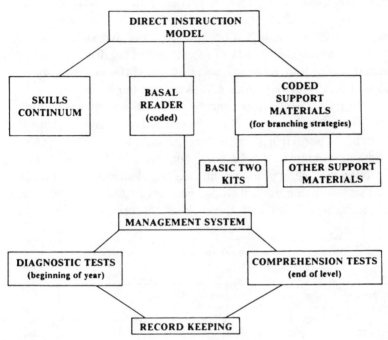

Figure 1. SER.

Immediate constructive feedback was to be an integral part of the model. Corrected materials were to include specific comments. The Socratic method was employed to lead a student to a correct answer; calling upon another child was not considered a positive strategy. Praise and constructive criticism are depended upon as part of the feedback, especially to the slow achievers. We should emphasize that this model reflected teacher effectiveness research available to the practitioner in 1978-1979.

The Evolution to a Specific Reading Focus within the Language Arts

As indicated earlier, the SER program had its origins in the Continuous Progress Program that had been an integral part of some of the Jefferson County elementary schools since 1959. On CPP, children worked on levels of reading, language arts, and mathematics in continuous progression through the elementary grades. The "average" child was expected to complete four levels in Grade 1, and three levels for each grade thereafter. Students were expected to function on identical levels in reading, the other language arts, and mathematics. Inevitably, it became apparent that student strengths were not homogeneous across subject areas; children had to be permitted to develop at varied paces in the different disciplines. By 1968, new CPP guides reflected this change in philosophy.

In 1972, Jefferson County mirrored the country's emphasis on behavioral objectives. Roger Farr and Jaap Tuinman (University of Indiana) participated in a federal grant to assist Jefferson County in the development of behavioral objectives in the area of reading. Through the CPP, specific reading skills had already been identified. Farr and Tuinman worked with the county to develop objectives that would be in concert with those skills. A series of criterion refer-

Language Arts Skills Building	Skills Instruction and Application in Reading*			Enrichment and Remediation	Total Time
40 minutes	30 minutes	30 minutes	30 minutes	20 minutes	
Penmanship	Developmental Reading	Independent Work	Independent Work	Enrichment 3 days per week	150 minutes daily
Spelling English	Group A (Average)	Group B (Slow)	Application of Skills Group C (Top)		
	Independent Work Application of skills	Developmental Reading	Independent Work	Remediation 2 days per week	
	Group A	Group B	Group C		
	Independent Work	Independent Work Application of Skills	Developmental Reading		
	Group A	Group B	Group C		

*Three developmental reading groups daily are suggested as a maximum.

Figure 2. Suggested schedule for language arts.

Condon and Kapel

enced tests was then developed to complete the program. The county director of testing monitored the process in pilot schools. The Stanford Achievement Test measured the general effects of the program. Through this test, the county sought assurance that the behavioral objectives, and resulting criterion referenced tests, reflected the learning and performance expected by a national broad based assessment instrument.

A new assistant superintendent was hired by the Jefferson County School District in 1978. One of his charges was to establish a management system for the language arts area. His first step was to organize a group to review CPP. The group found the reading program objectives sound and workable. The district administrators liked what had been developed.

Merger of county and city districts created some confusion in the implementation of the CPP. The behavioral objectives developed with Farr and Tuinman did not separate essential skill activity from enrichment activity. With a broader range of student ability and experience in a merged district encompassing innercity, suburban, and rural students, this knowledge became essential. Which skills should every student master? Allan Glatthorn (University of Pennsylvania) was recruited to help develop a workable taxonomy of basic reading skills.

A committee from the Jefferson County schools, consisting of key personnel in elementary curriculum and reading, worked under Glatthorn's guidance to isolate from the CPP the basic and sequentially structured reading/language arts skills. These specific skills were to become part of a skills continuum to be mastered by every student (see Figure 3).

The skills continuum was duplicated on large charts and sent to every school. All elementary teachers were encouraged to react to: 1) the importance of an identified skill, 2) its placement in the continuum, and 3) its appropriateness to specific grade levels. Teachers were asked to write directly on the charts and to be free and open with suggestions. The final compilation of skills is the result of much teacher input and consensus.

During this period of development and reorganization of the reading program, another consultant helped the reading committee

	Basic	Enrichment
Structured	The mastery curriculum—basic skills which require district coordination and careful curriculum development. Developed at a district level.	Knowledge not essential for all students, but requiring some loose coordination between levels. Can be developed by teaching teams and departments.
Nonstructured	Basic skills and attitudes which are essential but do not require careful curriculum development. Individual classroom teacher provides for as need arises.	Knowledge not essential for all students, not requiring articulation. Can be provided for by classroom teacher with large measure of student input.

Figure 3. Total school curriculum.

further define the county's concept of mastery. In addition, team members visited school districts with what had been identified as exemplary reading mastery programs in Washington, D.C., Denver, and Memphis to bring back ideas for the entire reading committee to consider.

In addition to developing specific skills and defining the mastery concept, the reading committee was assessing materials. The selection and purchase of new basal reading materials was slated for the 1979-1980 school year. The reading committee settled on the following:

1. A single basal was to be adopted for each school's developmental reading program.
2. Two series were identified as those basals most compatible with the Continuous Progress/Mastery Curriculum of Jefferson County.
3. A third series was designated for use with students not making satisfactory progress in the main series.

With these alterations in curriculum, class time allocation, and instructional practice, reading had been, in effect, "removed" from the language arts part of the curriculum. The teacher effectiveness research upon which the charges were based tended to focus on reading. To implement the research findings appropriately, separation of reading from language arts seemed sensible to the district.

Condon and Kapel

The Planned Impact of Teacher Effectiveness Research

The basic program began when the assistant superintendent charged the director of reading to create an ideal reading program. The resulting proposal formed the working model for SER.

Following the proclamation of board support, a rough outline of the SER program was circulated among the district's principals (refer to Figure 1). The principals agreed to make the Direct Instruction subset of SER a focal point of the entire system.

> Direct instruction applies to high levels of student engagement within teacher-directed classrooms using sequenced, structured materials....It refers to teaching activities focused on academic matters where goals are clear to students, time allocated for instruction is sufficient and continuous, content coverage is extensive, student performance is monitored, questions are at a low cognitive level and produce many correct responses, and feedback to students is immediate and academically oriented. In direct instruction, the teacher controls instructional goals, chooses material appropriate for the student's ability level, and paces the instructional episode. Interaction is characterized as structured, but not authoritarian; rather, learning takes place in a convivial academic atmosphere. (Rosenshine, 1978, p. 46)

A quote from the SER *Teacher's Guide* indicates an attempt to use Rosenshine's concepts, specifically direct instruction and sufficient and continuous time (see Figure 2): "The Direct Instruction Model and the two and one half hour block of instructional time serve as overlays of the entire program" (Jefferson County Public Schools, 1980a).

The next step was to locate a company willing and able to work with Jefferson County in creating the modules necessary to the SER program and its management system. A request for proposals from major publishing houses (Jefferson County Public Schools, 1979a) appeared in major national newspapers. The county accepted the bid of an established company that produced materials similar to those needed. Material was requested for delivery in two phases.

The first phase materials were for implementing the branching (remedial) strategies for grades K to 3. These materials were to be coded to the skills continuum for reinforcement of skills not mastered via basal reader. The publisher had a comprehensive decoding kit plus three comprehension kits on three consecutive levels; their own investigation assured the SER advocates that these kits contained strategies to teach effectively all the skills on the continuum that were to be mastered via direct instruction. Each lesson in the kits included teacher guided instruction material plus student follow up activities.

The publisher was also charged during Phase 1 with developing diagnostic tests for each grade through grade three, comprehension tests for each of the first ten levels, and a complete management system through grade three. A consultant from the publisher worked with Jefferson County personnel during the program development.

Phase II continued the process to include grades four and five. For the school year 1979-1980, most materials were completed for the primary grades. In 1980-1981, the kits and management system for grades four and five were in place. (At the present time, the complete management system is computerized by child and by class with the exception of end-of-level comprehension tests. These are still hand scored; teacher judgment is to remain an important component in the process—the instructor looks at the child holistically, rather than at skill mastery alone, prior to making a determination as to appropriate reading level. The diagnostic tests, which are skills oriented, require a minimum 75 percent mastery of material to reach a critical level.)

Implementation of the program

Teacher training began in Fall 1979. The intent was to train every primary teacher in the county in the use of the management system, the Direct Instruction Model, branching strategies, and the basal.

Two days of inservice before school opened laid the groundwork. The first year, two elementary schools served both as model schools and as inservice centers. Two more such centers were added the next year.

As each new phase of the program was developed, the publisher provided inservice training to the central office and regional personnel most involved with SER. These programs were conducted in one of the SER centers—*all* SER center faculty members were included in this first round of staff development instruction. They would then serve as the demonstration teachers for additional training sessions.

In the second step of the inservice program, SER teams from each school, consisting of one teacher from each grade level (K-3), were trained at a SER center through instruction and teacher observation. The teams then reported to the other teachers in their schools.

Plans to ensure the impetus of the new program seemed ample. In Spring 1980, videotapes were made to demonstrate and teach the SER components (the Direct Instruction Model, the management system, branching strategies, and use of the basal). In 1980-1981, the SER inservice model was extended to the intermediate grade teachers and to newly assigned primary grade teachers. The Board of Education commitment to the success of SER was quite apparent in their financial backing. Substitute teachers covered for teachers attending inservice programs. Each class received decoding and comprehension kits. Computerized printouts of diagnostic tests were made available on a monthly basis.

The program was evaluated yearly by the school district. Reading scores have improved as noted in Table 1.

Table 1

PERCENTILE SCORES ON CTBS (TOTAL READING)
FOR SER PROGRAM IN TWO GRADE LEVELS

			Year		
Grade	1979[1]	1980[1]	1981[1]	1982[2]	1983[2]
3	60	58[3]	58	57	64
5	56	58	60[3]	59	59

[1]CTBS form S (1971 norms)
[2]CTBS form U (1981 norms)
[3]First year of SER instruction

Most teacher response to SER has been positive (Jefferson County Public Schools, 1980b). Faculty were involved from the outset with the skills development. The Jefferson County Teacher Association had been apprised of every step. Inservice was continuous and considered to be thorough.

Parents, too, were made aware of the program. Brochures were distributed explaining SER and its components. Expectations were high in regard to its success.

Problems and Obstructions to Success

When the program began, the district initiated a weekly newsletter which has chronicled the implementation of SER and sheds light on this period of growth and evolution. We believe that the Direct Instruction Model, the district's articulation of teacher effectiveness, was never translated into practice. Through both the personal interviews and the review of newsletters, we could observe the changing focus of the Direct Instruction Model from an emphasis on total teacher controlled basic reading lessons to a more flexible approach which includes learning centers, games, and content area reading, and from a "center stage, top billing" to a "member of the chorus line."

In 1979, the weekly newsletter served as a morale booster for teachers who worried about the innovations in instructional practices and as a bulletin board. The inservice programs apparently left many practitioners confused and apprehensive. The newsletter attempted to allay those fears. One of the first newsletters begins with a quotation from Rosenshine: "What is not taught and attended to in academic areas is not learned." This type of statement in the newsletter, with the clear focus on direct instruction, left teachers feeling that there was a tightening in the instructional program. One source noted the sense of reprieve felt by the fourth and fifth year teachers who witnessed the anxiety of their peers in grades K-3 during the first year of implementation.

During the first inservice preparations, an entire newsletter was dedicated to Direct Instruction Model. In the introduction was the statement, "The SER Handbook states that the systemwide reading program is developed around a Direct Instruction Model" (SER

Update, Summer 1979c). The plan of direct instruction and the concepts gleaned from teacher effectiveness research were clearly in the forefront of this bold new effort.

The problems the teachers experienced in handling their uneasiness about the program were compounded by the shifts in the calendar for delivery of materials. Although the arrangements with the publisher had set August 1979 for completion of published materials and training of faculty, all the materials did not arrive until well into the year. The confusion and anxiety caused by this shift were reflected in the weekly newsletters which published teacher queries and remarks about the program. In September, one teacher question attended to in the newsletter was "When does SER begin?"

Without the new kits containing the branching strategies to correspond with the basal program, teachers wanted to use their old learning centers, games, and seatwork. These carryovers from pre-SER programs had been relegated to use outside of the 150 minutes dedicated to reading instruction and language arts. The first shift in direction away from the original tenets of Direct Instructional Model was in an October newsletter which stated that teacher made materials were acceptable provided they related to the mastery curriculum. The administration obviously could not ask teachers to "make bricks without straw" and chose to circumvent their own earlier edicts regarding direct instruction control and teacher made materials.

The nuts and bolts issues of testing, record keeping in the management system, and using the basal began to have primary emphasis as a survival orientation became prevalent in the absence of ordered materials. Seatwork became the focus of entire issues of the newsletter. The editors attempted to work direct instruction into the seatwork as much as was practical. (The teacher was not involved with direct control in this seatwork.) Such things as supplemental readers and library books were considered appropriate. Teachers were clearly allowing students' choice of task and providing little immediate feedback to student responses in these activities. (DIM was becoming quite diluted.)

By midyear, the teacher questions as reflected in the newsletter were concerned with materials, grouping strategies for classes with multilevels, and testing and management. The newsletter staff, however, was still clearly committed to pressing DIM into service. In the January 1980 issue, a dialogue appeared between a "solid direct instruction teacher" and a "bellyacher." The reasonable model teacher indicated how little she needed to change to use DIM and how all of her homemade materials could be included in the structures of the model.

Toward the end of February 1980 an issue focused on Mastery Learning, featuring comments by Benjamin Bloom regarding available time versus time on task, summative and formative testing, and process-product research kinds of testing strategies.

Interestingly enough, the next newsletter was not published until November of the next school year (1980-1981). The materials production lag was its focus and the issue was replete with promises of arrival dates. A review of the 1980-1981 newsletters reveals that while the teacher's manuals (prepared earlier) and much of the inservice material still mentioned Direct Instruction Model, DIM had been lost from the vocabulary of the newsletter writers. This could reflect changes in personnel which had occurred during the last half of the year in an attempt to pare down an enormous administrative structure, a carryover of the merged administrations of two school districts.

The remarks about teaching in the newsletters in 1981-1983 reflect the standard "...or how about this idea?" suggestions which teachers who assume the rights and responsibilities for their own classes can choose to accept or to reject. The hard line on implementation of documented effective teaching behaviors had become barely an echo with words like "cue the student to text location of answer." The mastery curriculum was apparently considered under control, and all of the suggestions in these editions had to do with enrichment, content area reading, and study skills ideas on specific units.

Interviews with teachers who have been in the classroom over the past four years suggest that the SER allocated time segment of a 150 minute language arts block (Figure 2) has endured as the single remnant of the heavy structure initiated four years before.

In 1982-1983, another series of staff retirements has left the district with only a handful of the original people remaining in positions which would affect teaching behavior, and most particularly Direct Instruction Model strategies and activities.

In the years since conception of SER, leadership, logistics of instructional materials distribution, and the experiences of life in the thousand plus elementary school classrooms have led us to question whether the DIM so central to SER was *ever* really implemented.

And So It Goes

Jefferson County has undergone many changes since the inception of the SER program in 1979 (See Figure 3). Mirroring other large urban areas, the system has had to deal with declining student enrollment and the resultant teacher retrenchment and reassignment. Added to these problems are the political pressures concomitant with school closings, a new school superintendent, paring down of administrative staff, and the everyday wrenches that foul the works of any organization.

The county is working hard to mesh the old and the new. SER, like all other programs, continues to change and adapt to new personnel and philosophy. The major change for the 1984-1985 school year was a proposed change in name. The SER title was dropped, and reading became a subset of the Jefferson County Language Arts Program, in an effort to extend the program through the middle school grades (6-8).

Although this does not indicate any overt change in philosophy or practice, it does represent a psychological shift in the valuing of the reading oriented research which formed the basis of SER and the DIM. One concern is the attitude of teachers toward the new title. SER has been a part of the school jargon for four years. Teachers are aware that it is a name change; however, they might also view it as a move away from the essence of SER. To quote one SER teacher: "Here we go again! They are always changing." Although most of the SER concepts are supposed to remain intact in the new thrust, it seems unlikely that the teachers were made aware of this. At this time, teacher effectiveness research, a driving force for promoting effective instruction, is no longer mentioned.

As has been indicated previously, SER was developed after a review of teacher effectiveness literature available in 1978. Much of

1959	1972	1975	1978	1979-1980	1980-1981	1981-1982	1982-1983	1983-1984
CPP Implemented	CPP Behavioral Objectives Developed	Merger of County and City	Reevaluation of CPP	Basal Adoption SER Approval	SER Extended to Grades 4 & 5	SER Continues	SER Continues	SER Subsumed by Jefferson County Language Arts Program
			Direct Instruction Model Research	SER Management System Developed: K-3	Management System Developed	Appointment of New Superintendent	Clinical Supervision Model Introduced to Principals	
				SER Team Inservice	Teacher Inservice Conducted			Clinical Supervision Inservice of Teachers
				SER Inservice of Primary Teachers				

Figure 4. Time line in growth and development of SER.

that literature reflected studies of primary students and there was little information gleaned which reflected upon the unique socioeconomic structure of the newly merged Jefferson County Public Schools. No attempt was made to update documentary research on or to alter methodology to reflect evolving knowledge of teacher effectiveness in the complex urban environment. One reading coordinator in the county who sees the SER program's direct instruction factor being eroded sees the county focusing on the curriculum material alone. The instructional process is a diminutive portion of SER application today.

What has caused the shift in balance away from teacher effectiveness and toward the management aspects of SER? One can only speculate as to the reasons. On a national level, we see a continued push toward mastery learning (Mendoza & Kossack, 1981-1982; Gardner, 1983). The conservative movement continues to intensify. "Teacher Proof" programs are gaining in popularity (Green, 1983; Justiz, 1983). The concept of teacher as facilitator is being replaced rapidly by the idea that material is central to learning. The coming of age of the microcomputer in education must affect this shift in attitude (Benderson, 1983; Melmed, 1983).

Locally, the district is completing the second year of a new superintendent. His basic charge to the school supervisory personnel is to become knowledgeable in and to practice the clinical supervision model similar to that reflected in the work of Hunter (Hunter, 1976; Cummings, Nelson & Shaw, 1980). Toward this end, all principals were trained during the 1982-1983 school year. Inservice sessions were opened to teachers during the summer of 1983 under the title of Teaching-Learning Process. Although this model potentially reflects teacher effectiveness factors inherent in the Direct Instruction Model, no effort has been made to couple it with the Direct Instruction Model of SER.

A cursory review of the past twenty five years of reading history in Jefferson County, Kentucky, could give the impression of a school district's coming full circle. In 1959, reading was an imbedded language arts component of the Continuous Progress Program. After a four year period as a separate entity, Specific Expectations in Reading, reading once again takes its place in the newly titled

Jefferson County Language Arts Program. One can only speculate as to what this will mean to achievement in the district. The individual classroom practitioner probably will not change either the focus or the intensity of instruction.

The practitioner uses the ingredients to "bake the cake," yet rarely has been included in, or advised of, the research basis of these waves of innovation. Carefully edited reviews of research are presented to the teacher as justification for innovation. "Take my word for it" becomes the accepted attitude. DIM, with its basis in the teacher effectiveness research, is no exception.

A reading committee conducted research on teacher effectiveness, adopted a model and strategies, and introduced them to teachers during inservice modules. Teachers were not apprised of the data behind the behaviors, nor were they guided in adapting techniques to direct instruction. Acceptable support materials arrived much too late to be of use to teachers working with new ideas. Almost immediately, the ideas to promote effective teaching in this new program became diluted.

As a teacher effectiveness factor, DIM was only a promise at its inception. Through no intentional act, the practitioner failed to value its worth; it was not a high priority element of SER for the teacher. The concrete matters of minute by minute teaching took precedence and the promise of the impact of the teacher effectiveness research was left unfulfilled.

What If?

Speculations about this program to implement the Teacher Effectiveness Research are in order. This area of research has yielded strong evidence to change teaching behavior. In this case, the teachers of Jefferson County were not compelled by the research.

1. What if the materials had arrived on time and the teachers had not had to fall back on their tried and true methods of instruction which did not necessarily reflect the DIM?
2. What if the inservice training had been as effective in changing teacher behavior as was initially hoped?

3. What if the administration had remained constant, and no shifts had been made in the key program personnel?
4. What if the time for the implementation of the program, the delivery of materials, and the phasing in of the various grade levels had been more realistic?
5. What if reading instruction had been kept separate from language arts in the program's most recent alterations?
6. What if no attempt had been made to merge elementary and middle school reading curricula?
7. What if teachers had been more involved from the beginning in the research, development, and implementation of SER?

Given what we know about the nature of the social and political sphere within which schools must operate, as well as the transitory nature of research in any field, we are inclined to conclude that the attempts to construct any state of the art in education are doomed to fail. There is no such status. Research is only a snapshot of one point of an everchanging dynamic.

The Jefferson County Public Schools attempted to make the snapshot from 1978 the goal of instructional change. If all of the "what ifs" had actually occurred, perhaps that goal may have been reached; SER, its Direct Instructional Model of teaching, and its generous prescribed structure for reading instruction may have been more clearly and measurably implemented. Still, the social and political spheres in Kentucky would have continued to evolve. The SER program would in effect have been obsolete when completed.

1. The human aspect of teaching would compel a teacher to alter, eliminate, or supplement the prescribed materials with personal choices.
2. The most carefully structured inservice training is still internalized by receivers based on their background of experience. It is impossible to have a one to one correspondence between objectives and learning.
3. Any social structure experiences change in key personnel. New administrators bring their own agenda to the positions. The average school superintendent in the major cities of this country serves less than five years. When

considering all of the assistant, associate, and deputy superintendents, the dynamics of any given administration are constantly in flux.

4. Time lines are estimates of the probable milestones along a path from inspiration to implementation. Flexibility moves toward rigidity as one moves from administrative decision making to instructional implementation. In attempting to abide by the time lines, teachers lost what perspective of the program they had.

5. The separation of reading from language arts allowed a focus which brought dedication of 150 minutes to language arts, with 110 of that specified for reading. The national rise of composition as a priority for all levels of students would surely have begun to undermine (appropriately) this bias by now.

6. Keeping the curricula in elementary and middle schools separate is administratively clean. However, it does not work in the best interests of children's language development. Pressure from the middle school to do a better job preparing students for the middle school curriculum would eventually affect implementation if not design of SER.

7. Involvement of teachers from the initial stages of development might have sustained the continuance of the structure for a longer period of time. Teacher attrition and change resulting from new learning, however, are bound to affect any program.

Finally, none of the speculations reflects the very nature of research. The SER program was pursued as if it were a culmination rather than an ongoing formulation. Since 1978, research in effective teaching has provided the educational community with information which was unavailable to the originators of SER. That information could have been the source of an everchanging implementation of teacher effectiveness research in the reading program. It was not. This, above all, is the lesson to learn from the Jefferson County experience.

Condon and Kapel

Notes

[1] The authors wish to acknowledge the cooperation which was generously offered by the employees of the Jefferson County Public Schools. From retired and practicing teachers, through supervisory and program development personnel, from individual school administrators to district level administrators, all of the professionals in this busy and vital school district made time, researched documents, and answered questions. We are proud to have been associated with them in our efforts to share these experiences with the larger professional community.

[2] This RFP, which includes a history of the SER program's development, was to solicit bids by publishers to produce management, testing, and instructional materials for the proposed program.

References

Becker, W.C. Teaching reading and language to the disadvantaged: What we have learned from field research. *Harvard Educational Review,* 1977, *4,* 508-541.

Benderson, A. (Ed.). *Computer literacy, focus 11.* Princeton, NJ: Educational Testing Service, 1983.

Berliner, D.C., and Tikunoff, W.J. The California beginning teacher evaluation study: Overview of the ethnographic study. *Journal of Teacher Education,* 1976, *27,* 24-30.

Brophy, J.E. Reflections in research in elementary schools. *Journal of Teacher Education,* 1976, *27,* 31-35.

Brophy, J. Successful teaching strategies for the innercity child. *Phi Delta Kappan,* 1982, *13*(8), 522-530 as cited in D.E. Kapel and M.B. Kapel, *The preparation of teachers for the urban schools: The state-of-the-art of preservice and inservice education.* New York: Eric Clearinghouse on Urban Education, Teachers College, Columbia University.

Cruickshank, D.R. Synthesis of selected recent research on teacher effects. *Journal of Teacher Education,* 1976, *27,* 57-60.

Cummings, C., with Nelson, C., and Shaw, D. *Teaching makes a difference.* Washington: Snohomish Publishing, 1980.

Durkin, D. *What classroom observations reveal about reading comprehension scores.* Technical Report No. 106. Champaign, IL: University of Illinois at Urbana-Champaign, 1978.

Gardner, D.P. *A nation at risk: The imperative for educational reform.* Washington, DC: National Commission for Excellence in Education, 1983.

Graves, D.H. Research update: What's new may not be good. *Language Arts,* 1977, *54,* 708-713.

Green, B.F. Adaptive testing by computer. In Ruth B. Ekstrom (Ed.), *Measurement, technology, and individuality in education.* Washington, DC: Jossey-Bass, 5-12, 1983.

Hunter, M. *Improved instruction.* California: TIP Publications, 1976.

Jefferson County Public Schools. *Request for proposals: Specific expectations in reading* (SER). Louisville, Kentucky: Jefferson County Public Schools, 1979a.

Jefferson County Public Schools. *SER: Staff development handbook.* Department of School Programs, 1979b.

Jefferson County Public Schools. *SER Update.* 1979c.

Jefferson County Public Schools. *SER: Teacher's guide.* Binghamton, NY: Gould, 1980a.

Jefferson County Public Schools. *SER: Interim report 1969-1980,* Report No. 28, 1980b.

Justiz, M.J. *Emerging themes and new partnerships for educational research in the '80s.* Paper presented at the Annual Meeting of the American Educational Research Association, Montreal, Canada, 1983.

Melmed, A.S. Productivity and technology in education. *Educational Leadership*, 1983, *40*(5), 4-6.

Mendoza, A., and Kossack, S. The State of Florida: A case study in governmental assessment legislation. *Action in Teacher Education*, 1981-1982, *3*, 17-24.

Rosenshine, B.V. Academic engaged time, content covered and direct instruction. *Journal of Education*, 1978, *160*, 38-66.

Stallings, J.A. How instructional processes relate to child outcomes in a national study of follow through. *Journal of Teacher Education*, 1976, *27*, 43-47.

Martha Rapp Haggard
Jennifer Reese Better

6

Effective Use of Instructional Time: The Cupertino Project

S taff development programs and inservice teacher education have become significant components in the efforts of local school districts to increase student achievement in reading. Little evidence exists, however, to suggest that substantial change in teacher behavior and in student achievement has occurred as a result of such programs. This appears to be due, in some measure, to the one-dimensional nature of previous approaches for study and improvement of teacher effectiveness and instructional practice: traditionally, research and training have focused, with shifting emphases, on one critical variable operating in the classroom to the exclusion of all others (Duffy, 1982). Recent research, involving both the process through which instruction occurs and the product of that instruction, suggests instead that many dimensions of the classroom must be studied simultaneously and affected in staff development programs to bring about desired change. From such research, new conclusions and, subsequently, new training approaches have emerged.

In the Beginning Teacher Evaluation Study, Fisher and others (1980) concluded that student achievement is directly related to the amount of allocated learning time (time available for learning to occur), amount of engaged time (time spent on task), and success of the student. That is, in this study, academic achievement was higher in classes where more time was allocated for instruction, and students spent a high percentage of that time at a task on which they were successful. In addition, specific teacher behaviors during instructional time — diagnosis, prescription, presentation, monitoring, and feedback — were found to contribute to student achievement. Related study findings indicate further that effective teachers 1) interact more with their students and provide a supportive environment for them (Stallings, et al., 1978); 2) group students for instruction rather than individualize (Stallings & Kaskowitz, 1972-1973), and 3) provide clear instructions to communicate academic and behavioral expectations (Evertson & Emmer, 1980). Based upon these research findings and others, Stallings and associates (Stallings, Needels, & Stayrock, 1979; Stallings, 1982; see Chapter 4 of this book) designed and implemented a series of inservice workshops to train teachers in the classroom conditions, teacher behaviors, and student activities that make most effective use of instructional time. This body of research and training program paradigm served as the foundation of the Cuptertino Union School District's involvement in the Effective Use of Instructional Time Project.

Cupertino Union School District is located at the center of the Silicon Valley in northern California, and serves over 12,000 students, kindergarten through eighth grade, in twenty four schools: nineteen elementary, four junior high, and one school for severely handicapped children. Teachers in the district are highly experienced (average experience is seventeen years), and most hold advanced academic degrees. Parents, as well as the educational community, have high expectations for student achievement. The board of education actively participates in curriculum development and implementation, and makes yearly fiscal commitments to district efforts to promote teacher excellence.

In the spring of 1982, three sources of district evaluation indicated a need for more effective teaching in the area of reading instruction: School Improvement Review results, standardized test results, and end-of-year personnel reviews. Although numerous inservice and support programs were already in place, teachers, administrators, and the board of education felt that implementation of a research based, multidimensional training program in reading instruction would be of substantial value to the district. The district then submitted a proposal to the David and Lucille Packard Foundation of Los Altos, California, for partial funding of a three phase project to increase effective use of instructional time: Phase I to provide intensive training for selected teachers and administrators in the effective use of instructional time; Phase II to prepare personnel trained in Phase I to expand the program to others in the district; and Phase III to continue implementation to within-district training for all remaining teachers and administrators. Funding was requested only for Phase I of the project, to be implemented during the 1982-1983 school year. Phases II and III are to follow during the 1983-1984 and 1984-1985 school years.

Four goals guided overall project planning and implementation:

1. To expand the knowledge and improve the skills of teachers in organizing and managing the classroom for effective instruction.
2. To provide administrators with methods to help teachers improve instructional strategies through analysis of engagement time.
3. To increase student achievement by increasing quality and quantity of the instructional time.
4. To improve demands on instructional time through revisions to the district infrastructure (i.e., board policies, district regulations, and local school agreements).

Goals one and two were the target areas of Phase I of the project.

Project Overview

Three strands of participation and training formed the core components of Phase I: Formal Observation Analysis—training for selected district personnel to observe and analyze classroom conditions and teacher behaviors relevant to effective use of instruction time; Inservice Instruction—training for teachers in activities and procedures which promote effective use of instructional time; and

Peer Observation—training for teachers and principals in informal observational techniques for analyzing peer use of instructional time.

School Sites

Seven elementary and three junior high schools were chosen to participate in the project by a selection committee composed of one teacher, one Complex Coordinator, and the Staff Development Coordinator, who also served as the Project Director. Before selection, all district schools were invited to volunteer for participation, and were chosen based upon the following criteria:

1. Title I elementary schools and all four junior high schools should have first priority.
2. Representation should include at least one elementary school from each Complex (a junior high school plus its feeder schools).

The criterion for strong involvement at the junior high level grew from school review reports indicating that the need for improvement in reading instruction was greater at the junior high level than the elementary level; the one junior high school that did not participate was excluded due to a variety of extenuating circumstances. Special consideration was also given for elementary schools undergoing unusual circumstances. For example, several schools were not included because they would be implementing new basal reading series during the project year; others were eliminated because they would be consolidating students into the school as a result of scheduled school closures.

Participants

Outside Consultants. Three educational consultants were contracted to assist in planning during the school year prior to project implementation. During the project, a consultant from the Stallings Teaching and Learning Institute conducted training sessions and assisted in monitoring project results.

Observer/Trainers. Three district staff members (two administrators and one teacher) were chosen to serve as observer/trainers in project classrooms. All three had strong academic training in reading or English, and all had taught reading at the elementary or junior high level.

Teachers. Two reading/language arts teachers were chosen from each participating school; at the request of one junior high school with an integrated language arts/social studies program, an additional social studies teacher was included, for a total of twenty-one teachers. Teachers were selected from a pool of volunteers at each school.

Principals. All ten principals from the selected schools participated in the project. District staff members were selected for their respective roles by the selection committee according to the following criteria:

1. A minimum of two teachers and the principal should participate from each project school.

2. Team members should have demonstrated interest in the project (e.g., attendance at the spring meeting, participation in writing school plans, evidence of leadership potential).

3. The participants should represent a balance of grade levels.

Outside consultants were contracted by the administration at the recommendation of the planning committee. As the project progressed, School Improvement Coordinators attached to participating schools were involved in an awareness workshop about the project in order to provide additional support for teachers, principals, and observer/trainers in their respective schools.

Project Implementation

The project began with an informational workshop for all participants conducted after school by the outside consultant. Because of the emphasis on translating theory and research into practice, approximately half of the workshops involved presentation and discussion of teacher effectiveness research. Special emphasis was placed on elements of classroom organization, behavior management, and instruction and monitoring techniques. The remaining time was spent on articulation of project strands and discussion of project goals, procedures, and expectations. Participant roles and their respective levels of required training were explained and clarified. Participants were given the option to withdraw from the project if its goals and procedures would not be appropriate for them or their schools. No one chose this option.

Strand 1: Formal Observation and Analysis

Following the informational workshop, observer/trainers met with the outside consultant for seven days of intensive training on formal classroom observation and use of the Secondary Observation Instrument. Training included lectures, role playing, analysis of videotapes, practice coding on computer forms, and comparison of observations. Emphasis was on objectivity and reliability within and across observers. At this time, they also learned methods for training teachers and principals to do informal peer observations.

Pretesting of classroom conditions and teacher performance was conducted by the observer/trainers in all twenty-one classrooms. Each teacher was observed three times for one hour of reading instruction at two-day intervals. The three observations for each teacher were done independently by the three different observer/trainers. Data from these observations were recorded on computer forms and compiled into Basic Skills Teacher Profiles by an outside firm contracted for that purpose. Following the final observation, observer/trainers met with individual teaches to discuss the profile and to identify each teacher's target growth areas. All observations and conferences were completed by the end of the first month of the project.

Posttesting was completed in the final month of school using the same procedures established for pretesting. Data from these observations were used as the basis for 1) comparison of individual pre-post project performance, 2) assessment of project effectiveness, and 3) future planning for Phases II and III of the project.

Follow up structured interviews were conducted by observer/trainers, and reading lessons were videotaped during the posttest period; however, these data were used primarily for refining plans for Phases II and III rather than as part of the posttest evaluation. The interviews were conducted to determine the impact of the project on individual teachers, their evaluation of project activities and procedures, and the needs they perceived as important to their own personal and professional growth. Videotaped lessons were collected to record teacher progress, provide opportunity for observer/ trainers to increase their observational skills, and establish a library of videotapes demonstrating effective use of instructional time.

Strand 2: Inservice Instruction

The outside consultant conducted monthly inservice workshops for project teachers. Teachers attended the two-hour sessions in small groups of six to eight because varying school dismissal times and other school related activities prohibited scheduling total group meetings. Instructional strategies were presented in the workshops through explanation, practice, and preparation of materials and activities for use in individual classrooms. The content of the monthly workshops focused on the following areas:

1. Classroom Management—use of homework, making assignments, routines, grouping.
2. Behavior Management—time on task, activity during guided practice, activity during independent practice.
3. Use of Instructional Time—allocated time, engaged time.
4. Classroom Interaction Patterns—teacher-pupil interaction, pupil-pupil interaction, pupil-teacher interaction, tone of interaction.
5. Instruction and monitoring—questioning techniques, levels of questions, checks for understanding, linking student experience and knowledge with new information, monitoring seatwork, reading in the content areas, direction giving.

Provision also was made for project teachers to enroll in available district sponsored staff development courses when appropriate to their needs. Individual inservice conferences were held between an observer/trainer and teacher when teacher needs were unique or of a personal nature.

During the course of the group session, project members realized that a substantial amount of classroom interaction was influenced by teacher aides and parent volunteers. School Improvement

Program Coordinators were subsequently invited to attend one of the training sessions, and encouraged to provide similar training for the adjunct staff, or to contract services of a district consultant through School Improvement Program funds.

Observer/trainers received monthly training from the outside consultant to learn classroom activities and instructional strategies designed to improve teacher performance in the targeted areas. In addition, they learned techniques for modeling effective instruction and coaching others toward improved performance. This was in preparation for their role as trainers in Phases II and III of the project.

Strand 3: Peer Observation

Peer observation was implemented concurrent with the instructional improvement strand. The outside consultant provided initial training in informal peer observation for all teachers and principals in a two hour workshop at the start of the project. During the training session, two areas were stressed: 1) observer attention to few (rather than many) classroom variables, and 2) focus on positive aspects rather than teacher/classroom needs. Additional training for principals occurred during six separate sessions. For both teachers and principals, the peer observation was considered a support function and not an evaluative tool.

Subsequent to the initial training session, teachers observed the other project teachers in their building at least twice. As with the formal observations, these took place during reading instruction and lasted one hour. At the elementary level, building principals often substituted in teachers' classrooms during the observation period; junior high teachers, for the most part, observed during their preparation period. Following each observation, the teachers met to share their perceptions of the instructional period and to clarify their interpretations.

Results

Statistical analysis of pre and posttest observation data and structured interviews is currently in progress, and will be used for formal evaluation of Phase I and continued planning for Phases II and III of the project. In the interim, informal analysis of project strand activities was carried out to obtain a general overview of immediate outcomes.

Strand 1: Formal Observation and Analysis

Pretest Basic Skills Teacher Profiles, obtained from formal observations by observer/trainers, yielded the following patterns of classroom conditions and teacher behaviors:

1. Reading instruction tended to consist of group discussion followed by independent seatwork in unvarying routine; although some variation was found from class to class, little was observed within classes.

2. Teachers did most of the talking, allowing minimal response from students. In classes where more student-teacher interaction did occur, it was generally in response to literal level questions.

3. Literal comprehension was the focus of a majority of teacher questions. Some inferential and open ended questions were asked, but no applied or evaluative questions.

4. Incorrect student responses were simply corrected rather than explored through clarifying questions or probes for explanations.

5. Many students were omitted from the discussion, with attention given most frequently to the most vocal students or those in need of discipline.

6. A great deal of time was spent on management tasks and discipline. Direction giving, movement from one place to another, establishing expectations, and correcting student behavior consumed a large part of instructional time.

7. Little monitoring of independent seatwork and a high rate of student off task behavior were observed.

Posttest profiles indicated the following:

1. Teachers provided greater variety of activities during reading instruction, and varied routine from day to day.

2. Student-teacher classroom interaction increased as teacher-student interactions decreased.

3. There were more inferential, applied, and open ended questions asked during instruction.

4. Clarifying questions and probes for explanations were more frequently used following incorrect student responses.

5. More students participated in discussions.

6. Time spent in classroom management and discipline decreased, and use of effective management techniques increased.

7. Increased on task student behavior was observed.

In interviews conducted after both pre and posttesting, teachers indicated that pretest observations were threatening, but that posttest observations were not. They expressed positive reaction to the computerized profiles from the pretest because of the specificity and the objective appearance of the form itself. They agreed that careful guidance was necessary for them to interpret the profiles—otherwise, it was "all just a bunch of numbers"—but were highly positive about the growth demonstrated on the posttest results. One teacher commented, "You just sort of read through your yearly evaluation because everything is always positive; but here, I could really see what my strengths and my weaknesses were."

Strand 2: Inservice Instruction

Teacher response to inservice activities was most positive for the areas of questioning techniques, classroom management techniques, and "sponge" activities for introducing variety and promoting critical thinking. Individual teachers generally rated those lessons highest which pertained to their own target growth areas. Interview comments revealed that this inservice was different and more beneficial than others they had attended because the monthly sessions allowed for presentation of many new ideas, the "personal" nature of the interaction in the workshops reduced anxieties, and the activities presented were both practical and research based.

All of the teachers indicated that they preferred attending sessions away from their own school sites (away from the phone, the work, and other distractions), and the small group classes. They stated that the small groups allowed high levels of participation in activities and comfort with one another, and gradually grew to be support groups as teachers tried new teaching techniques in their classrooms and conducted peer observations. Teachers gave a positive rating to cross-grade representation within the groups.

The inservice instruction considered most important by principals was the information they received to assist teachers in the effective use of time. In addition, principals stated they (unexpectedly) learned as much about the teaching of reading as they did about classroom management.

Strand 3: Peer Observations

Teacher response to peer observation was generally quite positive; some teachers reported initial reluctance and anxiety, but felt these were reduced after postobservation and inservice discussion. Areas felt to be most beneficial were 1) learning to focus on specific variables while observing instruction, 2) sharing perceptions and asking questions about the instruction during follow up discussion, and 3) perceiving insights about one's own teaching while observing and analyzing another's. Comments about peer observations frequently expressed surprise ("I found out they were doing the same things I was...[that] they don't have any magic over there," or "I couldn't believe how many kids I was missing in discussion! I thought I was including everybody. Now I'm working hard at improving that area"); and at other times, admiration ("I had always respected [her], but I had never sat in her class before. Now we really share a lot with each other").

Negative aspects of peer observation centered around organization of time within the school and provision for substitutes to allow the observations to occur. In some instances, observation time had to be shortened or postponed because a class could not be covered. Overall, the teachers agreed that peer observations should be continued.

The principals, also, were generally positive toward peer observation, with the suggestion that better provisions be made to allow them adequate time to observe and to substitute for teachers who are observing, or funds to hire substitutes. They were most pleased with the emphasis on observation for the purpose of support rather than personnel evaluation, and the opportunity they had to teach classes occasionally.

Conclusions and Recommendations

Phase I of the Cupertino project was intended to address the two goals of increasing teacher ability to organize for effective use of instructional time, and providing principals with skills to assist teachers in that effort. From the data analyses completed at this time, several conclusions can be drawn concerning the district's progress toward each goal.

Goal 1. To expand the knowledge and improve the skills of teachers in organizing and managing the classroom for effective instruction. Pre and posttest observation profiles suggest that this goal is being met. In the pretest condition, reading instruction appeared to be highly repetitious and routine, with little attention given to comprehension beyond the literal level or the logic behind students' responses. Furthermore, much of the time allocated for reading instruction was consumed by management tasks. After the inservice instruction and peer observation, however, improvement and growth were seen in each of these areas. Several features appear to be critical to this growth.

First, teachers need and want objective analysis of specific classroom behaviors as a means for assessing their own strengths and weaknesses. Furthermore, they require reassurance and proof of the nonpunitive nature of such evaluation. In this respect, the computer printed profile form itself was of value; it dehumanized the report, removing the *appearance* of subjectivity, and so allowed individuals to view their own behavior analytically. Once done, sensitivity to and willingness to accept inservice training were greater and the impact of the training was heightened.

Second, coordinated inservice training instruction, conducted over time and in small groups, creates an atmosphere for change. Through the coordination of an outside consultant, target areas were identified, instruction planned to meet specific needs, and adjustments made to meet changing needs. In monthly meetings, teachers could come back to the source of their new information to check, verify, or question if a lesson failed or a new technique did not work. Just as important, over time the teachers became comfortable with one another and developed into support groups, in which they exchanged ideas, gave suggestions, and shared anxieties. The net effect was increased willingness to experiment, to move away from old behaviors, and to implement new teaching and management strategies.

Finally, peer observation, conducted after training and guided by focusing criteria, increases teachers' abilities to analyze their own teaching behaviors and the classroom conditions they establish. Teachers in this study said repeatedly that they learned more about their own teaching while watching someone else teach than through any other activity. This was the result from insights gained in discussions following the observation, during which time each individual could learn how another person viewed a specific event. Such discussions led to introspection and analysis of an individual's own teaching, and decision making regarding the acceptance of new behaviors.

Goal 2. To provide administrators with methods to help teachers improve instructional strategies through analysis of engagement time. The results indicate that this goal, also, is being met. Principals reported learning a great deal in their inservice instruction, not only about classroom management, but about the teaching of reading as well. Principals were active and enthusiastic participants, attending workshops, scheduling released time, substituting, or finding substitutes whose efforts made it possible for teachers to participate fully in the project. Their role would seem critical to the success of any such teacher effectiveness training program.

Phase I of the Cupertino project appears to have been highly successful. Teacher behaviors and classroom conditions during reading instruction have changed to allow more effective use of instructional time. Principals have received training in methods for assisting teachers toward more effective use of time, and have participated in pivotal roles throughout the teacher training process. As with any research in progress, the full effects of this project will not be known for some time. Its ultimate success will undoubtedly be affected by the following variables: 1) the ability of observer/trainers to assume increasing responsibility for inservice instruction, 2) the ability of administrators to apply their knowledge of how to assist teachers in achieving more effective use of instructional time, 3) the responsiveness of the district to needs and changes indicated by results of the project, and 4) the mechanism established to sustain and support teacher change made during the project. Attention to these variables should serve to guide continued structuring and evaluation of the project, so that final results may provide new insight into effective means for implementing instructional change.

References

Duffy, G.G. Fighting off the alligators: What research in real classrooms has to say about reading instruction. *Journal of Reading Behavior*, 1982, *14*, 357-371.

Evertson, C., and Emmer, E. *Effective management at the beginning of the school year in junior high classes.* Austin: Research and Development Center for Teacher Education, University of Texas, 1980.

Fisher, C.W., Berliner, D.C., Filby, N.N, Marhave, R., Cahen, L.S., and Dishaw, M.M. Teaching behaviors, academic learning time, and student achievement: An overview. In C. Denham and A. Lierberman (Eds.), *Time to learn.* Washington, DC: National Institute of Education, 1980.

Stallings, J. *Using time effectively in classrooms.* La Honda, CA: Stallings Teaching and Learning Institute, 1982.

Stallings, J., Needels, M., and Stayrook, N. *How to change the process of teaching basic reading skills in secondary schools.* Final report to the National Institute of Education. Menlo Park, CA: SRI International, 1979.

Stallings, J., Cory, R., Fairweather, J., & Needels, M. *A study of basic reading skills taught in secondary schools.* Menlo Park, CA: SRI International, 1978.

Stallings, J., and Kaskowitz, D. *Follow through classroom observation evaluation, 1972-1973.* Menlo Park, CA: SRI International, 1974.

Gary A. Griffin
Susan Barnes

7

Changing Teacher Practice: A Research Based School Improvement Study*

I t is widely believed that research findings simply are not used as guides to school and classroom practice. Granted the assumption that educational research should ultimately lead to improved schooling, this failure to find research findings in use in schools and classrooms is a major disappointment, educationally and economically. Many reasons have been advanced for this condition: the reluctance of researchers to communicate their findings to constituent groups other than their research colleagues, the rigidity of school persons in terms of reconceptualizing the role of the teacher or the organization of schools, the "closed system" nature of many school settings, and the lack of rewards for changing behavior (Tikunoff, Ward, & Griffin, 1981). In short, in many settings the link between the research findings and the potential users of those findings is not developed to any sufficient degree.

The Changing Teacher Practice (CTP) study was conducted by the Research in Teacher Education (RITE) program of the Research

*The work reported herein was performed pursuant to a grant from the National Institute of Education, Department of Education. However, the opinions expressed herein do not necessarily reflect the position or policy of NIE and no official endorsement by NIE should be inferred.

and Development Center for Teacher Education as an attempt to develop such a link. The intention was to intervene in a selected school system at the level of the staff developer. This point of entry was chosen as a means to counter the argument that "outsiders can get the job done but the insider can't because of internal pressure, the informal system of the school, the history of the organization." The purpose of the study was to determine whether increasing staff developers' knowledge of two bodies of research—studies of teaching effectiveness and studies of successful school change—would affect classroom teaching and learning. In other words, would the increased knowledge of effective teaching and successful leadership behaviors result in the staff developers' adoption of successful leadership strategies, leading to an increased use of research based teaching behaviors in classrooms that would, in turn, increase on task student behavior? (For a more complete description of this study, the reader is referred to Griffin, et al., 1983.)

Description of the Study

The CTP intervention was presented to treatment group staff developers over a five day period three weeks before the opening of the 1982-1983 school year. The intervention contained four elements: research based teaching behaviors, research based staff development behaviors, relevant resources and materials, and a staff development planning booklet. Before turning attention to each of these elements, we must stress that the intervention was *not* a set of prescriptions for professional activity. It was designed as the provision of a set of options for instructional leadership, from which staff developers might choose the strategies and teaching behavior foci most aligned with their own systematic diagnosis of school and teacher needs. After the intervention staff developers began incorporating components of the RITE intervention into beginning-of-school staff development activities.

The teaching behaviors included in the intervention were identified from large scale, classroom based studies of "teaching effectiveness" where effectiveness was measured by student outcomes on standardized tests (Barnes, 1981; Good, 1981). This research focused in large measure upon classroom management or classroom instruction variables. The findings were translated into low inference, observable teaching behaviors such as "teacher breaks complex tasks into steps" and "teacher communicates consequences to students." The result of this translation was a set of 115 teaching behaviors which could serve to profile classroom teaching in this CTP intervention (Barnes, 1983). These teaching behaviors were organized into ten categories or factors (for factor analysis results, see Griffin, et al., 1983). The ten categories of behaviors reflected the research emphases on academic instruction — Planning and Preparation, Presentation, Interactions, Practice, Seatwork, Holding Students Responsible for Assignments — and on classroom management — Organizes the Classroom, Presentation of Rules and Procedures, Holds Students Responsible for Behavior, and Reactions to Students' Behavior.

The second major emphasis of the intervention was composed of research based staff development strategies found to be effective in facilitating school change (Edwards, 1981; Griffin, 1981). One strategy, organizational development, is based upon the assumption that organizations change as the people in them change (Dillon-Peterson, 1981). This strategy is characterized by a problem solving orientation, reflection and deliberation, and systematic use of available resources when addressing questions of organizational change. Another research based leadership strategy used in the intervention was Mutual Adaptation. Drawn from the work of Berman and McLaughlin (1978), mutual adaptation refers to the phenomenon, found in many settings, in which both the innovation and the characteristics of the setting change as an innovation is implemented. A third strategy included in the intervention was DDAE or the group process of dialogue, decision making, action, and evaluation, which occurs as a staff considers change (Bentzen, 1974). The final research based strategy shared with treatment group staff developers was the concerns theory detailed in work by Hall and Loucks (1978). This strategy focuses staff developers' attention upon the process of change as a personal experience, long term and developmental.

Providing treatment group staff developers with relevant resources and materials made up the third element of the intervention. Several teacher focused materials, like manuals and a demonstration videotape of classroom teaching, were previewed for treatment group staff developers. In addition, other resource materials for individual, independent study were presented to treatment group staff developers.

The fourth element of the intervention was a staff development planning booklet which directed staff developers' attention toward implementing suggestions shared in the first three components of the intervention. Treatment group staff developers first identified certain teaching behaviors as foci for future staff development efforts based upon their assessment of the need of the faculties. The planning booklet also gave the treatment group staff developers the opportunity to apply some of the research derived staff developer behaviors — diagnosing school regularities, providing for on call assistance and coordinating peer observations. By the conclusion of the intervention, the treatment group staff developers were more knowledgeable about the effective teaching and effective school change, as defined in certain bodies of research. They also had begun the process of designing staff development activities intended to move the research into practice in their own school settings.

In sum, the working hypothesis of the CTP study was that staff developers, when knowledgeable about research based effective teaching and research based leadership, would use the research based leadership behaviors when working with teachers and, in turn, the teachers would use the research based teaching behaviors in their classroom settings. Keep in mind that the intervention was provided only to the treatment group staff developers. RITE staff did not work with teachers.

The Setting and the Participants

The study was conducted in a large urban school district that was experiencing most of the problems of the 1980s: declining resources, shifting school populations, the need to provide equal educational opportunity to an increasingly heterogeneous population, legislative mandates to increase student achievement for some groups, and public pressure for "excellence." The district had spent many years vigorously trying to increase student scores on standardized achievement tests, primarily through the development and implementation of curricula in reading and mathematics based, in large part, on research findings. Further, the district had a history of attending to professional growth opportunities for teachers. Thus, contrary to many settings, this particular setting provided a rigorous test of the CTP strategy from the points of view of the problems faced by teachers and administrators and the historical attention that had been given to much of the same professional literature used in the CTP intervention. Regarding the latter point, it could be said that, in research terms, the district attempt was Treatment A and the CTP intervention was Treatment B.

The participants in the study were staff developers and teachers. Matched pairs of staff developers associated with elementary schools were nominated by the district using criteria of professional experience, role (principal or resource teacher), size and SES of school population, reputation of effectiveness, and willingness to participate in the study. Members of each pair were assigned to either treatment (N=5) or control (N=5) groups. From the teachers with whom the staff developers worked, two teachers were randomly selected for participation in the study. Thus, there were ten treatment teachers and ten control teachers.

The staff developer treatment and control groups were very similar. However, there was wide variation *within* the two groups. This was also true of teachers. The within group variation included years of experience, grade levels taught, nature of student populations, and professional development stage. Therefore, the CTP intervention encountered a wide, rather than a narrow, range of professional and site characteristics.

Data Collection and Analysis

Following the before-school intervention provided to treatment group staff developers, data were collected regarding staff developer behavior and teacher behavior. Treatment and control group staff developers provided the research team with self-reports of staff development activities and interactions in the form of journals. Teachers also provided self-reports of their interactions with staff developers and their participation in staff development activities. Using a low inference teacher observation instrument designed for the CTP study (Barnes, 1983), teachers were also observed teaching both reading and mathematics. Data collection began on the first day of the 1982-1983 school year and continued periodically over a six month period. Because observations of teaching behaviors occurred after treatment group staff developers had begun interaction with treatment group teachers, no baseline data on teaching behaviors prior to treatment were available. In addition, because staff developers decided to emphasize particular teaching behaviors based on their assessments of teacher needs, local variations were expected, encouraged, and did, in fact, occur. Due to this variation, predictable, cumulative treatment effects over time were not expected.

The journal entries were analyzed to determine the self-reported frequency of the research based leadership strategies. Four coders, trained to a .86 agreement level, worked in pairs to note the frequency of the leadership strategies. Disagreements were resolved through reexamination of the journal entries. Of 8,073 possible instances of coding agreement, 29 disagreements between coders were not resolved. These were not included in the analysis of staff developer behavior. For staff developers, treatment and control, the frequencies of research based leadership behavior were divided by the number of journal entries for each staff developer. This was necessary because of the differences in the number of entries across the staff developers. Thus, a mean frequency of research based staff developer behaviors was obtained for each participant. The frequency of each discrete behavior was also determined for each staff developer and for the treatment and control groups.

The frequencies of research based teaching behaviors, collected through the use of the low inference observation instrument noted above, were converted to rates per minute for each teaching behavior. Next, the teaching behaviors within each of ten categories on the observation instrument were averaged to produce means in each category for each teacher. Because the sample size of twenty teachers was small, mean rates were used to provide data that more closely approximated the normal distribution (Hayes, 1973).

The design used to analyze observed teaching data was a hierarchically nested, repeated measures design with five factors. One factor was the *treatment* factor with two levels, treatment and control. Nested within each treatment condition was the second factor, *staff developers*, with five levels. Staff developers were simply designated 1 through 5; no qualitative meaning was attached to those designations. Nested within each staff developer was the third factor, *teacher*, at two levels. The two teachers were again assigned number 1 or number 2 with no qualitative difference implied. Two factors were crossed with the other three; *time* (at three levels; time 1, time 2, and time 3) and *content* (level 1, mathematics; level 2, reading). These were included to account for systematic variation due to time and content differences rather than as factors of major interest.

These analyses allowed the RITE research team to test the effects of the intervention in terms of influence on both staff developer behavior and teacher behavior.

Outcomes

The outcomes of the CTP strategy can be examined in two ways, a research perspective and a client perspective. Each of these is discussed in turn.

Research Outcomes

Two bodies of research outcomes were pertinent for the purposes of this chapter: one related to research based leadership behaviors and another related to research based teacher behaviors.

Table 1 includes the frequencies of research based staff developer behaviors for treatment and control groups as well as for individuals within the two groups. The frequencies are presented as means (i.e., number of research based behaviors divided by number of entries as described above). The treatment group mean was slightly more than twice as high as the control group. The results of a Mann-Whitney test indicated that this difference was statistically significant at the .01 level. The within group means were also in favor of the treatment group in that the highest mean for the control group was lower than the lowest mean for the treatment group.

Table 2 includes the mean frequencies for each of the research based staff developer behaviors for treatment and control groups. These frequencies provide the substance of the difference

Table 1
MEAN FREQUENCIES OF ALL DESIRED STAFF DEVELOPER
BEHAVIORS PER JOURNAL ENTRY BY GROUP AND PARTICIPANT

ID#	Treatment	ID#	Control
1	5.12	6	3.70
2	5.44	7	2.33
3	8.78	8	1.66
4	8.14	9	2.85
5	6.43	10	4.15
	$\overline{x} = 6.47$		$\overline{x} = 3.05$

between the group means presented in Table 1. It can be seen that there were strong differences between treatment and control groups on certain of the behaviors and not on others.

The behaviors which accounted for the differences between the treatment and control group staff developers are of interest because they are, in great measure, characterized by 1) attention to the school as an organization; 2) reconsideration of the so-called isolation of teachers from the other teachers and administrators; 3) the need to adapt behavior and expectations according to observed school conditions; and 4) promotion of interactions within and outside the school environment. Taken together, the behaviors are ones that break down the perceived inadequacies of schools and school people to act together toward organizational goals.

Another observation about the staff developer behavior findings is that the greatest difference between treatment and control groups occurred for the leadership strategy which focused staff developer attention on interactions regarding teacher behavior. Schools have been criticized because they lack a "technical core" (Williams, 1982): that body of knowledge and skill used to accomplish the mission of the school, teaching. The CTP study accomplished the objective of providing staff developers with the research findings that can make up a technical core. And the treatment group staff developers did indeed demonstrate the use of that body of knowledge in their interactions with teachers.

The ten categories of research based teaching behaviors included in the CTP study, both as content for the intervention and as

Table 2

	Behavior	Treatment	Control
1.	Diagnose school and classroom specific regularities	.49	.27
2.	Provide teachers with opportunities to interact with one another about teaching and schooling	.25	.12
3.	Provide teachers with opportunities to observe one another and to discuss what was observed	.04	.02
4.	Provide teachers with opportunities to plan together	.11	.02
5.	Provide teachers with opportunities to implement their plans	.00	.00
6.	Provide teachers with feedback which is objective, concrete, and focused	.22	.12
7.	Use teacher time to deal with teacher problems, issues, and concerns (rather than with administrative, routine, or procedural matters)	.27	.26
8.	Interact with teachers in friendly and positive ways	.03	.02
9.	Adapt staff development behavior according to personal and organizational characteristics of "users"	.24	.05
10.	Demonstrate knowledge of "effective" teaching as revealed by research	.37	.05
11.	Provide in-classroom technical assistance (e.g., coaching) to teachers	.06	.03
12.	Provide teacher with specific, concrete resources	.29	.18
13.	Engage teachers in problem identification and solution formulation and testing activities	.16	.11
14.	Work with teachers on adaptation of teaching strategies according to the characteristics of students, the classroom, and the school	.24	.11
15.	Provide teachers with evidence that "teachers can make a difference" in pupil outcomes	.08	.02
16.	Link teachers to technical assistance outside the immediate school environment	.22	.09
17.	Communicate expectations clearly and precisely	.18	.12
18.	Diagnose individual stages of concern of teachers	.03	.00
19.	Formulate interventions based, in part, on teachers' stages of concern	.02	.00
20.	Provide consistent, ongoing assistance to teachers	.09	.08
21.	Include the building principal or resource teacher in activities	.17	.06
22.	Reflect upon the effects of his/her behavior and use that reflection as a basis for decisions about maintenance or modification of that behavior	.14	.06
23.	Focus on teacher behavior	.45	.09

objects of data collection, are noted in Table 3. The mean rates for each observation category were used to determine the degree to which the intervention was effective in influencing teachers through interactions with staff developers. These mean rates for each observation category for the treatment and control groups, as well as the grand mean, are also presented in Table 3. In the categories dealing with academics, the treatment teachers exhibited higher mean rates in Planning and Preparation, Presentation, and Holding Students Responsible for Assignments. Treatment teachers displayed behaviors related to Presentation twelve times more often then did control teachers. Behaviors related to Planning and Preparation were seen nearly twice as often for treatment teachers as for control teachers. Control teachers showed slightly higher mean rates for Interactions, Practice, and Seatwork.

A more consistent pattern was seen in the four observation categories related to classroom management. In each of those categories, the treatment teachers displayed higher mean rates. For two categories (Holds Students Responsible for Behavior and Reactions to Student Behavior) the differences were slight. For the other two categories (Organizes Classroom and Presentation of Rules and

Table 3

MEAN RATES OF OBSERVATION CATEGORIES
FOR TREATMENT AND CONTROL TEACHERS

		Grand Mean	Treatment Mean	Control Mean
Academic				
A.	Planning and preparation	.00667	.00865	.00489
B.	Presentation	.04255	.4831	.03739
C.	Interaction	.05041	.04692	.05354
D.	Practice	.00700	.00682	.00716
E.	Seatwork	.01456	.01291	.01640
F.	Holding students responsible for assignments	.01199	.01365	.01050
Classroom Management				
G.	Organizes classroom	.01142	.01591	.00740
H.	Presentation of rules and procedures	.00484	.00715	.00276
I.	Holds students responsible for behavior	.0098	.01102	.00905
J.	Reactions to students' behavior	.02671	.02741	.02608

Griffin and Barnes

Procedures), the mean rates of the treatment teachers were more than twice as large as those of the control teachers.

In summary, treatment teachers had higher frequencies of desired behaviors in seven of the ten observation categories. They consistently used research based teaching behaviors related to organizing and managing the classroom.

Statistically significant differences were in favor of the treatment group in two categories related to academics—Planning and Preparation and Presentation—and in two categories related to managing the classroom—Organizes Classroom and Presentation of Rules and Procedures. The other categories of research based teaching behaviors did not demonstrate statistically significant differences for either treatment or control group. In one category, Presentation of Rules and Procedures, a statistically significant time by treatment interaction did occur due to the extremely high frequencies exhibited by treatment teachers during the first observation period.

The teaching behaviors which differentiated between treatment and control group teachers were those which are fundamental to the act of teaching, planning, and presentation. Conventional wisdom, as well as studies of teacher planning (Yinger, 1982), supports the importance of that planning for student success in the classroom. Through presentation skills teachers explain new concepts, share ideas, arouse interest in further learning, and communicate knowledge. To increase these teaching behaviors significantly is educationally important. Because the teaching behaviors are neither exotic nor inconsistent with conventional classroom activity, it is not surprising that there were statistically significant effects for some categories of behaviors and not for others. Further, the intervention stressed matching content (teaching behaviors) of staff development activities to the assessed needs of the teachers. This resulted in differential emphasis of the teaching behaviors among the staff developers. Such variation in focus resulted in differences between categories which were emphasized and those which were not. Further, in light of the discussion of the school district's attention to research in teaching in recent years, a statistically significant difference between treatment and control groups for all categories would be surprising indeed.

The particular differences which emerged between treatment and control group teachers may have been closely tied to the resource materials shared by the RITE staff with the treatment group staff developers. One specific resource, *Organizing and Managing the Elementary School Classroom* (Evertson, et al., 1981), was particularly well received by both treatment group staff developers and teachers because of its practical, teacher derived suggestions for planning and implementing classroom organization. Another resource, *Teacher Manual: Missouri Mathematics Effectiveness Project* (Good, et al., 1977) stressed the importance of developing new concepts and skills through demonstration; for example, as part of a system of instruction in mathematics. Because classroom management and academic achievement are prevalent concerns in public schools today, the teacher oriented, immediately useable resources combined with training for staff developers in the related research resulted in a powerful intervention for certain kinds of teaching behaviors.

Client Outcomes

The effects of the strategy, in terms of practice, provide a chronicle somewhat different from a strictly research oriented one.

The participating school district officers were enthusiastic about the CTP strategy from the beginning. There was a high level of excitement about the possibilities before, during, and after the intervention and subsequent data collection associated with the research effort. Participant response from treatment group members was consistently positive. Participants testified that other staff developers in the district should have the same opportunity they had been provided.

When the study was completed and the findings were available, the district adopted the CTP intervention for 175 elementary and middle school principals and resource teachers. Part of the adoption decision was made on the basis of the findings of research. That is, the findings of the CTP study were positive enough to suggest the usefulness of the strategy for district purposes. A large part of the decision, however, appears to have been made on more practical grounds. The RITE research team suspects that the commonsense approach to leadership and teaching was compelling to district officials. The cost effectiveness of the strategy, in terms of financial resources, was undoubtedly attractive. In addition, the generalizability of the leadership behaviors to school improvement purposes other than teaching was also a likely factor.

Discussion

The CTP study was an attempt to introduce research findings into ongoing school settings as a means of improving instructional leadership and teaching. Admittedly, research findings that are available to the thoughtful practitioner do not nearly cover all of the activities associated with schooling and teaching. They do, however, provide a basis from which school leaders and teachers can make informed decisions and engage in reasoned action. Beyond what research tells school people is a world of schooling that calls for creative intellectual activity. The CTP intervention, in some regards, provided participating staff developers and teachers with a research based foundation upon which that creative activity could rest.

The two bodies of research that formed the core of the CTP intervention were findings from studies of teaching, and findings from studies of school and teacher change. The intervention was provided to treatment group staff developers who then worked with teachers. Rather than being a set of prescriptions, the intervention provided a body of information and the participating staff developers selected strategies and content that they felt were appropriate for their school settings, the teachers with whom they worked, and the students in the teachers' classrooms. Staff developer participants in the intervention were given time to engage in situation-specific planning and urged to use the results of that planning in their interactions with school faculty members. The CTP intervention was designed to test the notion that staff developers could accomplish school goals without participation by persons outside the system; the RITE staff did not interact with teachers except to observe in their classrooms.

Considerable talk and some activity has centered around the topic of the so-called "gap" between research findings and practice.

It has been assumed that the reduction of the ideological and temporal distances between what research discovers and what practitioners do are almost insurmountable. The CTP study, a deliberate attempt to bridge the gap, resulted in a set of desired outcomes that suggest that practitioners will use the results of research. Several implications can be drawn from the implementation of the CTP intervention.

First, practitioners in this study were neither disdainful of nor resistant to lessons learned from systematic inquiry. One can speculate that the reasons for their positive responses to the CTP intervention were based largely on the fact that the research presented was directly related to practice.

Second, the research provided a focus for doing the work of classrooms and schools. It provided conceptualizations of instructional leadership and teaching that were coherent and that could serve as rallying points around which to organize practice. Although obvious public emphasis is on improving schools, response from either research or practitioner regarding how to effect that improvement is less obvious. The CTP intervention seemed to provide bases for improvement activity, a welcome resource for school persons.

Third, the research was translated from the sometimes painful jargon of the research community into the more conventional language of schools. This translation was accomplished, in some instances, in print by the resource materials provided to participants and, in others, interpersonally by the RITE research team during the intervention. Although the study did not specifically address this issue, participant self-reports at the conclusion of the study testified to its importance in their decisions to adopt the strategy in schools and classrooms.

Fourth, the CTP strategy was conceptually and practically linked to ongoing processes and expectations in the school setting. As discussed earlier, the school district had in place activities and statements of purpose that were ideologically and theoretically aligned with the intentions of the CTP intervention at system, school, and classroom levels. As with other speculations, it can be surmised that this alignment was a significant system variable contributing to the overall success of the CTP strategy.

Fifth, the CTP strategy was not a set of prescriptions for action. That is, participants were not *required* to engage in certain practices. Rather, participants were expected to analyze their own situations, using a set of procedures and data sources, and then to make decisions and act upon their analyses. This is in marked contrast to improvement strategies that demand fidelity to a set of ideas or practices. The CTP strategy's demand was to consider and act upon the perceived match between school/classroom characteristics and a set of research based options for leadership and teaching practice.

Conclusion

The following statement appeared in the document that proposed the CTP study to the National Institute of Education.

> The story goes that George Washington Carver once prayed to understand the secrets of the universe. Despairing of an answer to so comprehensive a request, he modified his desire for understanding to the more modest dimensions of the peanut, thereafter contributing to scientific and economic advancement and successfully solving the problem of slippage in the jelly sandwich.
>
> Similarly, having despaired of understanding the secrets of producing effective teachers who will induce all students to become persons of all accomplishments and virtues; [RITE has] settled for understanding some processes by which most elementary teachers can be helped to teach most elementary students to demonstrate higher levels of skill in mathematics and reading.

As can be seen from this summary of the CTP study, that modest statement itself subsumed an ambitious purpose. The study, however, demonstrated the possibility of accomplishing large parts of the purpose and provided the groundwork for better understanding of the research into practice phenomenon.

References

Barnes, S. *Observer training manual for the CTP study.* Austin, TX: Research and Development Center for Teacher Education, University of Texas at Austin, 1983.

Barnes, S. *Synthesis of selected research on teaching findings.* Austin, TX: Research and Development Center for Teacher Education, University of Texas at Austin, 1981.

Bentzen, M. *Changing schools: The magic feather principle.* New York: McGraw-Hill, 1974.

Berman, P., and McLaughlin, M.W. *Federal programs supporting educational change. Vol. 8: Implementing and sustaining innovations.* Santa Monica, CA: Rand Corporation, 1978.

Dillon-Peterson, B. (Ed.). *Staff development/organizational development.* Washington, DC: Association for Supervision and Curriculum Development, 1981.

Edwards, S. *Changing teacher practice.* Austin, TX: Research and Development Center for Teacher Education, University of Texas at Austin, 1981.

Evertson, C., Emmer, D., Clements, B., Sanford, J., Worsham, M., and Williams, G. *Organizing and managing the elementary school classroom.* Austin, TX: Research and Development Center for Teacher Education, University of Texas at Austin, 1981.

Good, G., Grouws, D., Beckerman, T., Ebmeier, H., Flatt, L., and Schneeberger, S. *Teacher manual: Missouri mathematics effectiveness project.* Columbia, MO: University of Missouri, 1977.

Good, T. *Classroom research: What we know and what we need to know.* Austin, TX: Research and Development Center for Teacher Education, University of Texas at Austin, 1981.

Griffin, G. *An eclectic approach to staff development.* Austin, TX: Research and Development Center for Teacher Education, University of Texas at Austin, 1981.

Griffin, G., Barnes, S., O'Neal, S., Edwards, S., Defino, M., and Hukill, H. *Changing teacher practice: Final report of an experimental study.* Austin, TX: Research and Development Center for Teacher Education, University of Texas at Austin, 1983.

Hall, G., and Loucks, S. Teacher concerns as a basis for facilitating and personalizing staff development. *Teachers College Record,* 1978, *80,* 36-53.

Hays, W.L. *Statistics for the social sciences.* New York: Holt, Rinehart and Winston, 1973.

Tikunoff, W.J., Ward, B.A., and Griffin, G.A. Interactive research and development as a form of professional growth. In K.R. Howey, R. Bents, and D. Corrigan (Eds.), *School-focused inservice: Descriptions and discussions.* Reston, VA: Association of Teacher Educators, 1981.

Williams, R. Changing teacher behaviors: From symbolism to reality. In M. Defino and H. Carter (Eds.), *Changing teacher practices: Proceedings of a national conference.* Austin, TX: Research and Development Center for Teacher Education, University of Texas at Austin, 1982.

Yinger, R. A study of teacher planning: Description and theory development using ethnographic and information processing methods. In W. Doyle and T. Good (Eds.), *Focus on Teaching.* Chicago: University of Chicago Press, 1982.

Part Four
New Directions in Research on Effective Reading and Staff Development Efforts

S urely there is more to the effective teaching of reading than what has been revealed through process-product research. In this section of the book we move to consider alternative paradigms for research in effective teaching as well as staff development efforts directed toward effective teaching but not tied solely to the process-product literature. In the next chapter, Duffy and Ball describe the research literature on teacher planning and decision making leading to a discussion of the process mediating paradigm for the study of effective teaching. Roehler and Duffy's chapter reports instructional research derived from an interactive decision making framework. Calfee and Henry report a study of effective teaching and school improvement which is based on a conceptualized model for reading nstruction. Weisburg presents a review of the Madeline Hunter model for improving teacher effectiveness.

Gerald G. Duffy
Deborah L. Ball

8

Instructional Decision Making and Reading Teacher Effectiveness

A s previous chapters indicate, research on teacher effectiveness has been dominated by the process-product paradigm. The focus has been the observed behaviors of the teacher — what the teacher says and does in the act of teaching.

While such research is important, it suffers from a serious limitation. By studying only overt teacher behaviors, it precludes any examination of the less visible cognitive processes teachers engage in when teaching. In short, process-product research seems to ignore the mental life of teachers and the possibility that teacher thinking could be an important part of teacher effectiveness.

However, the newer research on teaching and teacher effectiveness has moved beyond the limitations of the process-product paradigm to study teacher thinking as well as teacher behavior. A major movement in this direction is research on teacher decision making.

Background

Decision making is often assumed to be an integral part of effective instruction. In the typical scenario, a teacher collects a variety of data about pupils, thinks about these data in terms of a theoretical orientation or a particular belief system, and then makes decisions about how to instruct. The decisions are reflective, involving selection from among alternative hypotheses based upon the data collected and the parameters of the teacher's theory or belief system. Hence, Kamil and Pearson (1979), representing reading, argue that the theoretical orientations of teachers result in differential decisions because "different models dictate different (and sometimes opposing) instructional methods." Cooney (1981) makes the same point about math education, saying that teaching

> Is a process of gathering information, making a diagnosis, and constructing a response based on that diagnosis. While much of this process may be quite automatic, some situations require conscious decision making. The act of generating and considering alternatives in constructing a response—that is, making an instructional decision—is of paramount importance in teaching. (p. 67)

Similarly, characterizing research on teaching generally, Clark and Yinger (1979) describe the teacher as

> Constantly assessing the situation, processing information about the situation, making decisions about what to do next, guiding action on the basis of these decisions, and observing the effects of the action on the students. (p. 247)

Positions such as these are based on two assumptions about teaching and teacher effectiveness. First, there are indeed alternatives from which classroom teachers can choose. Second, the teacher who is reflective in identifying such alternatives is more likely to be effective than the teacher who merely reacts or follows a teacher's guide.

Reading educators are particularly attracted to the concept of instructional decision making. They are uncomfortable with researchers (e.g., Rosenshine, 1981) who argue for the creation of "master developers" who write instructional scripts rather than for "master teachers" who make their own decisions, and with instructional programs such as DISTAR which seemingly leave little decision making to the teacher.

There are two explanations for this belief. One lies in the complexity of reading and of reading instruction. Reading educators believe that reading is not a one-dimensional skill that can be taught with scripts. Instead, reading involves a variety of cognitive processes, abilities, skills, and affective conditions which lead to a variety of outcomes. Further, the students are themselves complex, representing various knowledge backgrounds, experiences, abilities, and aptitudes. When the complexity of reading interacts with the complexity of students, a variety of potential instructional alternatives becomes possible. Hence, reading educators view instruction as a continuous selection from among alternatives.

The second reason why reading educators are drawn to the decision making model is their belief that teachers are professionals, rather than technicians. The tension which exists between these two kinds of behaviors is illustrated in Gage's *The Scientific Basis of the Art of Teaching* (1977). On the one hand, Gage argues for professional behavior when he writes that "no one can ever prescribe all the twists and turns to be taken as the...classroom teacher uses judgment, sudden insight, sensitivity, and agility to promote learning" (p. 15) and when he argues that teaching is an art which calls for intuition and improvisation as well as "departures from...rules, formulas, and algorithms." However, Gage also suggests technical behavior by describing the real role of the teacher as "bringing the student into...interaction with the instructional materials" and by claiming the materials, much more than teachers, are actually responsible for providing content coverage. This conflict between the teacher as a technician or a manager of the instructional environment, and the teacher as a professional who thinks and makes judgments is fundamental to understanding the position of reading educators. While the technician uses the science of instruction in relatively inflexible ways, the professional adapts scientific knowledge to meet the shifting demands of the instructional situation. Reading educators typically subscribe to the latter and, as a result, put a priority on decision making.

Surprisingly, however, there is little evidence that such teacher decision making is an important component of instructional effectiveness. Reviews of the teacher effectiveness research (Rupley, this volume; Brophy, 1979; Duffy, 1981; Medley, 1979) rarely mention decision making. Instead, the most heavily emphasized correlates of effectiveness are the amount of allocated instructional time, the amount of time in which students are engaged on task, the degree to which the teacher maintains an academic focus, the closeness with which the teacher monitors student response, and the pace maintained by the teacher to insure content coverage. In short, the focus is on efficient instructional management, either in terms of generating more instructional time or of keeping pupils engaged.

Similarly, there is little evidence of decision making in studies of classroom reading practices. For instance, Durkin's now classic study (1978-1979) of classroom comprehension instruction portrayed teachers "assessing" and mentioning comprehension, neither of which suggests that teachers make decisions or select from among alternatives. Similarly, Duffy and McIntyre's study (1982) of six primary grade teachers provided little evidence of instructional decision making. Instead, they report that the teachers "operated within the guidelines of the basal text and its affiliated workbook and, in effect, abdicated instructional decision making to these materials."

In sum, while reading educators believe in the importance of decision making, it has not yet been established as an important aspect of teacher effectiveness, and studies of practicing classroom teachers indicate that even effective teachers avoid reflective decision making during reading instruction. Despite this, we have recently learned some things about teacher decision making. This chapter examines these findings with a particular view toward reading teacher effectiveness. The existing research is reviewed and explanations for the lack of relationship between reflective teacher behavior and instructional effectiveness are suggested.

Research on Teacher Decision Making

Research on teacher decision making and on the cognitive processing of teachers is relatively recent. In addition to the review provided here, the reader may also wish to consult articles by Shavelson (1976, 1983), Clark and Yinger (1979), Brophy (1984), and Borko, et al. (1979), each of which provides a particular perspective for examining teacher decision making.

A variety of both laboratory (simulation) and classroom based studies has been completed to learn more about how teachers think. However, studying this "invisible" world of thinking presents significant methodological challenges. Four basic approaches have been used: video taping followed by stimulated recall, "think aloud" methods, policy capturing, and ethnographic case studies.

Stimulated recall interviews are used most frequently. In this process tracing method, teachers view videotapes of themselves planning or teaching classroom lessons and are asked to stop the tape whenever they wish to comment on or discuss thoughts or decisions occurring at the particular moment in the lesson. The researcher may also question or probe for thoughts and decisions.

The think aloud method, another process tracing approach, calls for teachers to talk into tape recorders as they plan lessons or make other preactive decisions (e.g., forming reading groups, selecting appropriate language arts activities). This method also may be followed by a stimulated recall interview as described above. The think aloud approach is most appropriate in studies of preactive teacher thinking since verbalizing one's thoughts during instruction interferes with the process of interactive teaching.

In policy capturing studies, teachers are given hypothetical descriptions of students or situations and are asked to report the judgments or decisions they make and the cues to which they attend in making such judgments. The approach has been used to study a variety of decision making situations, from management of student behavior to content selection.

Finally, ethnographic case studies of individual teachers have provided rich descriptions of teacher behavior which, in turn, lead to insights about the hidden world of thinking and judgment that lies behind observable teacher behaviors. These insights provide new hypotheses about teacher thinking during instruction.

Clearly, research on teacher thinking generally and on teacher decision making in particular is in an early stage. As such, the findings to date are constrained by the limitations of the techniques used by researchers. Despite this, useful research has been conducted. Typically, it has been divided into temporal phases. The *preactive* phase refers to decisions made when planning and thinking prior to instruction. The *interactive* phase includes the in-flight decisions made during instruction. Completing the cyclical process are decisions and reflections made in the *postactive* or evaluative phase (Jackson, 1968).

Studies of Interactive Decision Making

Because teacher effectiveness tends to focus on what teachers are doing when they are actually teaching, we consider first studies of teacher thinking during the interactive phase. Interactive thinking is particularly difficult to study because it occurs in the complex and busy environment of the classroom where thoughts cannot be examined at leisure and where the pace is often frantic. Such a climate does not lend itself to reflective and analytic self-consciousness. Despite this, several studies have examined interactive instructional decision making. Four representative ones are reviewed here.

McNair and Joyce (1979) studied ten teachers over a period of one school year as part of a larger project known as the South Bay Study. Using stimulated recall interviews, they interviewed each teacher on six different occasions. To learn more about the interactive information processing strategies that teachers use when making in-flight decisions, the investigators established a classification scheme for categorizing the teachers' concerns. Five major categories emerged: pupil, lesson content, procedures, time, and materials. In the course of the sixty stimulated recall interviews, the teachers mentioned a total of 1,249 concerns. Of these, 39 percent related to the pupils (e.g., their attitudes, behavior, and learning) and 32 percent were content related (e.g., facts and ideas, objectives and tasks). Concerns about direction giving, modifications of the normal routines, and scheduling procedures accounted for 15 percent of the total; materials accounted for 8 percent; and time concerns (e.g., pacing) accounted for 27 percent. In general, McNair and Joyce noted that the teachers focused on task completion rather than on thinking, and that there was little variation in thinking among the teachers studied.

Peterson and Clark (1978) reported similar findings in another stimulated recall study of teachers' interactive thinking. The major cue considered by teachers was student participation and involvement with tasks. Student attention took priority over the quality of the discussions. Of the organizational, cognitive, and affective objectives cited by teachers, the most prevalent was organizational, which involved "carrying out the plan" and in which decision making focused on management. Peterson and Clark concluded from their findings that teachers considered alternatives only when instruction was going poorly and that, even then, they rarely made a decision to change the strategy.

This finding about the press for carrying out a predetermined plan was further investigated by Morine-Dershimer (1979). She found that teachers have a set of expectations about their planned lessons which represents a comprehensive mental image of lesson activities and content. This mental image has a potent influence on teaching because interactive decisions are apparently made when the teacher observes discrepancies between the mental image of how the lesson ought to go and the reality of how it actually goes. Three decision points were identified. The first occurred when there was little or no discrepancy between the plan and reality, which allowed teachers to follow established routines. The second occurred when minor discrepancies occurred; teachers considered limited alternatives and made minor in-flight decisions or changes. The third type involved a critical discrepancy between the teachers' mental image and the actual lesson. In these cases, teachers typically considered the information available but then postponed making any decision to change rather than adapting instruction to meet these unanticipated discrepancies.

A fourth investigation examined how teachers cope with unpredictable student behaviors (referred to here as "critical moments"). Shroyer's analysis (1981) of four mathematics teachers' stimulated recall interviews revealed three types of teacher "moves" in response to critical moments: alleviation, exploitation, and avoidance. The most prevalent was avoidance (or what Morine-Dershimer called "postponement"). Shroyer concluded that teachers rely on routine behaviors in order to reduce the complexity of the classroom, that the absence of interactive teacher decision making is sometimes due to an inability to think of alternatives, and that the primary cause of teacher difficulty in dealing with discrepancies between plan and reality were 1) their limited knowledge of the content itself and 2) their limited "pedagogical repertoire" or set of alternative strategies for teaching the content.

These studies of interactive decision making indicate a preoccupation by teachers with activity flow and procedural concerns which suggests technical, rather than professional, teacher behavior. Interactive decisions aimed at promoting student understanding are strikingly absent.

Studies of Planning Decisions

Morine-Dershimer's concept of the teacher's mental image of a planned lesson suggests that what we can observe in the interactive stage of teaching is influenced by what teachers think about in the preactive phase. Consequently, we turn next to research on instructional planning.

Zahorik (1970) studied two groups of teachers to determine the effect of planning on actual instruction. One group of teachers was given two weeks to plan for a lesson, and was provided with objectives and an outline of the content to be covered. The other group was asked to reserve an hour of classroom time, but was given no further details about what they would be asked to do during that time. The teachers in both groups then taught a lesson, one group having planned for the instruction and the other teaching extemporaneously. The lessons were recorded and Zahorik analyzed them for differences in sensitivity of teaching behavior which he defined as "verbal acts of the teacher that permit, encourage, and develop pupils' ideas, thoughts, and actions." Zahorik found that the teachers who had not planned for instruction were more sensitive to and made more use of students' ideas and thoughts than those who had planned in advance. This suggests that the teachers who planned (and, presumably, created a mental image of a lesson) may have been less able to attend to cues which arise during the interactive phase. In contrast, the teachers who taught spontaneously tuned in more to such cues and, as a result, made more interactive decisions designed to encourage thoughts and ideas.

Zahorik's findings may be explained by other studies of planning which suggest that teachers' plans focus on establishing smooth activity flow rather than understanding. In one laboratory study, for instance, Zahorik (1975) found that, rather than considering objectives or purposes, most teachers decided on content activities first, while objectives were considered first by less than a third of the teachers. Zahorik concluded that the specification of objectives is not a focal point in preactive decision making.

Similarly, Peterson, Marx, and Clark (1978), in their study of twelve junior high school teachers, found that the teachers focused most on content, strategies, and activities during planning, with the least amount of time spent on instructional objectives. This pattern persists in other studies. In fact, Taylor (1970) found that teachers determined purposes for lessons by first selecting a particular activity and then deciding what the activity could achieve instead of selecting particular objectives and then determining activities. Again, the evidence points to a preoccupation with activity flow rather than attention to the promotion of student understanding.

Reading Research Which Relates to Decision Making

Some of the recently conducted reading instructional research has direct implications for teacher decision making. Three lines of research are of particular interest.

The first focuses on teacher decisions about establishing reading groups (Borko, Shavelson & Stern, 1981; Borko & Niles, 1982). Such studies are of the policy capturing type described earlier and, as such, are conducted in isolation from real classrooms and the constraints present in the instructional environment. While these studies provide a useful foundation regarding the thinking processes teachers *say* they use in forming groups, whether the findings are accurate reflections of how such decisions are actually made in practice is unclear (Duffy, 1982).

Another line of research focuses on teacher interruption behavior during children's reading and the way teachers respond to miscues (Allington, in press). Hoffman (1979) suggests that teacher feedback in response to reading miscues should be analyzed in three ways: 1) selectivity, or what to respond to; 2) timing; and 3) the nature of the prompt. He suggests that a teacher's decision to intervene when a student is reading may be based on the teacher's theoretical orientation to reading. For example, a teacher with a strong psycholinguistic orientation to reading may ignore miscues which do not distort the meaning of the text. Such decisions are thought to be independent of the basal text manual and are presumably aimed at promoting student learning. Similarly, the work of Harste and Burke (1977) is based on this hypothesis. However, research designed to test this hypothesis has failed to demonstrate an observable relationship between a teacher's theoretical orientation and instructional decision making. In fact, Hoffman and Kugle (1982) found the correlations between beliefs and teacher-student feedback to be small, ranging from a high of .33 to a low of .01, with most values below .20. This does little to support the contention that a strong relationship exists between teacher conception of subject matter and classroom instruction.

Duffy and Anderson (1982) found similar results. They set out to describe the relationships between a teacher's implicit reading theory held in the abstract and the teacher's actual practice. After a three year study in which three sets of teachers were observed for one year each, they concluded that decisions are not influenced as much by the teacher's theory as by the pressures of the instructional context. Specifically, the teachers focused on maintaining a smooth activity flow, on following the sequence prescribed in the basal textbook, and on providing "structure" for the low group students. These pressures took priority in the teachers' minds, and their implicit theories came into play only after being filtered though these priorities. The only time they selected from among alternatives was when establishing organizational procedures early in the school year (such as when forming reading groups). Once instruction was initiated, all the teachers seemed to follow the conception embodied in the basal text. The behaviors of the teachers were more technical than professional, and revealed little evidence of reflective decision making.

The third line of reading research examines teacher use of basal materials and has strong implications for the study of decision making. Most estimates indicate that 85-90 percent of American teachers follow one or another basal textbook and that in many cases the basal is mandated rather than selected by individual teachers. This places a severe restriction on instructional alternatives. In addition, Durkin's report (1981) that teacher's guides emphasize practice activities rather than instruction suggests a further restriction on the number of alternatives available. Shannon's study (1983) of why teachers so confidently use basal texts also has implications for decision making. The teachers he studied believed that commercial materials supplied the continuity, the instruction, and the assessment methods for their reading instruction. In Shannon's terms, teachers "reify" the basal text. In so doing, they rationalize their lack of instructional decision making and assign this function to the commercial text materials.

Summarizing the Decision Making Research

The findings from studies of teacher decision making do not support the assumption of a direct relationship between teacher decision making and teacher effectiveness. While it is intuitively sensible that such a relationship *ought* to exist, little evidence suggests that it does. Instead, the data suggest that teachers do not rely upon rational models to make decisions about developing student understanding but, instead, focus on procedural concerns regarding classroom organization and management. This apparently happens because of environmental conditions which encourage teachers to follow the prescriptions of the instructional materials in a technical, rather than professional manner and to be suppliers of activities and managers of the environment rather than explainers who develop insights and understanding. These findings are of particular concern to reading educators, who believe that a hallmark of the effective teacher is decision making regarding matters of reading content, interpretation of content, and selection of instructional strategies—decisions which are conspicuous by their absence in the research. In fact, based on data collected to date, one must conclude that effective teachers are effective because they generate a great deal of time on task through the use of effective management techniques, not because they select from among alternatives using a decision making model.

Discussion

The question that now needs to be answered is, "Why do the data indicate that classroom reading teachers make few instructional decisions?" We believe that effective teachers *do* make decisions but that we are not finding evidence of them because of our general lack of knowledge regarding what we are looking for and how to find it. We may not be sophisticated enough in our methodology to uncover all facets of teacher decision making and, given this condition, we cannot assume that decision making does not exist simply because we have not found it. Three illustrations of our lack of sophistication in the area of teacher decision making follow.

First, researchers may have made erroneous assumptions about how teachers make use of knowledge. A new literature on knowledge use in teaching suggests a contradiction between the reality of classroom life and the conventional view that formal knowledge provides a rational basis for conducting practice.

Consider the following examples. Schon (1983) states that an emphasis on solving classroom problems by rationally applying relevant knowledge disregards the prior importance of problem setting—that is, first making sense of the uncertainty, complexity, and parameters of the problem before seeking its solution. Similarly, during a one year return to classroom teaching, Cazden (1976) found unexpected and significant problems in trying to think "abstractly in the face of all that concrete reality." Finally, Lampert (1982) points out that many situations in actual teaching represent dilemmas having no solution (not problems which can be solved) and that, rather than solving problems as is assumed in the decision making research, teachers may instead learn to cope with dilemmas. All three examples suggest a conceptual and practical gap between what researchers and teacher educators believe the role of formal knowledge to be and the patterns of such knowledge use in actual practice. If such a gap exists, then the rational application model of knowledge use may prove to be an idealized and inappropriate one (Jackson, 1971; Lortie, 1975) which misleads teachers rather than helping them. For instance, if teachers are trained in the rational model and then find that it does not work in reality, they may reject formal knowledge as impractical and resort to trial and error, routinized behavior, or other strategies for making decisions (Feinman-Nemser & Ball, 1984). Hopefully, some may develop views of formal knowledge which are more helpful in teaching and in thinking about classrooms. If this is so, research may not be finding much decision making because the assumptions about how teachers use knowledge has been conceptualized and examined from a rationalistic perspective that does not match the reality of classroom life.

Second, researchers' examination of instructional decision making may not reflect the complexity of instruction itself and may not capture the kinds of decisions teachers make during instruction. For instance, our research may reveal only procedural decisions because we do not know what other kinds of instructional decisions to look for. We begin to see a broader range of possible decisions if we think in terms of two kinds of instructional concerns: *procedural* and *substantive* (see Fenstermacher, 1980 and Fisher, et al., 1978 for discussion of this distinction). *Procedural* decisions are those which have dominated the research to date and are primarily concerned with maintaining the activity flow through management of student behavior, time allocations, procedures (e.g., directions), instructional pace, quantitative monitoring of student responses, and completion of tasks. *Substantive* decisions, in contrast, are those decisions designed to promote student understanding of the content and the processes involved in reading, and include decisions about what to teach, interpretation of the content, exploitation of critical moments, qualitative restructuring of student responses, selection of alternative explanations or strategies, and affective responses to student interaction with content. Such substantive decisions can be further divided into content related decisions and decisions about pedagogical maneuvering. Content decisions are usually made in the preactive stage and focus on what to teach, the outcomes to emphasize, the materials to use, the examples and nonexamples which will serve as illustrations, and the demonstration or model to be provided. Pedagogical maneuvering decisions also focus on substantive issues, but they are issues which tend to occur during instruction when student responses indicate things are not going according to plan and alternatives must be selected spontaneously. They include the selection of alternative ways to model, of alternative illustrative highlighting, of redirecting students' responses to a task, and of terminating or continuing instruction for groups or parts of groups. Decisions about such substantive issues are seldom reported in the research. This may be because instruction itself has been imprecisely defined which has led, in turn, to unfocused observation of instructional decision making.

Third, we may not have found teachers making instructional decisions because we do not understand how teachers make sense of their workplace. Recent research of teachers and their work has emphasized the difficulty of working in classrooms (Shulman, 1981). Students are taught in groups of twenty-five or thirty, subtleties of social interaction must be negotiated and dealt with, and educational mandates must be followed. Hence, the typical classroom teacher must keep large numbers of students engaged for five hours or more in ways that the principal and parents perceive as appropriate "going to school" behavior, must "cover" the mandated basal text, and must prepare children to do well on a particular standardized test of reading achievement. Further, there are very real limits to the range of decisions teachers can make in this context. For instance, while reading educators often assume that teachers can choose the approach and materials to use, in reality such choices are seldom available. Teachers must use the mandated basal textbook and, if they want to use other alternatives (such as language experience), they must camouflage the alternative to look like the regular program. Because of these and other constraints, it is not surprising that teachers make few substantive instructional decisions. Instead, they strive to simplify a complex instructional environment and, when viewed from this perspective, their behavior is adaptive and sensible and the decisions they make under such conditions are those that the research indicates they are making: procedural decisions about which basal text reading group to assign children to; how to involve pupils in tasks; how to insure that their "mental image" of activity flow is realized; and, in response to reading miscues, how to expedite the smooth flow of instructional turntaking in the group. Decision making research may not have been based on an accurate understanding about what decisions teachers can reasonably make in classrooms and, as a result, has not produced accurate findings.

Conclusions and Future Directions

Certainly, the results from research on instructional decision making have been disappointing, particularly regarding the failure to establish a direct link between teacher decision making and reading teacher effectiveness. However, the absence of such findings does not mean that decision making is nonexistent or that teachers could not be made more effective by becoming better decision makers. Indeed, we believe that the most effective teachers are those who plan and who use the multitude of cues and insights which occur during interactive teaching to make in-flight decisions about how to make sense of the process of reading. Initial progress is being made in establishing a relationship between such decision making and effective reading instruction (Putnam & Duffy, 1983).

Perhaps Shavelson (1983) summarizes the decision making research best when he states that "a person's capacity for formulating and solving complex problems such as those presented in teaching is very small compared with the enormous capacity of some ideal model of rationality." Because of this, he suggests that teachers behave reasonably rather than rationally – that they are rational within certain limitations and constraints. This is quite different from the earlier stated positions of Kamil and Pearson (1979) and Cooney (1981) regarding the relationship between theoretical orientations, the generation and consideration of alternatives, and instructional decision making. The change reflects our growing understanding of the complexity of the teacher's work environment. As Shulman (1983) says:

> Teaching is impossible. If we simply add together all that is expected of a typical teacher and take note of the circumstances under which these activities are to be carried out, the sum makes greater demands than any individual can possibly fulfill.

Hamilton (1983) reinforces the same point when he says:

> Teaching and learning in most school classrooms differ profoundly from the teaching and learning embodied in such powerful images as Socrates in dialogue with his student, Emile with his tutor, or the psychologist shaping the behavior of rats and pigeons one at a time in the laboratory.

Hence, in continuing this aspect of teacher effectiveness research, two premises must guide our efforts. First, instructional decision making must be viewed through the lens of classroom realities and constraints and from the perspective of how teachers use knowledge. Second, we must intentionally look for instructional decisions which go beyond procedural concerns. Specifically, we must examine how teachers decide to maximize students' understanding of the content processes involved. If these two conditions are an integral part of the conceptualization and design of decision making research, we will soon be in a position to describe instructional decision making more fully and substantiate the relationship which exists between such decision making and reading teacher effectiveness.

References

Allington, R. The reading instruction provided readers of differing reading abilities. *Elementary School Journal,* in press.

Borko, H., Cone, R., Russo, N.A., and Shavelson, R.J. Teachers' decision making. In L. Peterson and H.J. Walberg (Eds.), *Research on teaching: Concepts, findings, and implications.* Berkeley, CA: McCutchan, 1979.

Borko, H., and Niles, J. Factors contributing to teachers' judgments about students and decisions about grouping students for reading instruction. *Journal of Reading Behavior,* 1982, *14*(2), 127-140.

Borko, H., Shavelson, R., and Stern, P. Teachers' decisions in the planning of reading instruction. *Reading Research Quarterly,* 1981, *16*(3), 449-466.

Brophy, J. Teacher behavior and its effects. *Journal of Educational Psychology,* 1979, *71*(6), 733-750.

Brophy, J. Implementing instruction. In G. Duffy, L. Roehler, and J. Mason (Eds.), *Comprehension instruction: Perspectives and suggestions.* New York: Longman, 1984.

Cazden, C.B. How knowledge about language helps the classroom teacher—or does it? A personal account. *Urban Review,* 1976, *9*(2), 74-90.

Clark, C.M., and Yinger, R.J. Teachers' thinking. In P.L. Peterson and H.J. Walberg (Eds.), *Research on teaching: Concepts, findings, and implications.* Berkeley, CA: McCutchan, 1979.

Cooney, T.J. Teachers' decision making. *Mathematics education research.* Alexandria, VA: Association for Supervision and Curriculum Development, 1981.

Duffy, G. Response to Borko, Shavelson, and Stern: There's more to instructional decision making than the "empty classroom." *Reading Research Quarterly,* 1982, *17*(2), 295-299.

Duffy, G. Teacher effectiveness: Implications for reading education. In M. Kamil (Ed.), *Directions in reading: Research and instruction,* Thirtieth Yearbook of the National Reading Conference. Washington: National Reading Conference, 1981.

Duffy, G., and Anderson, L. *Final report: Conceptions of reading progress.* Research Series No. 111. East Lansing, MI: Institute for Research on Teaching, Michigan State University. 1982.

Duffy, G., and McIntyre, L. A naturalistic study of teacher assistance behavior in primary classrooms. *Elementary School Journal*, 1982, *83*(1), 15-23.

Durkin, D. What classroom observations reveal about reading comprehension instruction. *Reading Research Quarterly*, 1979, *14*(4), 481-533.

Durkin, D. Reading comprehension instruction in five basal readers. *Reading Research Quarterly*, 1981, *16*(4), 515-544.

Feinman-Nemser, S., and Ball, D. *Views of knowledge in preservice curriculum.* Paper presented at the annual meeting of the American Education Research Association, New Orleans, April 1984.

Fenstermacher, G. On learning to teach effectively from research on teacher effectiveness. In C. Denham and A. Lieberman (Eds.), *Time to learn.* Washington, DC: National Institute for Education, 1980.

Fisher, C., Berliner, D., Filby, N., Marliave, R., Cahen, L., Dishaw, M., and Moore, J. *Teaching and learning in the elementary school: A summary of the Beginning Teaching Evaluation Study.* Report VII-1, 1978.

Gage, N.L. *The scientific basis of the art of teaching.* New York: Teachers' College Press, 1977.

Hamilton, S. The social side of schooling: Ecological studies of classrooms and schools. *Elementary School Journal*, 1983, *83*(4), 313-334.

Harste, J., and Burke, C. A new hypothesis for reading teacher research: Both the teaching and learning of reading are theoretically based. In P.D. Pearson (Ed.), *Reading: Theory and practice.* Twenty-Sixth Yearbook of the National Reading Conference. Clemson, SC: National Reading Conference, 1977.

Hoffman, J. On providing feedback to reading miscues. *Reading World*, 1979, 342-350.

Hoffman, J., and Kugle, C. A study of theoretical orientation to reading and its relationship to teacher verbal feedback during reading instruction. *Journal of Classroom Interaction*, 1982, *18*(1), 2-7.

Jackson, P. *Life in classrooms.* New York: Holt, Rinehart and Winston, 1968.

Jackson, P. Old dogs and new tricks: Observations on the continuing education of teachers. *Improving inservice education: Proposals and procedures.* Boston: Allyn and Bacon, 1971.

Kamil, M., and Pearson, P.D. Theory and practice in teaching reading. *New York University Education Quarterly*, Winter 1979, 10-16.

Lampert, M. *Learning about thinking from the perspective of the classroom teacher: A case study in collaboration with practitioners in educational research.* Cambridge, MA: Division for Study and Research in Education, Massachusetts Institute of Technology, 1982.

Lortie, D.C. *Schoolteacher: A sociological study.* Chicago: University of Chicago Press, 1975.

McNair, K., and Joyce, B. *Teachers' thoughts while teaching: The South Bay Study, Part II.* Research Series No. 58. East Lansing, MI: Institute for Research on Teaching, Michigan State University, 1979.

Medley, D.M. The effectiveness of teachers. In P. Peterson and H. Walberg (Eds.), *Research on teaching: Concepts, findings, and implications.* Berkeley, CA: McCutchan, 1979.

Morine-Dershimer, G. *Teacher plan and classroom reality: The South Bay Study, Part IV.* Research Series No. 60. East Lansing, MI: Institute for Research on Teaching, Michigan State University, 1979.

Peterson, L., Marx, W., and Clark, C. Teacher planning, teacher behavior, and student achievement. *American Educational Research Journal*, 1978, *15*(3), 417-432.

Peterson, P., and Clark, C. Teacher reports of their cognitive processes during teaching. *American Educational Research Journal*, 1978, *15*(4), 555-565.

Putnam, J., and Duffy, G. A descriptive study of the interactive decision making of one expert classroom teacher. Paper presented at the National Reading Conference, Austin, Texas, November 30, 1983.

Rosenshine, B. Speech on meta-analysis of teacher effectiveness research. Los Angeles: Invisible College of Researchers on Teaching, University of California, 1981.

Schon, D. *The reflective practitioner.* New York: Basic Books, 1983.

Shannon, P. The use of commercial reading materials in American elementary schools. *Reading Research Quarterly,* 1983, *19*(1), 68-65.

Shavelson, R.J. Teachers' decision making. In N.L. Gage (Ed.), *The psychology of teaching methods.* NSSE Yearbook, Part I. Chicago: University of Chicago Press, 1976.

Shavelson, R.J. Review of research on teachers' pedagogical judgments, plans, and decisions. *Elementary School Journal,* 1983, *83*(4), 392-413.

Shroyer, L. *Critical moments in the teaching of mathematics: What makes teaching difficult?* Unpublished doctoral dissertation, Michigan State University, 1981.

Shulman, L. Autonomy and obligation. The remote control of teaching. In L. Shulman and G. Sykes (Eds.), *Handbook of teaching and policy.* New York: Longman, 1983.

Shulman, L. *Educational psychology returns to school.* Invited address, G. Stanley Hall Lecture Series, American Psychological Association, Los Angeles, August 24, 1981.

Taylor, P.H. *How teachers plan their courses.* Slough, England: National Foundation for Educational Research in England and Wales, 1970.

Zahorik, J. The effect of planning on teaching. *Elementary School Journal,* 1970, *71*, 143-151.

Zahorik, J. Teachers' planning models. *Educational Leadership,* 1975, *33*, 134-139.

Duffy and Ball

Laura R. Roehler
Gerald G. Duffy

9

Studying Qualitative Dimensions of Instructional Effectiveness

T eacher effectiveness research is a relatively new endeavor. Its prevalent findings have emerged from process-product studies, a form of quantitative research which examines large numbers of teachers, counts overt teacher behaviors, measures student achievement growth, computes statistical correlations between teacher behaviors and student outcomes and, on the basis of these correlations, draws conclusions about which teacher behaviors are most effective in producing student achievement growth.

While this type of research has been instrumental in the study of teacher effectiveness, another type of research has emerged recently. This research is labeled "qualitative" because it is conducted with smaller samples of teachers and consists of microanalytical and nonstatistical analyses of teachers' instructional behavior as it has been captured on videotape or in transcripts of audiotapes. This chapter examines one example of this new direction in teacher effectiveness research.

*The work reported herein is sponsored by the Institute for Research on Teaching, Michigan State University. The Institute for Research on Teaching is funded primarily by the Teaching Division of the National Institute of Education, U.S. Department of Health, Education, and Welfare. The opinions expressed in this publication do not necessarily reflect the position, policy, or endorsement of NIE. (Contract No. 400-76-0073)

Looking Beyond Time on Task and Direct Instruction

The process-product research identified instructional time as the most important resource of schools. Studies conducted in the past ten years repeatedly report consistent, positive correlations (in the low to moderate range) between instructional time and student achievement (Bloom, 1974; Borg, 1980; Fisher, et al., 1980; Rosenshine and Berliner, 1978; Wyne & Stuck, 1979). As Wyne and Stuck (1982) state, "It appears that increasing the amount (proportion or percentage) of time students spend on tasks is a necessary condition for improved academic performance."

Because time on task is so important, there has been a recent emphasis on classroom management. Much research evidence indicates that teachers can create more time on academic tasks by managing students (minimizing disruptions), managing engagement (ensuring high amounts of time on task) and managing content (monitoring student progress) (Anderson, Evertson, & Emmer, 1980; Brophy, 1983; Brophy & Putnam, 1979; Kounin, 1970). Numerous specific techniques have been tested (Anderson, Evertson, & Emmer, 1980; Emmer, Evertson, & Anderson, 1980). When teachers employ such techniques well, the instructional time is used efficiently and students tend to learn more. When such techniques are not employed, the instructional environment is more loosely structured, time is used less efficiently, and less learning occurs. As Doyle (1983) says:

> Failure to attend to organizing and managing classroom groups can lead to a breakdown of academic work with predictable consequences for student achievement. Classroom management, in other words, is a central part of the task of teaching in classrooms. (p. 179)

The importance of time has also resulted in the use of direct instruction (Rosenshine, 1979). Central to this concept is the principle that effective teachers elicit a maximum number of student responses to a given task through content coverage, brisk pacing, high expectations, much practice, and teacher structured activities (Anderson, Evertson & Brophy, 1979; Barr, 1982; Good, 1983). When such techniques are combined with efficient classroom management, the result is more time on task and measurable differences in students' learning of basic skills, especially with low achievers (Brophy, 1979; Good, 1983). Rosenshine (1983) summarizes the importance of these findings:

> Students who receive their instruction directly from the teacher achieve more than those expected to learn new material or skills on their own or from each other. (p. 336)

However, as important as time on task is, management and direct instruction are not sufficient by themselves. As Good and Brophy (in press) note:

> An attentive, well-behaved class provides the opportunity for effective teaching and productive learning. What *use* teachers make of this opportunity, however, will be crucial in determining what and how much children learn.

The qualitative use of instructional time is the focus of this chapter. It examines how two teachers use essentially the same amount of instructional time and the same instructional format to obtain qualitatively different responses from students.

Background to the Study

The two teachers reported here (Teacher A and Teacher B) were among twenty-two teachers who participated in an experimental study of teacher instructional explanation, which was conducted in 1982-1983 (Duffy, et al., 1984). The study, influenced by recent findings regarding the strategic nature of reading comprehension (Brown, 1980; Paris, Lipson, & Wixson, 1983; Paris, Oka, and De-Britto, 1983), hypothesized that teachers of low group fifth graders who went beyond time on task by providing explicit explanations of how to use reading skills as strategies would produce students who were more aware of how to use skills strategically than the low group students in classrooms having equal time on task but less explicit explanations.

Both Teacher A and Teacher B were part of the Treatment group, both received training in how to provide explicit explanations of reading skills, both proved to be more explicit in their teaching than their control group counterparts, and the low group students in both classrooms were more metacognitively aware of the content of instruction than were the low group students in the control classrooms. As such, a relationship between explicit teacher explanation and student strategic awareness was established.

However, further study of Teachers A and B revealed an interesting phenomenon. Although both received high ratings for explicitness of explanation and both had students who were significantly more aware than students in control classrooms, the student interviews indicated that Teacher A's students were more aware of what they were doing with reading skills than Teacher B's students.

For instance, both Teachers A and B taught their low reading groups how to use context clues to figure out the meaning of unknown words. Following the lessons in both classrooms, the students were asked three questions: "What did you learn today in reading?" "When would you use it?" and "How do you do it?"

Note the qualitative differences in the responses. When Teacher A's students were asked to state what the lesson was about, they responded as follows:

Student A[1]: Our lesson was about finding the meanings of words that we don't know in a sentence and then using the context to help you.

Student A[2]: It was about knowing what the unknown word means by using the clues behind the word or in front of the word. Back or front. Then you can know what it means.

Student A[3]: The strategy we learned was about trying to figure out unfamiliar words from the known words around it.

In contrast, note the responses of Teacher B's students to the same question:

Student B[1]: Using the context when you don't know a word.

Student B[2]: To find out the meaning of the word.

Student C[3]: I remember that we are learning about context.

A similar qualitative contrast is apparent when students were asked "Why would context be useful in figuring out unknown words?" Note the responses of Teacher A's students:

Student A[1]: When you come to a word when you're reading, you would use that skill to find out that word that you don't know, if you don't know it. If you do know it, you don't have to use it.

Student A[2]: Okay, like if you're interested in math and you wanted to know a word so you can do your homework, you could figure it out so that you can do your homework right. And for me, if you just want to do pleasure reading, you can use it to find out what the word is so that you can know what they're doin' in the story.

Student A[3]: Like when we're reading in study hall and language arts, all you got to do is think back to what we did in reading and then try to figure out what the word means.

In contrast, note the responses of Teacher B's students to the same question:

Student B[1]: They help you find out more what the word is.

Student B[2]: When I come across a word that I don't know, I have to use the context rules that she gave us.

Student B[3]: So we can figure out words.

This contrast persists when examining student responses to the question "How can context clues be used to figure out the meaning of unknown words?" Teacher A's students responded as follows:

Student A[1]: Well, the strategy is to find the clues in the context or the surrounding sentences. Then you, once you have all the clues you think there are in sentences, you put them together with what you already know about that word—that one word that you don't know. Then you see if it makes sense, with those meanings that you put together. And that is the strategy.

Student A[2]: You think about the strategy that you learned so you can figure it out and the steps—find the words around it in the surrounding sentences, surrounding the word. Put the meanings together. You can do it pretty fast in your head if you know the strategy good. And put the meaning together in the sentence and you have a pretty good idea what that word means. And if you don't, you have to probably look it up in the dictionary or the glossary.

Student A[3]: Okay, to figure out the unknown word, there should be steps. Like, look for clues in the sentences and then put what you know together with the clues and then you'll know what the word is. Okay, then you read it into the sentence to see if it makes sense. Do you know what the word means?

In contrast, Teacher B's students responded as follows to the same question:

Student B[1]: Using the context, you don't know a word and you break it up into syllables and try to sound the word out and if you can't sound it out, break it up into syllables that you know and then say the word, and then if you can't do that, read it in the sentence, like. The words around it and, if you skip the word, you lose the meaning, so you shouldn't skip the word. Then, if you can't do that, you look it up in a dictionary or glossary.

Student B[2]: Go back and read the sentence several times. Figure out the words around it Pronounce it. I can't remember.

Student B[3]: I remember she told me to read it in the sentence and that is really all that I can remember.

Of course, the differences noted above may be attributable to differences in student language facility or other conditions. However, our experiences in interviewing the students do not substantiate such a hypothesis. Both Teachers A and B taught in the same large urban school district and had similar students with similar reading achievement scores; no apparent student differences would account for the differential interview responses. In search of a better explanation, we returned to the transcripts of each teacher's respective lesson on context to see if differences in student interview responses might be explained by what teachers said and did during the lesson. Analysis of these transcripts suggests that the qualitative differences in student interview responses may be a reflection of qualitative differences in what teachers said to students when explaining. These differences are presented in two categories: 1) findings about each teacher's initial explanation of context; and 2) findings about each teacher's explanations during instructional interactions following the initial explanation.

Initial Teacher Explanations

As Rosenshine (1983) says "although teachers are exhorted to ask higher level cognitive questions...teachers seldom demonstrate to their students how to answer such questions." A growing set of data indicates that such explanations and demonstrations are essential to effective instruction. Good (1983), for instance, provides experimental results which substantiate what he calls "active teaching." The core of such teaching is the development, or explanation, of the concept being studied. Other studies substantiate this position. Evertson, Emmer, and Brophy (1980) found that the most effective teachers use a presentation time to provide explanations and many examples; Pearson and his students (1984) indicate that direct explicit instruction is effective in teaching comprehension; and Duffy et al. (1983) report that teachers who are most explicit in explaining reading processes are most effective in producing increased metacognitive awareness in students.

It is intuitively sensible that teachers who provide good explanations will be more effective than teachers who do not explain, and that good explanations explicitly develop the concept under study. Indeed, Teachers A and B both received high ratings for the explicitness of their respective explanations of how to use context to determine word meaning. However, close analysis of the transcripts from the two lessons reveals three subtle differences in the initial explanations provided by Teachers A and B.

Differences in Statements of What Was To Be Learned and Its Usefulness

Both Teachers A and B made explicit statements in the introductory phase of the lesson about what was to be learned and the usefulness of the task. However, the two statements are qualitatively different. For instance, Teacher A began the lesson as follows:

> The skill is the one that you use when you come to a word that you don't know and you have to figure out what the word means. This is a skill you can use anyplace you read. When you read the newspaper, your social studies book, or your library book. Maybe even when you read the cereal package in the morning. Anyplace where you come to a word that is new to you, you can use this skill.

Teacher A's introductory statement emphasizes application of the skill, the problem it will solve and the context in which it can be used. Note, in contrast, Teacher B's introductory statement:

> Today we are going to do context clues. That means finding the meaning of a word. To find the meaning, look at the words around it. If we don't figure out the meaning, we lose the whole meaning of what we are reading. Context means finding the meaning of a word by using the clues around it. You lose meaning if you do not. The context will make your life easier. You won't be flipping through the dictionary everyday—or skipping. Don't skip.

In contrast to Teacher A's emphasis on use of the skill, Teacher B emphasizes what context is and mentions its use almost as an afterthought.

Teacher A's emphasis on usefulness dominates the explanation throughout. For instance, when she and her students were using context to determine the meaning of *despondent,* they found that *sad, lazy,* and *tired* were all possible meanings. Teacher A then provided this explanation of what to do when context is *not* useful:

> Well, how are we going to know? Is it "tired," is it "sad," or is this dog "lazy"? Could these clues make us think he is lazy? Or could they make us think he is sad? Or could they make us think he is tired? How are we going to know for sure what the word "despondent" means? This might be one time to turn to

Roehler and Duffy

the dictionary or the glossary. We're really not sure on this one, so we'll have to check. When you get to that point in your reading [when context clues give several plausible answers] and you can't figure out which one it is, that is the time to look it up. I just want you to know that when you come to a situation like this, you have to look the word up.

Both teachers were explicit at the onset of the lesson. However, Teacher A is explicit about the situations in which the strategy will (and will not) be useful. Teacher B, in contrast, focuses on what context *is*, rather than its use.

Differences in Presenting the Task as Problem Solving

Both Teachers A and B made explicit statements about how to use context and both modeled by thinking out loud for the students the steps of: 1) looking for clues in the context, 2) putting the clues together with what is already known to figure out what the word means, and 3) checking to see if the meaning that was chosen made sense. In this sense, both were explicit in their explanation of how to use context.

However, Teacher A always preceded these steps by focusing on how you decide that you don't know and how you select the appropriate "fix-up" strategy. As such, Teacher A always started her explanation of how to use context with 1) recognizing the problem (I don't know the meaning of a word), and 2) selecting a skill to help (context clues around the unknown word). She would *then* move to the specific steps of the context strategy itself. In contrast, Teacher B did not specify the problem that was to be solved or how the student was to select the correct strategy; she simply started with the steps of the strategy.

Differences in the Focus on the Mental Process

Both Teachers A and B made explicit statements about the mental steps one employs when using context to figure out a word meaning. However, there were sharp differences in the relative emphasis on the mental process as the lesson progressed. For instance, in the introduction and modeling stages, both teachers made frequent references to the mental steps to use (Teacher A devoted 87 percent of her talk in the introduction and 70 percent of her talk during modeling to the mental steps to use; Teacher B devoted 88 percent of her talk in the introduction and 71 percent in the modeling to the mental steps). As the lesson progressed, however, the relative emphasis on mental process changed considerably for Teacher B. She devoted only 5 percent of her talk to mental process during the interactive stage of the lesson and only 13 percent of her talk to mental process during the practice. Teacher A, in contrast, emphasized mental process throughout (67 percent of her talk during the interactive stage and 57 percent during the practice phase). In short, Teacher B did not focus on strategic mental processing throughout. Instead, she emphasized mental processing when she was demonstrating, but when students were trying to employ the strategy there was little reference to the mental processing.

Summary

Both Teacher A and Teacher B provided explicit initial explanations. However, Teacher A's explanations were qualitatively different. She emphasized, to a greater extent than Teacher B, the situational utility of the skill, how to recognize when to use it, and the mental process to use.

Teacher Explanation During Instructional Interaction with Students

Recent data indicate that, because different students interpret instructional explanations differently (Weinstein, 1983), teachers should follow explanations with a progressive series of guided responses which emphasize a conceptual awareness that leads to control in performing academic tasks. In this regard, Doyle (1983) argues for the importance of task selection. Good (1983) states that effective teachers "look for ways to confirm or disconfirm that their presentations have been comprehended by students" and Duffy, Roehler, and Book (1983) point to the need for teachers to provide spontaneous reexplanations, refocusing, and clarifying as they verbally mediate student understanding.

As with initial explanations, the instructional interactions of Teacher A and of Teacher B differ. Three examples are illustrative.

Differences in Moving Students to Independence

Students need to gradually assume responsibility for the mental processing in using the strategy. In Teacher A's lesson, after the introduction of information and the modeling, she structured a series of trials. She provided considerable direction in the first example, primarily by answering her own questions:

> I don't know what *upbraided* means. I have to figure it out. What do I do first? Look for clues. Are there any clues that might tell me what that means? Yes, here is a clue.

After carefully directing students through the first example in this manner, Teacher A moved from directives to questioning in subsequent trials:

T: You are reading and you come to that sentence. How are you going to figure out that word? Matt, what would you do first?

S: I would look through the context. I see *rage,* (inaudible).

T: Yes, "did not come" is a clue. When Jerry didn't come, whatever it was he caused, it was caused because he didn't come. Now you are thinking about what you know about when people don't come and people getting in rages. What do you suppose that means he was?

S: He was angry or mad at the person.

T: So, do you have a one word synonym that you could put there?

S: Mad.

T: How do you check to see if that makes sense?

S: When he didn't come, Jerry was so mad that he left in a rage.

T: Does that sound reasonable? Did he use all the steps to get that meaning? Yes. Let's try the next one.

Teacher A continued to present examples, gradually shifting to the students the responsibility for verbalizing now to determine the meaning of the unknown word. Gradually, she moved from directives to questions and, finally, to student independent use of the strategy.

Teacher B also structured a series of trials after the introduction and modeling phase of the lesson. However, rather than gradually shifting the responsibility to the students, she immediately had the students assume all the responsibility for deciding the meaning of the unknown word.

Differences in Verifying the Student's Use of the Mental Process

Another qualitative distinction between Teacher A and Teacher B was the tendency of Teacher A to verify student understanding at every step of the lesson. Even in the introduction stages, Teacher A asked for verification following her explanation:

> T: What is it that we are going to be working on?
>
> S: How to figure out words you don't know.
>
> T: How to figure out a word if you don't know it. Good. Why should we have this skill? Can we use it anyplace? Matt.
>
> S: You can use it in the newspapers, in books you read, anything we read.

This verification process was particularly noticeable during the interactive part of Teacher A's lesson when she attempted to get students to verbalize their mental processes. For instance, when a student provided only a word meaning and not the process used to figure out the word meaning, she said:

> T: Are you saying that *divulge* means *mention*? Oh, you jumped ahead to the end. You went through all the clues in your head and you are saying that this means *mention*. How did you know that? How did you figure out that it is *mention*?

Teacher A insisted that the student verbalize the entire mental process. This procedure was evident in all situations in which the students were trying out the new skill.

Teacher B, in contrast, did not have students verbalize the mental process in its entirety. She verbalized the individual steps for them, and the students responded only to her specific questions about one or another step in the process:

> T: Number 5, Annie.
>
> S: (Student reads sentence).
>
> T: Very good. Tell me what you know about the sentence, Annie.

S: (inaudible)

T: Tell me. Look at the sentence and tell me what they are talking about in the sentence. They are talking about something.

S: The club.

T: What kind of a club is it?

S: Secret.

T: A secret club. And they also have something else that is secret. What is that?

S: Password.

T: A password. So if you *divulge* the name of a secret club, you might as well tell the name of our secret password as well. So they are talking about something secret, and if it is secret, what don't you do?

S: Tell.

T: You don't tell. So would *divulge* mean (A) ask, (B) tell, or (C) forget?

S: B.

T: Would you check that and see if it is right?

S: (inaudible)

T: Make sense? Absolutely. Absolutely.

Students in Teacher B's classroom were not given the opportunity to verbalize the mental process in its entirety. They only verbalized pieces of the process.

Differences in Applying the Process in Concrete Situations

Another qualitative difference between Teacher A and Teacher B is the way they illustrated the usefulness of the strategy. Both tried to transfer the strategy to real text, but Teacher A emphasized the mental processing for determining unknown words from context when doing so:

We're going to continue practicing this skill now in our social studies book. I want to show you how it helps with social studies. In fact, we'll get a head start on our lesson for this afternoon. Turn to 351. Thank you. I know we read some of this yesterday. Let's go down to the bottom where it talks about tornados. The bottom, the second column. You know, when they write these social studies books, they think some of the words that they use fifth graders don't know, and they're the ones they print in the dark print. They're kind of guessing that you don't know these words. When you see one of those words in dark print, then you can use our strategy and help yourself to figure out what that may mean. Let's start reading down at the bottom. Read out loud for us, Terry.

Teacher A then proceeded to select unknown words in the text and had students verbalize how they used their context strategy to figure out the meaning. Not only did she provide opportunities for the students to experience the usefulness of the skill, she also emphasized the process used to get the word meaning.

Teacher B also provided opportunities to use the skill. However, student responses focused only on the word meaning, not on how the word meaning was determined.

T: We're going to do the next set. We are going to look at our book and we are going to read through the play, "Paddington the Bear" and we are going to figure out words that we don't know by using context. Terry, what is *concealed*?

S: Trapped.

T: It doesn't say in the sentence that he is trapped. What does it say there?

S: He's hidden.

T: He is hidden. He is down behind the parcels. Parcels hide him. Would you try to tell me what a parcel is? Look at the sentence. Another way to find context clues is to look at the pictures. Please tell me what a parcel is, Frank.

S: Surrounded by something.

T: Okay. Parcels. Look at picture number 1. Parcels and luggage are together. A parcel and luggage. What do you think a parcel is?

S: Boxes.

T: Boxes. Exactly. Right on the money. Okay, a parcel is a box. And if you can't figure it out by the words around it, the picture on page 209 certainly tells you that it is a parcel.

In contrast to Teacher A, Teacher B did not focus on the mental processing and she did not give the students the opportunity to verbalize how to do the mental process.

Summary

Both Teacher A and Teacher B were aware that individual students might interpret their explanations about context differently, that they would need to solicit responses from students to evaluate this restructuring, and that they would need to maintain a level of explicitness in doing so. However, Teacher A's interactions with students were qualitatively different than Teacher B's. She moved students gradually to independence, frequently verified the students' understanding of the mental steps of the strategy, and used concrete opportunities to illustrate the process as it was applied in transfer situations.

Conclusion

Qualitative analysis of the instruction of effective teachers (such as Teachers A and B) do not produce unequivocable findings of what distinguishes more effective from less effective teachers. For instance, our analysis does not "prove" that the qualitative differences in the instructional talk of Teacher A and Teacher B account for the qualitative differences in the interview responses noted at the beginning of the chapter. However, this does seem to be a reasonable hypothesis. Generating such hypotheses is the function of qualitative analysis. For instance, as a result of our analysis of Teachers A and B (as well as analyses of the twenty other teachers in our original study), we are now preparing to test the hypothesis that explicitness of explanation, like time on task, may be only a prerequisite condition to strategic student use of reading skills. In addition to time and explicitness, teachers may also need to emphasize the situational utility of the skill, the mental processing called for, its gradual internalization, its strategic placement within a repertoire of skills, and its retrieval at appropriate times.

The study of such qualitative distinctions of the instructional process is a new direction in teacher effectiveness research. Perhaps the greatest new challenge in teacher effectiveness will be the identification of such qualitative distinctions so that teachers can make better use of the instructional time which earlier research indicated was so important.

References

Anderson, L., Evertson, C., and Brophy, J. An experimental study of effective teaching in first grade reading groups. *Elementary School Journal*, 1979, *79*, 193-222.

Anderson, L., Evertson, C., and Emmer, E. Dimensions in classroom management derived from recent research. *Journal of Curriculum Studies*, 1980, *12*, 343-346.

Barr, R. Classroom instruction from a sociological perspective. *Journal of Reading Behavior*, 1982, *14*, 316-329.

Bloom, B.S. Time and learning. *American Psychologist*, 1974, *29*, 682-688.

Borg, W. Time and school learning. In C. Denham, and A. Lieberman (Eds.), *Time to learn.* Washington, DC: National Institute of Education, 1980.

Brophy, J. Classroom organization and management. *Elementary School Journal*, 1983, *83*(4), 265-286.

Brophy, J. Teacher behavior and its effects. *Journal of Educational Psychology*, 1979, *71*, 733-750.

Brophy, J., and Putnam, J. Classroom management in the elementary grades. In D. Duke (Ed.), *Classroom management.* Seventy-Eighth Yearbook of the National Society for the Study of Education, Part 2. Chicago: University of Chicago Press, 1979.

Brown, A.L. Metacognitive development and reading. In R. Spiro, B. Bruce, and W. Brener (Eds.), *Theoretical issues in reading comprehension.* Hillsdale, NJ: Erlbaum, 1980.

Doyle, W. Academic work. *Review of Educational Research*, 1983, *53*(2), 159-200.

Duffy, G., Roehler, L., and Book, C. A study of direct teacher explanation during reading instruction. In J. Niles and L. Harris (Eds.), *Searches for meaning in reading: Language processing and instruction.* Thirty-Second Yearbook of the National Reading Conference. Rochester, NY: National Reading Conference 1983.

Duffy, G., Roehler, L., Meloth, M., Book, C., and Vavrus, L. *The effects and some distinguishing characteristics of explicit teacher explanation during reading instruction.* Paper presented at the annual meeting of the National Reading Conference, Austin, Texas, 1983.

Duffy, G., Roehler, L., Vavrus, L., Book, C., Meloth, M., Putnam, J., and Wesselman, R. *A study of the relationship between direct teacher explanation of reading strategies and student awareness and achievement outcomes.* Paper presented at the annual meeting of the American Educational Research Association, New Orleans, 1984.

Emmer, E., Evertson, C., and Anderson, L. Effective classroom management at the beginning of the school year. *Elementary School Journal*, 1980, *80*, 219-231.

Evertson, C., Emmer, E., and Brophy, J. Predictors of effective teaching in junior high mathematics classrooms. *Journal of Research in Mathematics Education*, 1980, *11*, 167-178.

Fisher, C., Berliner, D., Filby, N., Marliave, R., Cahen, L., and Dishaw, M. Teaching behaviors, academic learning time, and student achievement: An overview. In C. Denham and A. Lieberman, (Eds.), *Time to learn.* Washington, DC: National Institute of Education, 1980.

Good, T. Research on classroom teaching. In L. Shulman and G. Sykes (Eds.), *Handbook of teaching and policy.* New York: Longman, 1983.

Good, T., and Brophy J. Research in school effects. In M. Wittrock (Ed.), *Handbook of Research in Teaching.* New York: Macmillan, 1983.

Kounin, J.S. *Discipline and group management in classrooms.* New York: Holt, Rinehart and Winston, 1970.

Paris, S., Lipson, M., and Wixson, K. Becoming a strategic reader. *Contemporary Educational Psychology,* 1983, *8,* 293-316.

Paris, S., Oka, E., and DeBritto, A. Beyond decoding: Synthesis of research in reading comprehension. *Educational Leadership,* 1983, *41,* 78-83.

Pearson, P.D. Direct explicit teaching of reading comprehension. In G. Duffy, L. Roehler, and J. Mason (Eds.), *Comprehension instruction: Perspectives and suggestions.* New York: Longman, 1984.

Rosenshine, B. Content, time, and direct instruction. In H. Walberg and P. Peterson (Eds.), *Research on teaching: Concepts, findings, and implications.* Berkeley, CA: McCutchan, 1979.

Rosenshine, B. Teaching functions in instructional program. *Elementary School Journal,* 1983, *83*(4), 335-352.

Rosenshine, B.V., and Berliner, D. Academic engaged time. *British Journal of Teacher Education,* 1978, *4,* 3-16.

Weinstein, R. Student perceptions of schooling. *Elementary School Journal,* 1983, *83*(4), 287-312.

Wyne, M., and Stuck, S. Time and learning: Implications for the classroom teacher. *Elementary School Journal,* 1982, *83*(1), 67-75.

Wyne, M.D., and Stuck, S. Time on task and reading performance in underachieving children. *Journal of Reading Behavior,* 1979, *11,* 119-128.

Robert Calfee
Marcia K. Henry

10

Project READ:
An Inservice Model for Training
Classroom Teachers
in Effective Reading Instruction

I mprovement in student literacy remains a fundamental challenge for American public education. Despite the concentration on instruction in the basic skills (reading and mathematics) by local schools; the infusion of state and federal funds for research and development on reading instruction; and the earnest efforts of practitioners, indicators of reading performance indicate that many youngsters leave high school unable to read with sufficient fluency to meet the demands for literacy needed for survival in modern society. The high dropout rate is one indication of the problem; the findings of the National Assessment of Educational Progress provide fine grained detail. The pattern is one of improvements in the lower grades and the lower level skills over the past decade, coupled with declines at the upper grades and higher level skills (NAEP, 1981).

This chapter describes efforts to improve reading instruction through a school improvement program, Project READ, developed by a research team at Stanford in collaboration with several elementary schools in the Bay area. For the school faculties, the goal has been to improve the quality of education provided to youngsters. For the university team, the goal has been to determine the validity of theoretical principles based on recent findings in the area of cognitive psychology (cf. Slavin, 1984, for a related point of view).

We begin the account with a description of the present situation in the public schools, followed by a review of the theoretical principles on which the Project is based. [This chapter is a companion piece to an earlier review (Calfee, 1981) that explored the relations between research on cognitive psychology and educational practice; the reader might find it helpful to consult this article for additional background.] The chapter then provides some details on the development of the Project, and concludes with observations about the effects of the methods for instruction. Our purpose is not to highlight empirical findings—these will be available in future reports. The reader will probably gain more from the chapter by focusing on the validity of the argument about the relations between thinking, learning, the curriculum of the school, and the methods of instruction. If this argument is not sound, then empirical data will have little relevance. To put it another way, while there are many ways to raise scores on objective tests, some may make more sense than others.

The Present Situation

In this section, we briefly describe the present state of reading instruction. The account is impressionistic—a detailed and heavily referenced survey is not the intention. The sketch begins with the student and then considers the teacher, the principal, and the school as an organization unit.

The Student

Most children enter school eager, willing, and motivated to learn. They are excellent candidates for education, for training in the formalities that contrast with the "natural" experiences of early childhood. On entry to school children differ in ability, previous experience, and developmental level. Children who have spent a year or more in preschool enter readily into the give and take of the academic and social interactions appropriate to school; less experienced children hold back. This diversity in students (and in the objectives of the school) presents both opportunities and problems for the teacher. As things now stand, differences in entering ability are typically amplified by the process of education. This spread between students with low and high entry level scores on readiness tests tends to become greater over the years of schooling.

The Teacher

One cannot consider the education of groups of children without considering the role of the teacher. Today's teachers have generally been provided little in the way of an explicit conceptual framework for promoting student achievement. Duffy (1977) found that only one teacher in ten showed evidence of a strongly held belief system about reading. We do not intend by this statement to add further to the abuse presently being heaped on the teaching profession; teachers' conceptions reflect what they have been taught in schools of education, by presentations in textbooks, by the content of teachers' manuals, by the scope-and-sequence charts common throughout administrative guidelines, and by the lists of objectives in testing programs used to assess the outcomes of reading instruction. Perusal of these sources reveals a general lack of coherence. Teachers and students alike are having trouble comprehending material that is diffuse, scattered, and lacking in thematic focus.

The Principal

The principal plays an especially significant role in the effectiveness of a school (Edmonds, 1985). The principal's task is a relatively new one. The "principal teacher" of the 1900s has been gradually transformed into today's "principal" and something important may have been lost along the way. The position has taken on the responsibilities of school management, instructional supervision, and community relations (Blumberg & Greenfield, 1980; Calfee, 1981). The task has increased in both size and complexity. Schools are larger, demands for services are greater, and the margin for error is smaller (our comments apply to the elementary school; the situation for the secondary school is even more exceptional). The resulting conflicts mean that principals seldom fulfill their potential as individuals and they are unable to satisfy their varied clients. For present purposes, the most significant point is the importance of providing a framework for curriculum and instruction that is sufficiently simple to sustain the principal in the role of instructional leader in spite of the other presses on time and energy.

The School

Many programs for improving education focus on the teacher. The teacher is certainly the sine qua non. But the teacher is part of a collective. The school may be the smallest autonomous unit for the modern educational system: "It is the school that establishes the structure within which teachers and students must function, and that establishes a territory distinct from the rest of life" (Eisner, 1979, p. 280). The interactions among the various actors within the school are quite strong compared with the weaker interactions among schools, and between schools and the district administration. A particular school may lack coherence as a unit—this is often a sign of trouble.

Thinking and Learning

The previous section dealt with the major actors in the educational enterprise. Here we will address the foundational elements of that enterprise.

Thinking

Thinking is the most basic skill for survival in modern society. The past two decades have added substantially to our understanding of the nature of thought. The mind is actually quite a simple device in its basic architecture (cf. Calfee, 1981 for a review). *Long term memory* provides virtually unlimited space for the storage of experience. As long as an event has received attention, it is likely to be recognized subsequently. If the event has been linked to a more substantial structure, then one can remember it almost at will. *Short term memory,* the aspect that we are consciously aware of when we "think" about something, is far more explicit. Here is where the organization of experience takes place. This part of the basic architecture has one noticeable feature—its capacity is quite limited, such that no more than half a dozen distinctive elements can be thought about at any one time.

Calfee and Henry

These findings about the basic architecture of the human mind have practical implications of considerable significance. First, they support Bruner's contention (1966) that almost anything can be taught to almost anyone if a way can be found to capture attention, and if the information can be properly organized. One can expect differences in the rate of learning between individuals, and acquisition of knowledge does not lead immediately to proficiency. Proficiency takes practice, and practice takes time. The comment does not imply that knowledge is the only guide to action; motivation, distractions, conflicting and incomplete evidence all intervene between knowledge and behavior. These considerations notwithstanding, research on human information processing suggests that we should be able to teach virtually every child of normal intelligence how to read, not in the sense of minimal competence, but to reach a level of literacy adequate to meet the challenges of modern society.

The limited capacity of short term memory puts a caveat on the preceding proposition. If a broad domain of knowledge and skill like reading is to be taught so that most individuals can acquire and employ it, the domain must be organized as a simple, coherent representation. To be sure, an individual may learn a domain that is complicated, but only with considerable effort and time, and with the consequent likelihood that many individuals will fail to persevere in the effort to make sense of the complexity. Simplicity and coherence are important for both teacher and student. The teacher who lacks a parsimonious account of a subject matter will have no basis for deciding what is important and what is inconsequential. Students who fail to comprehend that which is hard to comprehend will quickly decide they are poor learners, and may retreat from the struggle.

Learning

Some years ago, research on learning focused on the distinction between all or none and incremental learning (Calfee & Atkinson, 1965). Incremental learning was a slow process in which performance improved by small increments following each study opportunity. All or none learning, in contrast, was more a matter of sudden insight. The student might go for a few trials with no apparent improvement, and then a single study opportunity would do the trick—a link would be established with previous learning, after which performance would be virtually perfect.

The debate about the validity of the two models of learning was not resolved in favor of one or the other. Rather, it was found that 1) the models described different situations (all or none learning was more typical of simple verbal learning by college students, whereas incremental learning was characteristic of complex "skill" learning, and learning by subhuman organisms), and 2) models were developed that combined the two processes, which permitted estimation of the relative contribution of insight (attention?) and rote learning in a given situation.

Research on learning has been on psychology's back burner for the past decade (Greeno, 1980). Learning remains a major consideration in education, however, and cannot be disregarded even if it is temporarily out of style for experimental psychologists. We (Calfee, 1983) have found it useful to translate the preceding distinction between learning styles into a contrast between *learning by doing* (incremental learning) and *learning by knowing* (all or none learning).

Learning by doing, the college of hard knocks variety, comes from repeated experience, is based on trial and error, and typically entails little explicit awareness of what has been learned. Learning by knowing, the school based variety, comes from teaching, may be virtually instantaneous (the "aha" reaction), entails organization of the information for efficient presentation, and often focuses on a clearly articulated and explicit understanding of what has been learned.

Both types of learning are valid, depending on the situation. The educated person is capable of employing one or the other or both methods, and takes advantage of the interplay between the two styles. A major goal of schooling is to transmit to the student the most significant facets of our cultural heritage, knowledge that is most efficiently transferred through learning by knowing. In addition, the school teaches the student how to acquire knowledge in this fashion (learning to learn, if you will, of a special variety). The school needs to ensure that youngsters learn to do certain things (including reading, writing, and calculating) and to do these well. The current emphasis on specific objectives and training through drill and practice supports this goal.

Equally important, the school needs to teach children how to learn by knowing. This style is at issue in the acquisition of "higher level thinking," and is vital if the individual is to keep pace with the shock waves of new knowledge sweeping over modern society.

The Curriculum of the School

The curriculum, the course of study, comprises the cultural domains viewed by society as sufficiently valuable to pass on to succeeding generations. This body of knowledge, after several centuries of slow accretion, is now expanding exponentially. Where education was once limited to a small elite, it is now an important element for productive livelihood for virtually all citizens in modern societies. Finally, where the content of the curriculum was once the focus, it is increasingly important to pass on the structures and processes as well as the content; knowing *how* is at least as important as knowing *what*.

Coherence and parsimony were important features of the classical curriculum. Present day curriculum frameworks have taken on a more piecemeal, splintered appearance. A glance at the list of objectives in the typical scope-and-sequence chart is sufficient evidence to support this claim. The pressures for accountability and the design of testing systems have led to an increasing emphasis on those skills that can be objectively specified and behaviorally assessed. The various subject matters have taken new shape as a collection of relatively low level skills. Subject matter areas that bear a close relation to one another are treated as distinct entities, unrelated in either content or approach.

For instance, reading and language arts, domains that should be mirror images, are treated as separate disciplines in many classrooms: separate textbooks, taught at different times, and assessed by different techniques and with different priorities in the accountability hierarchy. While one hears frequent pleas for "integration of reading and language arts," and while programs exist for bringing together the areas of reading, writing, speaking, and listening (e.g., Moffett, 1968), the classroom reality presents a melange of activities in which it is virtually impossible to identify the overarching themes that bring order to the technical use of language for thinking and communicating. The rhetoric (the academic discipline that provides the foundation for the study of reading and the language arts) has been lost in the shuffle of specific objectives.

Instruction: The Lesson

The Socratic dialogue provides one model for instruction. The instructor designates the topic, and then through a series of guiding questions leads students to explore the topic and their reasoning about it. A more recent version of this model is found in the various techniques for small group discussion (Gall & Gall, 1976; Calfee & Sutter, 1982).

The lecture method provides a didactic alternative to discussion. The teacher talks and students listen. This approach has the virtues of efficiency and predictability. In small group instruction, the teacher can effectively involve only a handful of students at any one time—ten to fifteen seems the practical limit. While the teacher has the responsibility to keep the discussion oriented toward a particular topic, the small group's path in dealing with that topic is necessarily subject to a degree of uncertainty. In contrast, a lecturer may deal with hundreds of students, and can control completely the direction of the presentation.

The advantages of the small group discussion procedure are that the teacher has far more information about the nature of the students' thinking on the topic, and can provide timely feedback and guidance in understanding. It takes considerable knowledge and perseverance to benefit from a lecture; in a word, it helps to be educated. Small group procedures are more appropriate for the student who is in the process of being educated. We propose that a major goal of elementary education is to lead children from the conversational skills that they bring from home into possession, by sixth grade, of the ability to enter into a formal discussion of a topic and to have some sense of when each style is appropriate.

The typical reading lesson in today's classroom is a rather curious mix. To the degree that the teacher follows the guidance provided by the basal reading manual, here are the characteristics of the lesson. First, within a given lesson the teacher covers a range of topics—vocabulary, discussion, oral reading, and questions about the text. Second, teachers do most of the talking (Dunkin & Biddle, 1974), often because the questions being asked require relatively low level factual responses. Once the basic facts have been provided in the answer, what else is there to say? Third, any open-ended discussion tends to be the outgrowth of conversational or story telling experiences ("Have you ever been to a zoo?") which have neither the process nor the structure of formal small group discussions.

This account is understandable if one examines the materials for instruction and for training teachers. Textbooks on language in the classroom provide only cursory treatment of small group discussion, and the questions in basal manuals generally elicit answers that are quite brief (the questions are often followed by the answers, or else by the statement that "answers may vary").

The teacher led lesson is only a fraction of the time spent in reading instruction for most elementary students. For each minute spent with the teacher, the student spends another two or three minutes laboring over worksheets to practice various skills, or working through the tests that are included in the curriculum or are mandated by external agencies for assessment of literacy. These activities require independent work by the student and, as conducted, provide no opportunity for sharing ideas in an open forum.

A Conceptual Framework for Reading Instruction

Efforts to improve the effectiveness of reading instruction in the schools have taken various stances. The method of instruction and the content of the program are perennial favorites (Chall, 1967), giving us the debates between direct instruction versus individualization, or between phonics versus look-say or meaning based approaches.

Time has been identified as a critical factor. Allocation of sufficient time, assurance that the students are actually engaged in study, and providing materials appropriate to the students' preparation, all appear to have some influence on test performance (Denham & Lieberman, 1980). As Goodlad (1984) has pointed out, time is important, but only when the task is also considered: "Increasing the days and hours in school settings [and, we would add, the engagement] will in fact be counterproductive unless there is, simultaneously, marked improvement in how this time is used" (p. 283).

More recently, attention has focused on the role of organizational factors at the school level. Some schools have better than expected reading scores; they also tend to have strong leadership, a focus on instruction in the basic skills, and a strong assessment program, among other features (Edmonds, 1985; Brookover, et al., 1982; Carnine & Gersten, 1984). While critics have pointed out weaknesses in this research (Purkey & Smith, in press), the basic themes have a ring of reasonableness. How we should alter these factors at the local school level and which are causes and which are effects are not clear.

Each of these efforts, and others that might be mentioned, focus on one or another of the several dimensions that make up the program of reading instruction at the local school. None provides a coherent representation of the curriculum of reading, nor any conception of the relation between teaching and learning adequate to direct the design of an instructional program.

The starting point for Project READis the development of a parsimonious and coherent theoretical framework for representing the various elements of a reading program. Students, teachers, and principals—the human actors in this enterprise—are all "thinkers;" they all have the capabilities for long term storage of information described earlier, and all are subject to the same limitations of short term memory. If all are to work together toward a common end, they must share a common conception of reading instruction, a conception based on a small number of distinctive and separable components, each of which can be divided into a small number of subcomponents, and so on.

This hypothesis (for such it is) contrasts in at least two ways with conventional practice. First, it presumes that such a simple description is possible. Most reading experts emphasize the complexity of reading instruction. Certainly a lot of "stuff" is covered under this rubric, and one can find perspectives from which the domain appears quite complex and idiosyncratic. We propose that a simple representation is possible, within which the major elements of reading instruction are clearly and simply related to one another. If such a representation is possible, then it has the advantages of promoting cohesiveness and providing the various participants with a shared conception and a common language. Second, to the degree that they address curriculum as an issue, most existing programs tend to focus on detailed objectives without regard for the big picture. Learning that *f, ff, gh,* and *ph* can each take the pronunciation /f/ is helpful to the reader, but it is far more important for the reader to understand the contexts in which this correspondence obtains, and reasons behind the variations. The practice today is to teach the correspondences in a rote fashion, without ensuring that either teacher or student have a fundamental understanding of the nature of the English spelling-sound system (Venezky, 1970).

A Model of Reading

What is a reasonable basis for a simple representation of reading? The answer, which is actually quite straightforward, takes its foundation from the *rhetoric*, the set of techniques designed over the past two millenia for the effective formal use of language, and most easily reviewed by sampling any of the better texts for the first year college English course (e.g., Brooks & Warren, 1972). A more detailed discussion of this matter can be found elsewhere (Calfee & Drum, in press). The following sketch presents the main themes.

Four fundamental components form the basis for the reading curriculum, and hence the foundation for the representation of reading in the mind of the competent reader (or reading instructor):

Decoding. The translation of the printed word into a pronounceable equivalent.

Vocabulary. The assignment of meaning to a word, where meaning entails access to a network of associations.

Sentence and paragraph comprehension. The "bottom-up" aspect of comprehension (Rumelhart, 1977) in which a relatively limited amount of text is parsed into a small number of functional units (subject, predicate, topic sentence, elaborations, for instance).

Text comprehension. The organization of a complete text according to one or more of the genres used to create texts (narratives, descriptions, sequential accounts, and persuasive writing).

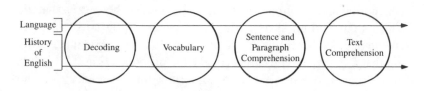

Figure 1. Elements and themes in reading instruction. Tying the elements together in this model are the themes 1) the relation between natural and formal language and 2) the role of the history of the English language in the evolution of written English (after Calfee, 1983).

These four components, which are laid out in Figure 1, are distinctive in their content, in the structures for describing them, and in procedures for analysis. It is undoubtedly for these reasons that they have been distinguished by rhetoricians, and these are also valid reasons for representing them as separable components of a reading model. Rhetoricians typically disregard decoding, presumably because of a focus on the accomplished reader, for whom decoding has become a highly automated skill. Moreover, in placing sentence and paragraph comprehension under one rubric, we are for simplicity clustering two areas that are typically separated in the rhetoric.

As indicated in Figure 1, having divided the reading curriculum into four domains, we then tie the components together with two unifying themes. First, reading stands in parallel with other forms of language usage. The linguist in studying language under the headings of phonology, morphology, and syntax is nonetheless aware of the wholeness of language in normal usage, and similarly for reading. Second, we must consider the historical development of the English language in order to understand features that cut across all of the four components, for this perspective makes sense of the

Calfee and Henry

spelling system, the formation of vocabulary, and certain aspects of the grammar.

This brief account will frustrate some readers while enlightening others, but the representation of the reading curriculum presented can serve as a foundation for comprehending the broader goals of reading instruction, and for making sense of the large array of specific objectives found in the typical basal reader. It provides a basis for lesson design, and for aiding the teacher in setting priorities. It gives teachers and students a set of concepts—a metalanguage—for discussing the formal analysis of language, which we view as one of the fundamental outcomes of reading instruction.

The Teacher and the Lesson

The componential approach can be applied to other aspects of reading instruction. In designing Project READ, we used the method for analysis of the teacher's task, and of the events in a reading lesson.

What is the job of teaching? Figure 2 displays seven elements identified as significant and distinctive components of the teacher's role (Calfee & Shefelbine, 1981). While the Project touches on each of these components to some degree, the major focus is on the curriculum and materials. In many respects, basal materials today replace clear conceptions of the curriculum. By separating these two elements, the teacher is able to cast a critical eye on the materials, and to determine the appropriateness of a basal lesson for meeting various instructional objectives.

The other elements are described in more detail in the reference. Two themes cut across the set of components—the individual students who make up a class and the range of unique features that distinguish this collective, and the passage of time, both long and short term. A complete discussion of these topics would take us beyond the purposes of the present chapter. The important point is the approach to teachers—"How can you represent your task as a teacher so that it is comprehensible, and so that you can communicate effectively with colleagues about this task?" The model provides one answer to this question, an answer that most participating teachers have found useful.

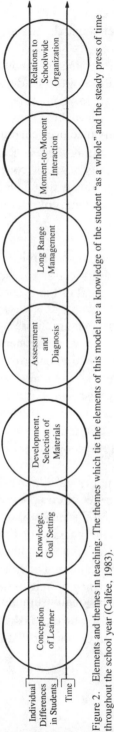

Figure 2. Elements and themes in teaching. The themes which tie the elements of this model are a knowledge of the student "as a whole" and the steady press of time throughout the school year (Calfee, 1983).

What are the essential components in a lesson? To a degree, the answer to this question depends on the kind of lesson. For a lecture, the components may be slightly different than for a small group discussion. We have considered only the latter format, and have concentrated our efforts on the temporal dimension. The components may seem unduly simple and straightforward; we can only remark that they represent an advance over current practice.

First, a lesson should concentrate on a single focal topic. More specifically, we propose that for effective instruction in elementary reading, the lesson should cover only one of the four components of the reading model. The teacher might decide to analyze a narrative. In this case, the lesson would begin with a quick reading of the story, followed by a discussion of the plot, the characters, and perhaps the creation of a story map. The same text might serve as the basis for a vocabulary lesson. If the story is about the adventures of a family during a hurricane, then the development of a semantic web around the topic of "stormy weather" might be the lesson. Or if the basal lesson includes a worksheet on the long-short distinction between vowels, a separate lesson would focus on this topic, bringing in a variety of patterns to illustrate the contrast.

The rationale for this hypothesis is quite straightforward. If the student is to internalize the four component model, then the lesson must highlight these components. If in each lesson the student darts first to one component and then to another (a little vocabulary, a little decoding, a little literal detail) then the student may understandably miss the point.

Once a single focus has been decided on, the other facets of the lesson fall out quite directly. In the *opening*, the teacher states the point of the lesson, the goal to be achieved. "We are going to analyze a story." "We are going to see what 'communication' means." Next, in the *middle game* or discussion segment, the teacher initiates student thought and talk about the topic, asking leading questions with a variety of possible reactions, bringing the students back to the topic when necessary, occasionally summarizing, and recording on the board the results of the discussion. The *closing*, which is seldom found in most lessons, is a time to review what has been discussed, both the content ("We talked about 'communication'.") and the structure ("We made a matrix of types of communication—

newspapers, radios, and so on—and the features of each—cost, audience, and length of message."). Finally, *follow up activities* provide practice and reinforcement of the discussion. A fifth grade class might be divided into groups, and each assigned a communication medium for further research.

The components are, as noted, quite simple. Nonetheless, this model, while not necessarily unique, provides a conception that lends coherence to the daily routine of the "reading lesson," a coherence that is often missing in today's elementary classroom because of a lack of guidance in preservice training and in the basal manual. (A quick scan through seven reading texts shows only one referring to "lesson" in the index; the reference is to the steps in the typical basal reader.)

Project READ: A Plan for School Change

Project READ is a response to several problems in contemporary reading instruction, many alluded to previously. Schools lack a coherent social organization; teachers are not provided a coherent conception of reading or reading instruction; textbooks present a piecemeal curriculum; principals are trained in management more than instruction; inservice programs focus on limited problems of the individual teacher, and are generally of short duration.

In contrast, Project READ begins with a conception of reading and reading instruction designed to give the teacher an understanding of the overall goals of reading, a conception that also fosters communication by all members of the faculty as well as the principal, and that provides the staff a framework for independent decisions about how to use the basal reading program. The school is approached as an organizational entity; the Project is designed not only for individual teachers but for a schoolwide effort—most if not all of the teachers in a building. The Project promotes the idea of small group learning by students, and the same principle seems likely to work with teachers. There appear to be advantages when teachers become aware of the activities of colleagues in grades other than their own; continuity from year to year becomes smoother when teachers and students are proceeding down the same track.

Finally, a school based approach provides the context for engaging a "champion" at the building level; when a critical mass of teachers is working on the same project, the principal or a resource teacher naturally serves as a liaison or support person. Finally, the Project is a long term program. The design calls for activities that provide support and guidance during a yearlong phase-in.

The remainder of this section describes the practical aspects of the Project. First is an account of the materials that present the theoretical framework, and aid in the translation of the theory into classroom practice. Next is a discussion of the methods for engaging a school. Last is a description of the stages in the training process.

Materials

The Book. The Project began as a collaborative enterprise between a team of university researchers whose investigations of tests had led to a critical examination of teaching practices and the content of basal reading materials (the end result was considerable confusion about the underlying design principles) and the principal and faculty of a nearby elementary school who, in spite of high test scores, were dissatisfied with the reading program. After a weeklong workshop, both groups agreed that a better foundation for reading instruction could be created from the conceptual framework presented in the earlier sections of the chapter. At the conclusion of the workshop, which was held in the early summer, the university team was asked to develop a notebook containing the conceptual materials, along with some generalized lesson plans which had come to be referred to as *scripts* in the course of the workshop. This notebook was developed during the summer, and was entitled *The Book* (Calfee & Associates, 1981). Although considerably revised and still viewed as a draft, it is a document of great significance for the Project.

The first section of *The Book* contains background information on the theoretical foundation of the Project. Next comes a selection on pragmatics—tips about implementation of the Project, largely generated by teachers who have participated over the past few years. Then come four sections, one for each of the major components of the reading model. Each section begins with additional

THE BOOK: Components of Reading Instruction
Table of Contents

Introduction

Guidelines for Using Scripts

Decoding
> Overview
> Regular Short Words
> Structural Analysis for Decoding
> Syllabication
> Compound Words

Vocabulary
> Overview
> Webbing
> Weaving
> Structural Analysis for Word Meaning
> Dictionary
> Words in Context

Sentence and Paragraph Comprehension

Comprehension
> Overview
> Story Strucure: Narrative
> Expository Structure: Description
> Expository Structure: Sequence
> Expository Structure: Argument and Persuasion
> Analyzing Text

Test Taking

Listening and Discussion

Assessment

Integration of Components

Figure 3.   Table of Contents of *The Book* (Calfee & Associates, 1981).

background information on the component, along with several scripts of sufficiently widespread importance to warrant inclusion (Figure 3). Within the domain of vocabulary, for instance, five scripts are listed:

> *Webbing.* A technique of free association followed by clustering of the associates, used by many teachers already, though seldom incorporated in the basal lessons.
>
> *Weaving.* An extension of the webbing principle, in which the concept of matrix and hierarchical structures is added to the rather primitive associational form.
>
> *Structural analysis.* A technique for decomposing a complex word into its underlying parts, as in *inter-nation-al;* morphographics.

Calfee and Henry

Dictionary. The basic tool for finding out about words. How does this device work, and what are the differences between dictionaries, thesauruses, and encyclopediae?

Words in context. For the experienced reader, more words are acquired by occurrence in context than through any other means; how this process operates, and how students can be aided in taking advantage of the process.

Script	Comprehension of Story Structure: Narrative

AIM:
STUDENT'S PREREQUISITES:
STUDENT OUTCOMES:
TEACHER'S PREPARATION:

Opening
    Probe for purpose

    Probe for structure

Modal
Middle Activity
    ANALYSIS OF
    STORY ELEMENTS
        Characters
        Setting
        Time
    IDENTIFICATION
    OF EPISODES

Closing
    Probe for content,
    structure, and process

Figure 4.   Sample script from *The Book* (Calfee & Associates, 1981).

Each script contains four items (Figure 4):

A statement of purpose and rationale for the teacher.

Opening. A pronouncement to the students of what is going to be taught, and why.

Middle activity. The problem solving segment, which includes a small number of leading questions.

Closing. A review of what was learned in the way of content and structure, how the learning might be applied in other settings, and the process used during the lesson.

In addition to this basic framework, each script has a number of additional features. The Modal Middle activity is the approach to the problem that supplies the greatest support to the students in solving the problem. Other middle activities are suggested that place greater demands on the students in the group. Following each script are lists of important patterns (e.g., variant forms of the narrative grammar) and chalkboard examples (how teachers can use the board to support the oral discussion).

The intention is not to put words into the teacher's mouth, but to provide a generic model of a discussion on a particular topic, which the teacher can then adapt to a variety of situations. Indeed, the scripts are intended to be applicable to a wide range of grades and student ability levels, and to fit most existing basal series, while also accommodating tradebooks and texts from the various content areas.

Lesson critiques. With appropriate training and *The Book* as a guide, classroom teachers can adapt most basal lessons to follow the Project conception of reading instruction—if they can find enough time. Aye, there's the rub!

To solve this problem, our staff came up with two ideas. The first, the *microscript,* looked good on the surface. We would examine a basal lesson, decide how it might be most effectively scripted, and prepare one or more descriptions of how to conduct a lesson on a particular topic. These were labeled microscripts because the description had to be written tightly enough to fit into the white space in the teacher's manual. These synoptic lesson plans were quite successful because they reduced preparation.

The problem was time. We determined that teachers were quite capable of planning these aids, but each lesson still took from two to four hours to review and write up. Seven grade levels, 180 days in the school year—the task amounted to a rewriting of the teacher's manual, which was not our purpose.

The second effort we have labeled the *lesson critique*. A research assistant or a teacher looks for problems and possibilities. The process is actually quite straightforward, once one becomes familiar with a particular series. The first step is to examine the text. Does it read well, what is the genre, what are the opportunities for vocabulary, sentence and paragraph comprehension, and decoding? What is suggested in the basal that can be used as is for analysis? What about the worksheets? Which ones have promise? Can the "back of the lesson" suggestions be incorporated in some way? The lesson critique brings the results of this investigation together in a one page review, with suggestions for scripts and follow up activities. Teachers are provided with a professional synopsis, and then left to make their own decisions. This approach has proven to be quite popular. Teachers prefer to have the freedom to make decisions to suit the situation. And the cost of preparing a critique is substantially less than for a microscript. An example of a critique is shown in Figure 5; the accompanying basal materials have not been reproduced because of the space limitations, but the basic principle should be obvious.

Approaching the School

This brief section is included to indicate the variety of ways in which a school change project can be initiated and sustained. Project READ began in one school with a reflective and concerned principal, who had identified a pervasive problem, who sought out resources to deal with it, who encouraged the faculty to experiment with the Project, and who personally supported the implementation of the activity. In turn, the university research team concentrated its energies on the development, installation and refinement of the concepts and procedures in that school.

Subsequent extensions of the Project have taken several forms. In one district, the central administration identified several schools as target sites. Principals varied in their enthusiasm for the Project, and in their ability to support its implementation. In gen-

Really Are Dragons   Level 12/Gr 5

Background: The text for this lesson is a rather rambling exposition about "real dragons," i.e., large lizards. The passage, which is unmarked, is basically descriptive in form, but to untangle the pieces the *Text Analysis Script* is recommended. After a brief introductory aside, the main point is presented in the second and third paragraphs on SE 186 — there is a basis in reality for the legends about dragons. The "large fish" (possibly a coelacanth?), the Loch Ness monster (bad example, because it is a legend itself!), and finally the Komodo dragon, which is the real point of the passage. Notice that the main topic is restated at the bottom of SE 186, after which the next three passages discuss the Komodo dragons — where they live, how they were discovered, the museum expedition to study the beasts, and then the ending question (a good one), "What about dragons in our part of the world?" As noted, the passage wanders rather badly, but the main points should be relatively easy to pull out.

Follow Up and Additional Activities: Monsters — dragons, lizards, serpents, snakes, real and legendary — there ought to be a basis in these topics for library research, with writing and graphics galore. If possible, locate some Oriental paintings and scrolls; how do these compare with contemporary comic books, with the paintings of Hieronymous Bosch, and the like?

The Vocabulary activity (TE 261) can be extended by a *Weaving Script* for discussion of Skillpack 68. The "unrelated" category is uninteresting, and "Go-Together" might be changed to "Related in Other Ways." The analysis of words in this latter category might lead to interesting discussion in its own right. You might select words from the text to analyze in this "weave."

An aside — the following lesson on "Math Reading," like others in this series, is quite general and provides no specifics about how to analyze *math* texts per se.

2/84 — Calfee

Figure 5. An example of a critique.

eral, and consistent with the prevailing literature, effective support by the principal is a significant determinant in the installation and support of a program, especially when resources are limited. The Project is "working" in half of the target sites in this district.

In another district, the Project was adopted under auspices of a teacher center program run by the local teachers' association. In each of the three schools in this urban setting, a teacher specialist received training in the Project concepts and procedures. The teacher specialist was then responsible for followup of individual teachers after the Project director presented workshops. Although there has been no followup of the effects of the Project on student performance in this setting, this approach seemed to have a substantial impact on the target teachers. Evaluation of this activity was

Calfee and Henry

outside of our purview, but our impression was that the separation of staff development from the school administration caused problems and diminished the effectiveness of the Project for the school as a whole.

More recently, the Project is being installed at several sites remote from the Bay area. The principal and one or more resource specialists are introduced to the concepts and procedures and provide followup support of the Project. We cannot yet determine the value of this model, but it appears to be a sensible allocation of resources and responsibilities.

District and school level administrators are often on the lookout for promising programs to improve reading performance. Some seem naturally adept at enticing, cajoling, or jollying their faculty into experimenting with new ideas. We suspect that many program developers have experienced situations in which the administration is ahead of the faculty—the presentation of a project prefaced by an enthusiastic introduction is greeted with skeptical and cold responses by the school faculty. The characteristics of Project READ have allowed us to conduct a show-and-tell activity that has proven quite effective in hurdling this barrier. After initial contact with an interested principal, we suggest a series of demonstration lessons with children at various grade levels: Relevant faculty can then observe the technique being employed with their own students. The demonstration is followed by a brief presentation of the concepts, with an opportunity for discussion of the Project. Thus far, this approach has proven the most effective way of encouraging a serious consideration of the Project by a school faculty.

These ruminations should be considered outside the context of the Project as a formal entity. We include them in this report because we could find relatively little literature on how a school with the potential for change is identified, approached, wooed, and won (some thoughts on this matter can be found in Louis, 1981, pp. 182ff).

The Implementation Sequence

This is a section on practical matters. As the Project has evolved over the past four years, a training model has taken shape.

The basic elements are these.

Initial training. A school faculty that has decided to take on the Project goes through a three day workshop which allows enough time to present the basic concepts and procedures adequately.

Demonstration lessons. Teachers are skeptics, and rightly so. Whatever the intellectual response to the workshop sessions, demonstrations of the procedures in the classrooms of several teachers have proven extremely valuable.

Observation and feedback. Eventually, if the Project is to become a reality, the individual teacher must put the procedures into practice. Well established practices of convention are hard to overcome, and we feel that once a teacher has decided to try a new approach, someone must be present to observe the event, to provide feedback and support, and to help plan the next occurrence.

Follow up workshops. We have found it valuable, after the initial training session, to plan followup sessions at intervals of two to three months. Project READ gives the teacher a great deal of responsibility, much more than is apparent at first glance. There is a tendency to worry about "whether I'm doing it right." Some concepts are easier to implement than others; story grammars are exciting to introduce to students because they are gaining mastery over something they already know, but exposition is another matter. An inservice day can be a productive experience for a school faculty.

The end-of-the-year session. Here we must speak from limited experience. The first school to go through the Project set a standard that may be hard to follow, but it merits description nonetheless. The final session of the year included a retrospective of the Project by the school faculty, an extraordinarily professional review of the strengths and weaknesses of the activities with suggestions for improvement, and a prospective plan for the school for the next year. Whether that event can be consistently expected is speculation, but it is congruent with the general principles of the Project, which emphasize explicitness, reflection, and formality in communication.

Calfee and Henry

Evaluation of the Project

We have collected various kinds of data from Graystone Elementary School, the site at which the Project was developed. These data are of limited value. Self-evaluation is somewhat like serving as your own lawyer; while better than no evaluation at all, it is by no means completely trustworthy. Graystone was also unusual in that we were able to concentrate substantial resources in support of the school staff during the first year.

Nonetheless, these findings provide an opportunity to present an evaluation plan of the sort that we think appropriate for assessing this type of project, and the results are generally encouraging. As this chapter is being written in the spring of 1984, we are collecting additional data from a larger sample of schools, and activities are underway for an independent evaluation of the impact on a new cohort of schools that will enter the Project in the fall.

Outcomes for the Teacher

Project READ is primarily a staff development activity, and so we begin by asking how it affects teachers. We collected data before, during and after the workshop. Teachers were observed and interviewed conducting reading lessons with various scripts. Teachers also filled out "script logs," a one-line account of any lesson during which they used a script. End-of-year interviews have sought an overall account of the effects of the Project on the individual teacher, on students, and on the school as a whole. The publisher of the basal series in place at Graystone has sought out the teachers' reactions to the series, and the Project staff has independently asked for critical analyses of the series.

Several themes emerged from this collection of information. The pre-Project interviews are consistent with the findings of others. Teachers generally have trouble articulating a clear conception of reading instruction. They often refer to the basal series as the foundation, and they tend to follow the path laid out by the basal lesson. With experience, some teachers explore sideroads and turn to supplementary materials and texts.

Initial response to the three day workshop is cautious. The ideas are unfamiliar, the emphasis on theory disturbs the practically minded person who has to deal with thirty students on Monday, and the implicit criticism of existing practice does not go down well, no matter how supportively phrased. By the end of the first day, many teachers feel overwhelmed by the range of new ideas, stimulated by the challenge, but skeptical about the applicability of the ideas in the classroom. During the second and third days, after simulated application in the workshop exercises, the concepts become clearer and the attitudes more positive. Some teachers comment that they already employ many of the ideas in the Project. Since many of the practices are the result of interactions with practitioners, this comment makes sense. Our role in the Project is to create a "package" for the foundation concepts, and to provide a rationale that is comprehensible and communicable.

With support from the principal or some other local "champion," the Project is implemented. The use of scripts as the lesson plan is a gradual process. After the preliminary demonstrations, a teacher may plan one script a week for several weeks. In most instances, teachers begin using scripts for the majority of their reading lessons by the end of the year. The driving force behind this change is the student response.

Three themes have appeared in the end-of-year comments. First, teachers report an increased sense of professional effectiveness: They can explain what they are doing; they feel more confident that their approach to reading instruction is on the right track; and they think that students are more engaged in learning. Second, they are finding greater professional satisfaction in their relations with other members of the school faculty; many have also commented positively about the collaboration with a research team. Finally, they are more satisfied with the reading curriculum and with the instructional approach, and with the outcomes for students.

Faculty had the following kinds of observations to make about various aspects of the Project: One saw *The Book* as "a philosophy of teaching reading that can be used in a practical way." Another found the year long process a valuable design for staff development, and noted that the concepts provided a way of "extending the students' thinking skills that can be used in many areas of the curriculum." Observations in the classroom have shown that scripted lessons are commonplace in language arts, but also in social studies, science, and even mathematics. A fourth grade teacher noted the value of a "ready vocabulary to discuss reading instruction with parents and peers."

Outcomes for the Student

The program appears to affect students in three ways. First, the discussion methods are effective. The amount of student talk has increased, the quality of student involvement has improved, and students appear to enjoy the greater opportunity to participate. Teachers have shared the jargon with students, so that the latter talk about "doing a script lesson," generally with approval and even enthusiasm.

Second, students are becoming more adept at formal speaking and writing. Expressive skills are improving; students are writing more, they are writing longer passages, and they are better at explaining what they know. Writing samples provided by Project teachers show that most of the writing is at the paragraph level or above, with several projects that entail outlining of extended texts and "reports" of several pages.

Third, the scores on standardized tests have improved at Graystone during the two years of the Project (Figure 6). The school serves an upper middle class neighborhood, which shows up in the pattern of 1981 scores—students are about one grade level ahead of the expected value at the end of first grade, and are two or three grade levels ahead by the end of fifth grade. At the end of the first year of the Project, scores had improved by one-half grade level or more at most grades in all three areas of the test battery. The improved performance was sustained during the second year of the Project, despite a substantial reduction in the amount of support by the Project staff. We are not presenting data from a controlled experiment, and so do not claim that the Project has caused the increase, but the Project certainly has not harmed performance on this index.

Summary

Slavin (1984), using Carroll's model of learning as a point of departure, has noted that many of the disappointments in instruc-

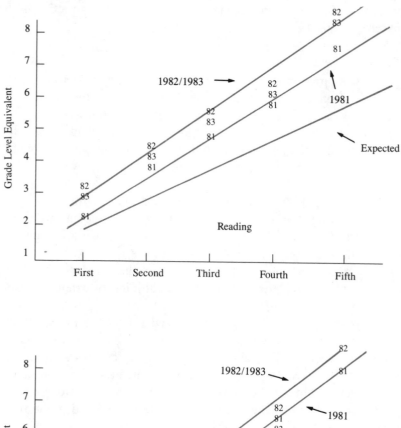

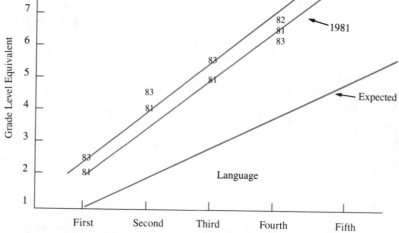

Calfee and Henry

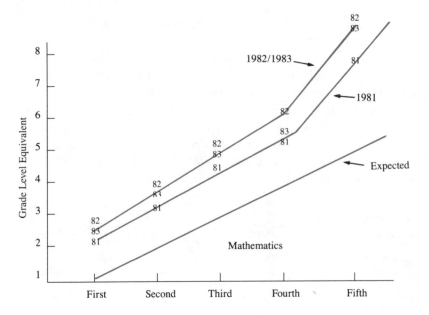

Figure 6.   Longitudinal analyses of Standardized Test Scores, Graystone School, 1981-1983.

tional research may result from a narrow focus on one or another of the significant components in classroom instruction. The principle seems an important one. Efforts to improve instruction with too limited a vision of the classroom may fail, not because the ideas are poor, but because the effects are lost in the welter of other factors.

Project READ can be viewed as an "experiment," not in the sense of the classical experimental versus control group paradigm, but more in the "trying out" interpretation of the word. Its unique features include the emphasis on coherence and parsimony as a basis for the reading curriculum, and the importance of the teacher as an informed professional with a significant decision making role in classroom instruction. Metacognition is an active area of psychological research at present. We would propose that the chief task of teachers is to train students in the skills of reflective analysis that are at the heart of metacognitive activities. They will be unable to carry out that task unless they take a similar stance with regard to their work as instructors.

When the Project began four years ago, the district's major concern was to help high school seniors pass the minimum competency tests. Within that context, our proposal to the collaborating teachers seemed more radical than it does today: "The basic skills needed for survival in modern society are thinking, problem solving, and the ability to communicate; reading and language arts are simply 'covers' for teaching those skills." This statement still captures the essential spirit of the Project.

References

Blumberg, A., and Greenfield, W. *The effective principal.* Boston, MA: Allyn & Bacon, 1980.

Brookover, W.B., Beamer, L., Efthim, H., Hathaway, D., Lezotte, L., Miller, S., Passalacqua, J., and Tornatzky, L. *Creating effective schools.* Holmes Beach, FL: Learning Publications, 1982.

Brooks, C., and Warren, R.P. *Modern rhetoric,* (shorter third edition). New York: Harcourt Brace Jovanovich, 1972.

Bruner, J.S. *Toward a theory of instruction.* Cambridge, MA: Belknap Press, Harvard University, 1966.

Calfee, R.C. Cognitive psychology and educational practice. In D.C. Berliner (Ed.), *Review of research in education.* Washington, D.C.: American Educational Research Association, 1981.

Calfee, R.C. The mind of the dyslexic. *Annals of Dyslexia,* 1983, *33,* 9-28.

Calfee, R.C., and Associates. *The book: Components of reading instruction.* Unpublished manual for reading teachers, Stanford University, 1981.

Calfee, R.C., and Atkinson, R.C. Paired-associate models and the effects of list length. *Journal of Mathematical Psychology,* 1965, 2, 254-256.

Calfee, R.C., and Drum, P.A. Research on teaching reading. In M. Wittrock (Ed.), *Third handbook on research on teaching.* Chicago: Rand McNally, in press.

Calfee, R.C. and Shefelbine, J.L. A structural model of teaching. In A. Lewy and D. Nevo (Eds.), *Evaluation roles in education.* New York: Gordon and Breach, 1981.

Calfee, R.C., and Sutter, L. Oral language assessment through formal discussion. *Topics in Language Disorders,* 1928, *2,* 45-55.

Carnine, D., and Gersten, R. The logistics of educational change. In J. Osborn, R.C. Anderson, and P. Wilson (Eds.), *Foundations for a literate America.* Lexington, MA: Lexington Books, 1984.

Chall, J. *Learning to read: The great debate.* New York: McGraw-Hill, 1967.

Denham, C., and Lieberman, A. (Eds.). *Time to learn.* Washington, D.C.: U.S. Department of Education, 1980.

Duffy, J. *Project description: Teaching conceptions of reading projects.* Unpublished manuscript, Institute for Research on Teaching, Michigan State University, 1977.

Dunkin, M.J., and Biddle, G.J. *The study of teaching.* New York: Holt, Rinehart and Winston, 1974.

Edmonds, R. Characteristics of effective schools: Research and implementation. In J. Osborn, R.C. Anderson, and P. Wilson (Eds.), *Foundations for a literate America.* Lexington, MA: Lexington Books, 1985.

Eisner, E.W. *The educational imagination: On the design and evaluation of school programs.* New York: Macmillan, 1979.

Gall, M.D. The use of questions in teaching. *Review of Educational Research,* 1970, *40,* 707-721.

Gall, M.D., and Gall, J.P. The discussion method. In N.L. Gage (Ed.), *The psychology of teaching methods.* Seventy-Fifth Yearbook of the National Society for the Study of Education. Chicago: University of Chicago Press, 1976.

Ginn Reading Program. *Teacher's edition.* Lexington, MA: Ginn, 1982.

Goodlad, J.I. *A place called school.* New York: McGraw-Hill, 1984.

Greeno, J.G. Psychology of learning, 1969-1980: One participant's observations. *American Psychologist,* 1980, *35,* 713-728.

Louis, K.S. External agents and knowledge utilization: Dimensions for analysis and action. In R. Lehming, and M. Kane (Eds.), *Improving schools: Using what we know.* Beverly Hills, CA: Sage Publications, 1981.

Moffett, J. *A student-centered language arts curriculum, Grades K-6: A handbook for teachers.* Boston: Houghton-Mifflin, 1968.

National Assessment of Educational Progress (NAEP). *Three national assessments of reading: Changes in performance 1970-1980.* Report No. 11-R-01.

Purkey, S.C., and Smith, M.S. Effective schools: A review. *Elementary School Journal,* in press.

Rumelhart, D.E. Understanding and summarizing brief stories. In D. LaBerge, and J. Samuels (Eds.), *Basic processes in reading: Perception and comprehension.* Hillsdale, NJ: Erlbaum, 1977.

Slavin, R.E. Component building: A strategy for research based instructional improvement. *Elementary School Journal,* 1984, *84,* 255-269.

Venezky, R.L. *The structure of English orthography.* The Hague, Paris: Mouton, 1970.

11

Renée Weisberg

The Madeline Hunter Model of Teacher Effectiveness

A ccording to Madeline Hunter, if you want to find out why a baseball team is losing badly, you don't look at its scores. You watch the team as it plays. Then you analyze its actions in order to improve its performance. Reading scores reflect how students have performed in a specific task, but scores do not tell *why* students have performed that way. To analyze students' reading behaviors in order to remediate their reading difficulties, observe them when they are reading and answering questions about their reading.

Hunter answers the questions "What does a successful teacher need to be able to do? and "How do you know when a teacher is doing it with the students?" in her clinical theory of instruction (1977). Called Instructional Theory into Practice (ITIP), the theory is based on a synthesis of research in teaching and learning and on an analysis of teachers' instructional decision making, conducted primarily at the Laboratory School of the University of California at Los Angeles. In Hunter's model, teachers' decisions are the independent variable because Hunter believes that, in the teaching learning interaction, the only variable teachers can control is their own behavior.

Hunter based ITIP on several assumptions.

1. Because teachers can control instruction, they should be accountable for their instructional decisions.
2. When teachers plan instruction which has an identified objective, student achievement will probably increase.
3. When teachers use known principles of learning, they will be able to improve students' motivation to learn, to teach more, to increase retention, and to teach students how to apply what they have learned in appropriate situations.
4. Students can only learn whatever is the next step to what they already know. If new information is too far removed from what is presently known, learning will not be effective.
5. If teachers are aware of *what* they do well and *why* they are doing it well, they will try to continue to improve their teaching performance.
6. Although artistry in teaching cannot be taught, the art of teaching is based on sound principles of learning. Hunter quotes photographer Ansel Adams, who said, "You can have a craft without an art but you can't have an art without a craft."
7. Because Hunter views ITIP as only the *how*, not the *what* of teaching, she believes it is generalizeable across all content areas, school organizations, different learning and teaching styles, and students of all ages.

According to Hunter, ITIP is not a formula. Instead, it identifies the principles of learning upon which to base instructional decisions. Hunter feels the need to explain this because of her concern about those practitioners who eagerly adopt the model but blindly follow it to the letter as if it were the only "right" way, without seeing it as just a vehicle for enhancing teachers' instructional decision making and their continued professional growth.

The Hunter Model and the Directed Reading Activity

A superintendent in one school district which has implemented the model compares the Madeline Hunter Model of Teacher Effectiveness to the Directed Reading Activity. He believes both instructional models are basically teacher directed, that both require teacher decision making concerning the learning objective, and both are based on the concept of diagnostic teaching—the teacher's ongoing observations of the learner during the lesson to insure that learning takes place.

Readiness

Readiness, the first step in a Directed Reading Activity, is also the first step in the Hunter Model. Questions the teacher must ask before actually teaching are: "What is the learning objective?" "Where is the learner in relation to the learning objective?" "What must the learner do in order to learn this?" "What principles of learning are appropriate for this learning?"

The learning objective must be at the correct level of difficulty for the learner. According to Hunter, if the lesson is too easy or too difficult, no learning will take place, either because it is already known, or because it is too different from what the learner presently knows, making the effort to learn too great. This view reflects Hunter's principle that learning is incremental (Hunter, 1979). Prior knowledge determines to a large degree what the learner can learn next. Therefore, the teacher must diagnose the learner's state of readiness in relation to the learning objective and to the content of the lesson.

Eberwein (1974) found differences in the reading achievement of disabled readers who were informed of the behavioral objectives of their reading tasks and those who were not informed. Achievement differences were attributed to differences in student awareness of what an acceptable reading performance was.

In a review of fifteen studies on the relationship of behavioral objectives to achievement, Walbesser and Eisenbert (1972) found little difference in student achievement between students who were told and those who were not told the behavioral objectives for the lesson. When third and fourth graders participated in setting their own goals, Powers (1970) found they had significantly higher scores on tests of reading skills than students who did not set goals.

Whether there are learning hierarchies in reading was questioned by Roudabush (1974). He proposed a statistical model of a hierarchical structure, but cautioned that his results were subject to measurement errors because of his research methodology. He concluded that there were some reading skills that were prerequisites for others, although he did not find a single "contingency relationship" (p. 414).

Duchastel and Merrill (1973) reviewed research studies on the impact of behavioral objectives on learning outcomes. In a group of studies which compared learning outcomes between groups of students who had received instruction with established behavioral objectives and groups without behavioral objectives, results showed positive effects in half the studies and no differences in the other half in immediate posttests. In another group of studies which investigated the effects of behavioral objectives on the type of learning—factual versus conceptual—only one study out of seven found positive effects of objectives on achievement. An investigation of learner characteristics indicated that knowledge of behavioral objectives reduced anxiety in highly anxious students. Duchastel and Merrill concluded that, although few main effects of behavioral objectives on student learning are evident, interactions definitely exist among individual differences in the learner, the text, and the task.

Diagnosing the lesson's content from the learner's point of view requires the teacher to perform a task analysis in order to become aware of prerequisite learnings, as well as the incremental and sequential steps needed to learn the content of the present lesson. For example, before children can do initial consonant substitution with phonograms, they must already have learned the consonants. The teacher who tells children they must pause in their reading when they see a period because it means the end of a sentence, without finding out if the children know what a sentence is, has not done a task analysis from the learner's point of view (Durkin, 1979).

Collins (1978) cautioned that a task analysis in reading has to question appropriateness of instructional procedures, the purpose of the task (reading for pleasure or reading for instruction), the learner's interest and motivation, the importance of the skills to the reading process, and the teacher's awareness of the assumptions of the author about the prior knowledge of the reader.

Additional readiness for the teacher requires the selection of the relevant principles of learning which will enhance successful achievement of the lesson's objective. Among the questions the teacher would ask which reflect Hunter's principles of learning are: "How can I help motivate the learner?" "How can I increase the amount and rate of learning?" "How can I improve retention of what is to be learned?" "How can I insure transfer of learning to new situations?"

How Can I Motivate the Learner?

Implicit in the readiness stage of a Directed Reading Activity is the importance of motivating the reader to want to read the text. In Hunter's view, to create an environment which can increase motivation, teachers should insure some degree of successful performance by the students and should relate each learning activity to the students' internalized goals. In this way, learning is behavior that fills a need.

Hunter believes that no one can really motivate another person because motivation is a state of need within a person. Motivation causes behavior that will fulfill that need. Hunter's point is that teachers can help students become aware of the need for learning.

An aspect of motivation a teacher can control is the degree of student interest in the lesson. To make learning interesting to students, Hunter suggests relating the lesson's content to the student's life. When teaching main idea to teenagers, Hunter would use paragraphs dealing with teenage concerns rather than paragraphs about photosynthesis or the Civil War.

The degree of vividness with which a lesson is presented is another motivating factor under a teacher's control. By vividness, Hunter means novel or different approaches in the readiness part of a lesson.

A motivational variable called "success" is especially important in preventing reading problems. Hunter believes that when students have successful experiences, their interest in those activities increases. Conversely, students will not be motivated or interested in those activities in which they have not experienced success.

For activities to be motivating, teachers must select activities at a moderate level of difficulty so that students perceive that success is possible. To Hunter, the successful student is the one most highly motivated to learn.

When students are aware of the results of their performance, Hunter believes they will be motivated to improve. Hunter cautions that feedback must be both specific and positive to be motivating. Commending a student who is doing better in identifying the main idea and then showing the student how to find the main idea in those paragraphs that were incorrect is feedback which is both specific and positive.

The bottom line in motivation is meaning. Effective reading teachers know how to help students bridge the gap between what they are reading and some aspect of their own lives.

Motivation and its relation to reading achievement was investigated by Koenke (1978), McNeill (1977), and Carver (1971). Koenke reviewed research which found that motivation improved when the reading specialist and the teacher planned cooperatively and individualized instruction to meet students' needs, not just their instructional levels. Other studies reported by Koenke indicated that when expectations for success were maintained, students modeled their behavior on others and set high standards for themselves. The effect of different reading materials on students' motivation showed that children's own writing was a motivating force in reading instruction.

McNeill (1977) discussed research which indicated that extrinsic rewards have a negative effect on motivation, but that students are positively motivated when they perceive their behavior as self-initiated. His conclusion was that students will be less motivated when they are reading because the teacher sets the purpose or asks the questions. Instead, McNeill calls for instruction which helps students set their own goals in reading. As an example, he cites Singer's research called "active reading."

Carver (1971) investigated how much disabled readers' improvement in reading ability was due to their increased motivation and how much to the instructional method used. Four groups of disabled readers were each taught with a different teaching approach for seven months. Children in all four groups received consistent warm approval regardless of their behavior or their reading improvement. At the end of the seven months Carver found that students in all groups improved significantly and no differences could be attributed to instructional method used.

How Can I Increase the Probability that the Lesson Will Be Learned?

Lesson Content Should Have Meaning to the Learner. The interaction of the task to be learned with the learner can increase or decrease the probability that learning will take place. To Hunter, the meaningfulness of the material to the learner is the factor in the task itself which can increase learning. It is easier to learn words that go together in some way than to learn lists of unrelated words. Although meaningfulness is rarely an all-or-nothing situation, the effective teacher must analyze the lesson to relate concepts in the present lesson to the particular group's past experience.

Knowledge about students' prior knowledge to activate pupils' schemata has been researched and reported by Bobrow and Norman (1975) and Rumelhart and Ortony (1977). Pearson and Johnson (1978) state "Comprehension is building bridges between the new and the unknown" (p. 24).

Teacher Guidance Increases Learning

In a Directed Reading Activity, the students' first reading of a passage is silent but not independent. In this *guided* silent reading the teacher helps students use their word recognition skills to unlock new words. The teacher provides as much guidance as is necessary.

In the Hunter Model, teacher guidance is recommended at the beginning stages of the lesson to increase the amount and rate of new learning. Teachers then lessen that guidance as learners begin to master the new learning.

Positive and Negative Influences on New Learning

A student who has already successfully learned something related to the new lesson should transfer that prior knowledge to the new learning. Past learning will increase chances for learning the new material successfully. Children who have begun to learn to read and who feel they are good readers will have positive feelings about learning more. Their past repertoire of reading skills, however rudimentary, will enhance their learning of additional skills.

On the other hand, when past learning has been perceived as a failure, these negative feelings will interfere with new learning. When past learning interferes with present attempts to learn, negative transfer is operating. When direct teacher guidance is not available as students are learning, new lessons may be learned inaccurately, thus interfering with the next task and perpetuating errors.

Active Participation of the Learner

The active participation of the learner is a crucial variable in increasing the amount of learning that will take place. Hunter cites two types of participatory learning: overt and covert. Overt learning is observable: students writing their answers on a test or answering questions orally in class. Covert learning is not observable: students thinking of answers, for example. Hunter suggests a combination of covert and overt participation. In a Directed Reading Activity, asking students to read silently is enjoining covert participation. Some are reading; some may be daydreaming. However, following the silent reading, if students are asked to raise their hands when they have found a specific sentence or write an answer to a specific question, their participation or lack of it will be observable.

How Practice Influences Learning

An effective teacher never has students practice a skill without being aware of three factors: the part of the lesson to be practiced; the right length of a practice session; and how often to schedule practice sessions. In the Hunter model, the amount of the practice lesson depends upon how much material is needed to maintain meaning. When practicing newly learned words, for example, students need a context which provides meaning and aids retention.

The right length of a practice session is the shortest time needed to improve learning and maintain attention. Because students make errors, the first practice sessions should be short to avoid fatigue and to discourage students from making more errors.

The scheduling of practice sessions is clear-cut in this teacher-effectiveness model: mass practice at the beginning, review in the middle of the lesson, and review again at the end of the lesson or the end of the day. The amount of time a new skill is practiced is less important than the schedule of the practice sessions. Hunter believes follow up practice is essential for retention. Because the largest amount of forgetting occurs after the skill is no longer practiced, practice should occur the day after a lesson is taught, and the third and fifth days after that. Something that is learned well and practiced often is not likely to be forgotten.

Level of Aspiration

To help students become proficient learners, teachers must increase students' awareness of how well they are actually doing. Students who know they can learn will be motivated to learn more. To help overcome the lack of motivation in students with reading problems, teachers should break tasks into manageable units, select tasks the students can achieve, and reinforce students when they do achieve. Positive reinforcement should be a regular and conscious aspect of effective teaching.

Teaching to Increase Transfer

To enable students to apply new learning in appropriate situations is the goal of effective teachers. It is an important answer to the first question Hunter's model raises: "What is it that effective teachers need to be able to do?" First, students have to be able to identify what in their previous learning is applicable to their present task. They must also see some similarity in the two situations. Next, students must be taught how to identify and label invariant elements in the previous learning and the new one. For example, the reader who knows *ate* can be helped to identify *late* and *gate*. Using several instances of the same element, students can develop categories having the same properties. They need what Hunter labels "a set to perform," a strategy that will help solve their present problem. They can then be led to form generalizations of the underlying principle. The generalization is transferable to new situations. Students must first learn a concept before they can generalize and transfer it. To Hunter, when teachers teach for transfer, they help students learn how to learn.

Research in transfer of training in reading instruction has focused on transfer of word recognition abilities, differences in transfer of different reading abilities, and some underlying abilities needed for transfer. Research in the transfer of decoding abilities was reviewed by Richardson and DiBenedetto (1977). They concluded that for beginning readers, training in decoding abilities transferred effectively to new letter combinations and to unknown words, but that transfer depended on the degree of mastery pupils achieved during training.

Three word recognition strategies, graphophonic, structural, and contextual, were investigated for their transfer effectiveness by McNeill and Donant (1980). Second, third, and fourth grade subjects were able to apply each word recognition strategy to new words in each category after training. They concluded that students need multiple word recognition strategies which they can use according to the demands of the task.

Onmacht and Fleming (1977) investigated which reading abilities transferred to subsequent reading abilities. If certain skills are required for transfer to higher level skills, which skills are needed at different stages of learning? Results indicated that some reading abilities which are needed for transfer at some stages are not the same abilities needed at other stages. For example, the ability to apply morphological rules seemed to differentiate good and poor readers in first and second grade but was not an important difference between good and poor sixth grade readers. In addition, learning for transfer based on a skill hierarchy cannot be specified to account for either reading ability or reading disability.

Spiro's discussion of thinking (1977) in the acquisition of new information in school describes why new information does not always transfer. Often the student is unaware of how this new information could transfer to life outside of school. Learning is often compartmentalized because students have come to expect they will be tested on discrete information. Spiro believes there is not usually an effort made to relate new information to previous knowledge, to build "bridges between the new and the unknown" (Pearson and Johnson, 1978). Does Hunter's principle of teaching—selecting the objective at the correct level of difficulty—and her belief that learning is incremental support Spiro's and Pearson and Johnson's view?

Research on critical components in Hunter's definition of effective teacher behavior was reported by Heath and Nielson (1974), Kyriacou and Newson (1982), Medley, Soar, and Soar (1975) and

Medley and Mitzel (1959). Heath and Nielson (1974) reviewed studies which attempted to discover the teaching skills that led to improvement in student achievement. Among the studies they analyzed critically were fifty studies of Rosenshine and Furst (1971). After examining the criteria used for student achievement, the statistical analyses of results, samples used, and how teaching behavior was defined, Heath and Nielson concluded that teacher behaviors which influence achievement have not been empirically demonstrated. In addition, because content taught and type of student were variables which had not been studied, the question was raised about possible different teacher behaviors needed for effective teaching when teaching different types of students and different content areas.

Kyriacou and Newson (1982) reviewed research in four areas related to Hunter's Model of Teacher Effectiveness. The first area, teacher characteristics, the basic ingredient in the Hunter Model, has been extensively researched, but Kyriacou and Newson conclude in their review that generally studies have not investigated how the same teacher characteristics—the ability to use higher level questions, for example—may actually differentially affect students. Brophy and Evertson (1974) did find an interaction between SES of students and the effect of the level of questioning on student achievement.

The second area, research on classroom interactions during teaching, is related to Hunter's Model of clinical supervision. Kyriacou and Newson believe that research on systematic observation of classrooms is subjective and has limited generalizability. For example, what the observer concludes may not agree with teacher or student perceptions of the lesson's effectiveness.

Kyriacou and Newson object to time on task studies of student activities during lessons because student behavior is the criterion for achievement instead of the means to the end, which is student learning.

The use of gain scores as a criterion of teacher effectiveness, the fourth area, has its own difficulties. For example, what unit of analysis measures gain? Many aspects of student behavior which have improved (such as attitude, motivation, appreciation of subject matter) are often overlooked. Suggestions are made for descriptions of the lesson by the observer, questionnaires for students and teachers to assess perceptions of the lesson's effectiveness, and feedback to teachers to develop awareness of the process of effective teaching related to their own teaching contexts.

Medley (1975) raised important questions about components of the Hunter Model and presented research for consideration. First, Medley questioned the use of student gain scores to measure teacher effectiveness. He questions their validity in the long term and raises concerns about teachers who would teach facts which are measured on the tests. Medley cites research which suggests that direct instruction can raise pupil achievement up to a point. After that, continued teacher control results in decreased pupil gain and in a lowered self-concept (Soar and Soar, 1972). Medley cites other research which suggests an interaction effect on student gains in reading, teacher-directed lessons, on the SES of the students (Soar & Soar, 1973, Brophy & Evertson, 1974). Differences in pupil characteristics also interacted with self-selection versus teacher controlled lessons, SES of students, and student motivation.

Medley and Mitzel (1959) examined the relationship among teacher effectiveness variables, student achievement in reading, and teachers' self-ratings of their performance. They found that pupil achievement and teachers' self-ratings were related to teachers' effectiveness in teaching reading. Professional personnel in Pennsylvania and Virginia believed teachers were more effective in teaching reading since the implementation of the Hunter Model. Teachers in Pennsylvania who were interviewed said they had more confidence in their ability to teach reading, often because the staff development program reinforced teaching behaviors they had been using.

Case Study of the Hunter Model

There is a small school district in eastern Pennsylvania which lies in a valley surrounded by rolling green hills. The area is primarily rural and small town, not suburban; has no malls or shopping centers; and no decline in its pupil population of 3,200 who are enrolled in its three elementary schools, its one middle school, and one high school. Its 16,200 residents are mostly middle class, although there are two low income pockets, a trailer park and a low cost housing area. An expanding industrial park nearby provides many jobs. The values of the community reflect its Pennsylvania-German heritage. Hard work, discipline, and support for education are prized. These values result in excellent teacher-parent relations and in an annual budget of ten million two hundred thousand dollars, a per pupil expenditure of $3,187.50. The community is stable. When polled a few years ago, all members of the school board had been born in the area and had lived there all of their lives.

The peaceful sleepy look of the valley contrasts sharply with the well-organized administrators responsible for the school district's policies and procedures. In this stable community, administrators never seek change for the sake of change itself, but they are always alert to changes to bring about teacher effectiveness.

In 1977, the dynamic superintendent of the school district attended a meeting of the American Association of School Administrators at which Hunter's Teacher Effectiveness Model was presented. The superintendent immediately saw its potential for improving instruction in the district and arranged for selected administrators, school board members, and three teachers to observe the model in action in Virginia. A second group of teachers later spent a week of inservice in Virginia and they presented the program to the rest of the staff. The teachers were asked, without the administrators present, to vote on whether to adopt the model. It was overwhelmingly accepted. The school board then voted to fund a staff level program to implement the model to help pay for substitutes so that teachers could participate in the program.

Subsequently, the coordinator of staff development took more courses in the psychology of effective teaching based on the Hunter Model. He also attended seminars with Madeline Hunter and with the Director of Professional Development in Long Beach, California, where the model had been adopted. The district's professional staff development program was organized and was awarded a Title IV-C grant of $71,955 to help fund the program's first three years.

Implementation of the Hunter Model in a Pennsylvania School District

In 1979, after the teachers voted to adopt the Hunter Model of Teacher Effectiveness, the director of staff development began implementing the program. The first decision was that staff participation in the program be entirely voluntary.

During the first year, 35 percent of the staff volunteered. Typical trainee groups of twelve to fifteen consisted of elementary teachers, middle school and secondary teachers, a principal, and some central office administrators.

A training cycle lasted six weeks. Each Monday a different aspect of the Hunter Model was introduced and modeled. Participants then practiced the specific learning of that day. The staff development director observed the staff and provided specific feedback. Tuesday through Friday, the teacher participants practiced the specific objectives of the week in their own classrooms. At least one day that week each participating teacher was observed, and provided feedback in a conference. Just as teaching to a specific objective is a basic principle of the Hunter Model, so too was conferring about a specific objective part of the director's responsibility.

The content of each week's learning was based on a major principle of Hunter's Teacher Effectiveness Model. The four instructional skills that form the structure of the program follow.

1. The teacher can select an objective at the correct level of difficulty.
2. The teacher can teach to an objective.
3. The teacher can monitor the progress of the learner and make the necessary adjustments.
4. The teacher can use the eight principles of learning: mental set, closure, covert behavior, overt behavior, motivation, reinforcement, retention, and transfer.

Week 1. Teaching to an Objective

The teacher learns how to generate in the student observable behavior to find out if the student has achieved the learning objective. The four components in this lesson are: explanation, questions, activities, and response to the learner.

Explanation tells the student what is to be learned. Explanation should be varied, interesting, and, if possible, creative in order to capture the interest of students at the beginning—the Hunter principle of vividness.

Questions must be asked when teaching to an objective in order to check for the learner's understanding. The questions must be relevant to the lesson's objective. Teachers learn to ask questions at different levels of difficulty and complexity. Bloom's taxonomy of knowledge, comprehension, application, analysis, synthesis, and evaluation serves as a framework for the development of questioning techniques. Competency in using Bloom's taxonomy in questioning and in the selection of a learning objective at different levels of difficulty is the basis for the second week's staff development session.

Activities provided by the teacher are of two kinds. The first is guided practice, which follows after the teacher explains the lesson and teaches it. Teachers are taught to monitor learning so the dependent guided practice activities gradually develop into the second kind of activity—the independent activities. Teachers are taught how to provide additional practice activities with students who need more time to master the learning objective.

Response to the learner should use the language of the learning and be specific. Responses such as "Terrific" and "Great," while positive, are not couched in the language of the learning. "Yes, Joe, that word is 'biped' " or "Yes, Jan, 'Petroleum is an important product of Mexico' is the main idea of that paragraph" are direct, specific, reinforcing teacher responses which use the language of the lesson to be learned.

Week 2. Bloom's Taxonomy

Set and Closure. Because the staff development director believes strongly that students should be taught to think beyond the literal level, he uses a pamphlet based on Bloom's taxonomy. Each page represents a level of the taxonomy and is divided into four sections. The first section explains in eight to ten different ways exactly what that level is. The second section provides the teacher with the vocabulary needed to formulate questions or statements at that level. Examples of what students would do at a particular level are given in the third section, called Student Learning. The fourth section lists sample questions or activities so teachers can use the descriptors and the vocabulary to plan specific learning activities. The use of this brochure is an excellent example of a staff development program actually doing what it says teachers should do: model, demonstrate, practice, and apply.

Anticipatory Set and Closure, two of Hunter's eight principles of learning, are also developed in the second week's session. Anticipatory Set has three parts: 1) a statement of the learning by the teacher; 2) involving the learner through teacher questions; and 3) relating the lesson to the learner's past experiences, to present needs, or to some possible future concerns.

In Closure, the teacher summarizes the lesson and involves the learner at the conclusion of the lesson. In the Hunter Model, the teacher helps learners see similarities in elements of their learning and to form rules or generalizations. When learners can restate what was learned in their own words, or can summarize key aspects of the lesson, then Closure has been successful.

Week 3. Task Analysis

Does the teacher select an objective at the correct level of difficulty? To do this the teacher first has to be aware of what a student already knows about the target material. Second, the teacher has to understand the sequential development of the content, its prerequisites, and the steps the student must go through to learn the present lesson.

The five steps in analyzing a task are: 1) identify the objective, 2) brainstorm, 3) weed out nonessential learning, 4) sequence, and 5) form diagnostic questions. This analysis is based on Hunter's view that learning is incremental and predictable.

Covert and Overt Behavior. Because covert behavior cannot be observed, teachers are taught to generate overt behavior in their students. Raising their hands when they have a solution to a problem is an example of students' overt behavior. Covert behavior precedes overt behavior since thinking about an answer must precede the act of answering. Teachers can increase student involvement by asking a second student to agree or disagree with the first answer. When students know they have to hang in and evaluate their peers' responses, a great deal of both covert and overt behavior can take place. The teacher can also tell the whole class to think about the answer to a question and then say, "I'll ask one of you to answer it."

Week 4. Monitoring and Adjusting the Progress of the Learner

Teachers monitor and adjust student progress by having students participate actively in the lessons. Teachers can tell where a learner is in relation to the lesson's objective and often adjust a prepared lesson to meet the present needs of some learners.

For example, when teaching a lesson in alphabetizing to the second letter, after generating overt behavior in students the teacher realizes that students cannot learn the task. The teacher understands that alphabetizing to the first letter is prerequisite for the present lesson and proceeds to teach alphabetizing to the first letter.

Week 5. Motivation and Reinforcement

Motivation. This staff development program provides its teachers with six ways to improve students' motivational level. The first is using novel teaching approaches in the readiness stage or through a seldom-used approach in other parts of the lesson. This element is termed "vividness."

Teaching at the correct level of difficulty, the second way, can motivate students to feel they can learn successfully, because lessons are neither too easy nor frustratingly difficult.

The third element is creating a desired atmosphere in the classroom. When the tone is obviously warm and pleasant, when the expectation for success is obvious to students, motivation to learn is enhanced.

Providing specific feedback to students about the results of their performance is the fourth factor in increasing student motivation.

The fifth element is called tension, that is, a concern for learning. Staff training focuses on how to develop this concern for learning without creating anxiety.

The last element is rewarding students for successful achievement. This district believes most students can be rewarded for something they have achieved and that not just top students should be rewarded. However, rewards offered indiscriminately are discouraged.

Reinforcement. Three types of reinforcement are taught through classroom simulation: positive reinforcement, negative reinforcement, and extinction. When reinforcing positively, the teacher provides feedback the student wants to see or hear either verbally or nonverbally. Negative reinforcement is feedback which the student may not want to see or hear, but which the student needs to stop behavior which is detrimental to learning. This staff is encouraged to go from negative to positive reinforcement. For example, instead of saying, "Sam, stop shouting out your answers and interrupting others," teachers practice saying, "Sam, when you think you have the answer, sit up tall and I'll know." The staff is also trained to ignore some behavior in order to weaken it and eventually stop it. This type of reinforcement is called extinction.

Week 6. Retention and Transfer

Retention. The crucial question all teachers ask is "Have the students learned anything?" Usually students are tested to see how much they have remembered. In this district the issue of retention is addressed by training teachers to use five variables taken directly from the Hunter model.

First, when students learn something very well in the first place they are more likely to remember it. Second, a pleasant atmosphere helps students remember. Third, teachers are trained to be sensitive to what students already know that can transfer positively to what they are supposed to learn. The fourth variable emphasizes students' prior knowledge in the readiness part of this lesson, called *set*. The staff is trained to relate present lessons to knowledge the students already have. Practice, the fifth variable, is applied in short sessions, using small segments of new material as long as segmenting the lesson does not destroy meaning. Practice sessions are scheduled immediately after teaching and throughout several days that follow.

Teaching for Transfer. In the Hunter Model teaching for transfer is a critical principle of learning, in essence helping students form generalizations which are transferrable to new situations. In this district teachers learn how to help students 1) see the similarity between the present lesson and something they already know, 2) practice forming associations between the two lessons, 3) achieve a degree of mastery so new information will be remembered, and 4) identify critical attributes which are similar in each situation.

Clinical Supervision

Several factors are essential in this staff development program that may not be part of most inservice programs. First, the theory underlying each component of the program is explained or described. Second, every component is modeled. Third, the professional staff has a chance to practice in simulated sessions and in the classroom. Feedback is given during practice. Feedback in the form of clinical supervision is also provided during the entire week when teachers are observed in their classrooms applying their new teaching strategies.

The conference which follows each observation has an objective based on the specific teacher effectiveness principles developed in each Monday's staff development session. In these conferences, supervisors help teachers identify what was effective, consider alternative effective practices, identify ineffective behaviors, and evaluate potential for improvement.

The Effectiveness of the Program: Inside and Outside Views

The View from Inside. Interviews with the reading specialists of the school district revealed the effectiveness of the program from the insiders' point of view. The middle school reading supervisor feels the staff development program has helped her know what to look for in classrooms and has helped the teachers know what she is looking for. She feels that knowing the instructional skills that are the heart of the Hunter model in no way stifles teachers, but helps them realize what they want to accomplish.

Since teachers have participated in staff development they now use their judgment when following lessons in basal reader teacher's manuals. They teach to students' needs instead of simply following the manuals.

A continuing problem, however, is teaching reading comprehension, especially higher level thinking skills. While teachers are cognizant of Bloom's taxonomy, and of thinking skills above the literal level, translating their knowledge into instructional practices remains a goal.

The Chapter 1 reading specialist implements his staff development training through the task analysis he does when teaching reading skills to students in his program. The reading specialist's ability to analyze the skills he teaches in relation to their sequential development and to the readiness of the students has strengthened the program's effectiveness, according to him and to the reading supervisor.

At the elementary level, the two reading specialists interviewed see differences in classrooms after the staff development training. First, they sense teachers are more aware of what they're doing, even though the curriculum is the same. Second, they see more structure in the classrooms, in that teachers are better able to monitor the learning that is going on. Teachers use teacher's manuals and workbooks more selectively, a difference which was also reported in the middle school.

The biggest change at the elementary level, according to the reading specialists, is in the teaching of reading comprehension. They reported increased development of readiness for learning; better motivation for each lesson; better assessment of the state of the learner; greater awareness of relating the lesson to the prior knowledge of the learner; more consistency in setting a purpose for reading, and increased use of a statement of learning, that is, the lesson's objective.

The bottom line is that teachers feel more professional. This statement was reported by all the reading specialists interviewed, by supervisors, and by central office personnel.

The View from Outside. The effectiveness of the staff development program was evaluated by a team from the Pennsylvania State University in 1981, after the program had been in effect for two years (Thompson & Flanagan, 1981). Questionnaires concerning approximately thirty-eight practices, attitudes, and beliefs were sent to all personnel who had completed the staff development program. To gather additional data, evaluation team members also observed several of the Monday staff development sessions plus ongoing staff development activities.

Training was found to be the strongest stage in the staff development program. The opportunities for participants to practice new techniques during training, the responsibilities given teachers of becoming inservice leaders, and the development of discussion groups or learning teams to review their training were three main reasons given.

Planning was the second strongest stage selected because of this program's specific defined objectives and the support services provided.

The weakest stage in the program was readiness. Needs seen in this area included a need for increased trust and communication in working relationships. There was also a need for collaboration among teachers, administrators, and parents in the development of goals for school improvement and in an evaluation of current school practices to assess their congruence with school improvement goals. The positive side of readiness was the leadership of administrators and school principals in getting staff development activities underway.

Concern was expressed about motivating professional staff who resist participating in the training program. If participation had been required, these professionals may have been too resentful to benefit from the program. When some don't participate, however, the entire school staff cannot communicate effectively nor have the same professional goals related to teaching and learning.

At this writing, 150 of the 165 professional staff have voluntarily participated. Most of the holdouts have been senior high or middle school content area teachers who see themselves primarily concerned with their discipline and feel no need to adopt a new perspective on the teaching-learning interaction.

The Pennsylvania State University evaluation team concluded that this district's staff development program is a strong one. The program has influenced positively the participating staff, who perceive themselves as effective educators who can and do enhance learning in the students they teach.

Reading, the main concern in the primary and elementary grades, is taught through a Directed Reading Thinking Activity approach, which this district's reading specialists believe is the most useful instructional framework for the application of Madeline Hunter's Model of Teacher Effectiveness.

Data Based Results from Three School Districts Which Have Implemented the Hunter Model

The Pennsylvania School District

These results of the reading comprehension subtest of the Stanford Achievement Test are districtwide for each grade level.

	Grade 2	Grade 4	Grade 6	Grade 8
1977 (before program)	3.4	5.5	7.1	8.9
1979 (after first year of progress)	3.8	5.9	6.9	9.6
1982 (latest figures)	3.9	6.1	7.9	9.7

The Virginia School District

These results were reported as percentages of students in fifth grade reading on or above grade level, based on the SRA Reading Test administered since the program was adopted.

1976 — 44 percent
1977 — 46 percent
1978 — 53 percent
1979 — 54 percent
1980 — 60 percent

The California School District

Test results in reading were reported from 1972 through 1976. Results were stated as the "difference in median months gained between pupils taught" by teachers who had been trained in the staff development program based on the Hunter Model and those pupils whose teachers had not been trained (1976). No test names were reported except to note the tests were standardized tests. The number of teachers and aides in grades varied from 136 teachers and aides participating in 1974 to 49 teachers and aides participating in 1973. Total funds for training also varied each year. No explanation was offered for the gains in median months in grade four each year in contrast to the gains shown for grade three only in 1974 and 1975. The report of the program states that pupils whose teachers participated in the training program made greater test score gains than pupils whose teachers were not trained. Nevertheless, these results can only be reported, not interpreted.

			Grade		
	2	3	4	5	6
1972			+4		+6
1973	+1		+1		+2
1974	+5	+1	+5	+3	
1975	+1	+1	+3	+5	
1976			+2	+2	+2

Conclusions

Eisner (1984) questioned whether research results inform practice or influence practice. What is the relationship between what educational researchers do and what teachers do? Does research in education provide heuristics only and not specific rules to be followed? To make instructional decisions, is a research based theory required? Often we change practices because the new ideas seem intuitively compelling and not because we have "data-based" conclusions (p. 449). How can research inform instructional practice? We need an intimate knowledge of life in the classroom, not tightly controlled laboratory studies which Eisner characterizes as transferring results of rat and pigeon learning into classrooms. We need to look at research on teaching to discover if a generic set of skills is generalizable to all teachers.

Baker (1984) acknowledges that research is sometimes based on theory and sometimes on practice. She believes the acceptance of new ideas often depends less on the idea than on the credibility of the one who proposes it and on the medium of transmission. In the three school districts which have implemented the Hunter Model, strong leadership and ongoing staff development will assure that new practices will not deteriorate from neglect. There is a need, Baker states, to find what is useful to practitioners, to investigate practice in schools, and to use many-faceted inquiries, for we need different viewpoints to see the truth—or the truths.

Zumwalt (1982) describes two major trends in research on teaching and proposes a third view. The first trend, process-product, usually describes classroom processes and related teacher behaviors in terms of educational outcomes. The research is usually correlational. Its appeal is strongest in the present atmosphere calling for teacher and school accountability. Results are used for prescription.

The second major trend in research on teaching is labeled descriptive. This research is concerned with the context of the classroom in which instructional practices are described qualitatively, with few attempts to generalize or to imply any immediate payoff in student improvement.

The third view proposed by Zumwalt is that of a deliberative orientation (p. 226). In this view, the decisions a teacher makes can be enhanced by research data but data are only one influence. Experience and insights, together with descriptive data, can help a teacher reflect on management skills and on bases for decision making. Zumwalt believes we can't substitute research results for the teacher's own need to solve instructional problems individually. Classrooms are not context free. The goodness of research findings seems to be determined by the values and beliefs of the user and the contextual demands of the teaching. This does not imply that teachers do not need skills to teach. However, they also need judgment. Teachers need general descriptions, not specific prescriptions. Research on teacher effectiveness has to help teachers use new information about teaching and learning. Instead of giving teachers simple answers, educational research has to help them discover the questions to ask.

The two major questions basic to Hunter's model can be restated as "What does an effective reading teacher have to do?" and "How do you know when the teacher is being effective?"

Among the criteria specified by the International Reading Association Guidelines for the Successful Preparation of Reading Teachers (1978), the effective reading teacher has to diagnose the learner's strengths and needs; the learner's prior knowledge as it relates to the requirements of the present lesson; the learner's motivation and interests; and the concepts, language, and word recognition abilities needed to comprehend the present lesson. The teacher also must be knowledgeable in ways to develop and present the lesson in the light of what is known about the learner. Practice and feedback must be provided to assess learning. The learner must be provided with strategies to monitor learning, to aid retention and recall. Generalizations should be arrived at, for these are the tools needed for application and transfer.

How do you know when a teacher is being effective? Perhaps the real questions are: Do the students understand what they are reading? Are they readers?

The author acknowledges the contributions of the administrators and staff of the Upper Perkiomen School District, Pennsylvania.

References

Baker, E.L. Can educational research inform educational practice? Yes! *Phi Delta Kappan,* 1984, *65,* 453-455.

Bobrow, D.G., and Norman, D.A. Some principles of memory schemata. In D.G. Bobrow and A.M. Collins (Eds.), *Representation and understanding: Studies in cognitive science.* New York: Academic Press, 1975.

Brophy, J.E., and Everston, C.M. *Process-Product correlations in the Texas teacher effectiveness study.* Final report. Austin, Texas: University of Texas, 1974.

Carver, C. *Motivation versus cognitive methods in remedial reading.* Paper presented at the meeting of the International Reading Association, Atlantic City, 1971.

Collins, A.M., and others. The analysis of reading tasks and texts. Technical report no. 43. Washington, DC: National Institute of Education, 1978.

Duchastel, P.C., and Merrill, P.F. The effects of behavioral objectives on learning: A review of empirical studies. *Review of educational research,* 1973, *43,* 53-67.

Durkin, D. What classroom observations reveal about reading comprehension instruction. *Reading Research Quarterly,* 1979, *14,* 481-533.

Eberwein, L. Effect of behavioral objective information upon remedial reader performance. Paper presented at the annual meeting of the Southeastern Regional International Reading Association, Louisville, Kentucky, 1974. (ED 132 533)

Eisner, E.W. Can educational research inform educational practice? *Phi Delta Kappan,* 1984, *65,* 447-452.

Guidelines for the professional preparation of reading teachers. Developed by the Professional Standards and Ethics Committee of the International Reading Association, 1978.

Heath, R.W., and Nielson, M.A. The research basis for performance-based teacher education. *Review of Educational Research,* 1974, *44,* 463-484.

Hunter, M. Appraising the instruction process, a clinical theory of instruction, 1973. *Resources in Education.* Washington, DC: ERIC Clearinghouse on Teacher Education, 1977.

Hunter, M. Diagnostic teaching. *Elementary School Journal,* 1979, *80,* 41-46.

Hunter, M. *Motivation theory for teachers.* El Segundo, CA: TIP Publications, 1967.

Hunter, M. *Reinforcement theory for teachers.* El Segundo, CA: TIP Publications, 1967.

Hunter, M. Six types of supervisory conferences. *Educational Leadership,* Journal of the Association for Supervision and Curriculum Development. Washington, DC: NEA, 1980.

Hunter, M. *Teach for transfer.* El Segundo, CA: TIP Publications, 1971.

Hunter, M. Teaching is decision making. *Journal of Educational Leadership,* October 1979, 62-67.

Hunter, M. *Teach more—faster!* El Segundo, CA: TIP Publications, 1969.

Hunter, M. The teaching process and the learning process. In Eli Seifman and Dwight Allen (Eds.), *Handbook for teachers.* Glenview, IL: Scott, Foresman, 1971.

Koenke, K. Motivation and reading. *Language Arts,* 1978, *55,* 998-1002.

Kyriacou, C., and Newson, G. Teacher effectiveness: A consideration of research problems. *Educational Review,* 1982, *34,* 3-12.

McNeil, J.D. Research directions and the design of reading instruction. *Journal of Reading Behavior,* 1977, *9,* 405-409.

McNeil, J.D., and Donant, L. Transfer effect of word recognition strategies. *Journal of Reading Behavior,* 1980, *12,* 97-103.

Medley, D.M., and Mitzel, H.E. Some behavioral correlates of teacher effectiveness. *Journal of Educational Psychology,* 1959, *50,* 239-246.

Medley, D.M., Soar, R.S., and Soar, R. *Assessment and research in teacher education: Focus on PBTE.* Washington, DC: American Association of Colleges for Teacher Education, 1975.

Newport News Public School, Newport News, Virginia. *Five year goals and outcomes.* Graphed information presented in a division handout.

Onhmacht, F.W., and Fleming, J.T. On the differential transfer of abilities to reading. Presented at the Reading Association of Ireland, University College, Dublin, Ireland, 1977. (ED 160 987)

Pearson, P.D., and Johnson, D.D. *Teaching reading comprehension.* New York: Holt, Rinehart and Winston, 1978.

Powers, J. Goal-setting behavior, achievement in reading, and attitude toward reading associated with individual goal setting conferences. University of Wisconsin at Madison, Research and Development Center for Cognitive Learning, Report No. TR-142-2. Washington, DC: Office of Education, 1970. (ED 047 921)

Richardson, E., and DiBenedetto, B. Transfer effects of a phonic decoding model: A review. *Reading Improvement,* 1977, *14,* 239-247.

Roudabush, G.E. An empirical structure for reading objectives. *Journal of Reading Behavior,* 1974, *6,* 403-419.

Rumelhart, D.E., and Ortony, A. The representation of knowledge in memory. In R.C. Anderson and R.J. Spiro (Eds.), *Schooling and the acquisition of knowledge.* Hillsdale, NJ: Erlbaum, 1977.

Soar, R.S. *Follow-through classroom process measurement and pupil growth, 1970-1971.* Gainesville, FL: Institute for Development of Human Resources, University of Florida, 1973.

Weisberg

Soar, R.S., and Soar, R. An empirical analysis of selected follow-through programs: An example of a process approach to evaluation. In I.J. Gordon (Ed.), *Early childhood education.* Chicago: National Society for the Study of Education, 1972.

Spiro, R.J. Remembering information from text: The "state of the schemas" approach. In R.C. Anderson, R.J. Spiro, and W.E. Montague (Eds.), Hillsdale, NJ: Erlbaum, 1977, 137-165.

Thompson, S.R., and Flanagan, K. *A report of the study of the utility based staff development program of the Upper Perkiomen School District.* Pennsylvania State University, 1981.

Walbesser, H.H., and Eisenbert, T.A. *A review of research on behavioral objectives and learning hierarchies.* Columbus, OH: Center for Science and Mathematics Education, Ohio State University, 1972. (ED 059 900)

Zumwalt, K. Research on teaching: Policy implications in teacher education. *Eighty-First Yearbook of the National Society for the Study of Education.* Chicago: University of Chicago Press, 1982.

Part Five
Policy into Practice: The Special Case of the Special Reading Teacher

T he field of reading education has a history of involvement in meeting the needs of the students experiencing difficulty in learning to read. Indeed, the professional community of reading educators experienced its greatest growth spurt during the 1960s as the Federal Government focused attention and directed resources to help solve the problems of disadvantaged children failing in school reading programs. Federal involvement was so massive and arose so rapidly that out of necessity major policy decisions were made at the national, state, and local levels that shaped the face of compensatory reading instruction around the country. Most of these policy decisions were made in the absence of research or even tradition to guide them. What do we know about effective reading instruction in compensatory settings? Are policy, practice, and research consistent in the way they deal with effective compensatory instruction? In this section of the book Allington reports the results of his efforts to answer these basic questions.

12

Richard L. Allington

Policy Constraints and Effective Compensatory Reading Instruction: A Review

T he largest compensatory educational effort in the United States is the federally funded Title I of the Elementary and Secondary Educational Act of 1965 (ESEA) now revised as Chapter I of the Educational Consolidation and Improvement Act of 1981 (ECIA). (For purposes of simplicity, I will refer to both programs as Title I.) In the 1982 fiscal year, the federal government allocated almost $3 billion of Title I funds to about 13,000 school districts (Stonehill & Groves, 1983). This funding was allocated "to provide financial assistance to local education agencies serving areas with high concentrations of children from low income families to expand and improve their educational programs" (Kirst & Jung, 1980, p. 4). Nearly 90 percent of all school districts receive some funding and in these districts nearly 20 percent of the elementary school students receive some services. Of those students served by the Title I program, 85 percent receive instruction in reading or language arts for between two and one-half (Allington, 1980) and three and one-half hours per week (National Institute of Education, 1977b), the vast majority in pullout compensatory instruction classes.

After nearly two decades of Title I services, critics of the program now abound. Cooley (1981) argues "On balance, Title I is not producing the level of achievement impact that people had hoped it would have" (p. 300). Levin (1977) suggests that "the ostensible inability of Title I programs to create even a nominal impact on student scores in basic skills seems to be endemic to the program" (p. 156). Kaestle and Smith (1982) note that Title I achievement "gains are modest in comparison with the original promise of Title I" (p. 398). Doss and Holley (1982) present convincing evidence that the dismantling of the traditional Title I program structures, including special class reading teachers, will produce a more positive effect on achievement than modifying it.

The development, implementation, and evaluation of Title I programs have produced controversy and a large literature on policy issues that have affected education agencies at federal, state, and local levels. The controversies on various facets of program policies are wide ranging and well summarized elsewhere (e.g. McLaughlin, 1975; Vanecko, Ames, & Archambault, 1980). However, because of the unprecedented size of the program, the impact of Title I policies on the delivery of compensatory reading instruction has been enormous. The current structure of compensatory reading programs has seldom been guided by research on effective instructional practice and more often influenced by policies designed to ensure compliance with program regulations. In this review, I attempt to describe current practices in compensatory reading programs, offer evidence on how such practices evolved, identify program features that may be problematic, and suggest ways to redesign compensatory reading instruction to enhance its effectiveness. Special problems such as overlaps of Title I with PL94-142 and interference of Title I with the local core curriculum also will be discussed.

The Delivery of Instruction in Compensatory Programs

Program Structure

The most popular program structure for the delivery of clinical/remedial instruction is the pullout class. According to Glass and

Smith (1977) 84 percent of remedial reading instruction is offered on such a basis in which children leave the regular classrooms to go to a second location, usually within the same school building. They note no observable differences between the majority who are pulled out and the minority who receive remedial instruction in their regular classrooms, suggesting that students are not pulled out because of differentially prescribed instructional needs.

If students are not pulled out based on some differential instructional needs criteria, why do most remedial students go to another location for remedial instruction? The most commonly cited reason is that such a program structure results from overly "conservative and restrictive interpretations" of federal program regulations (Vanecko, Ames, & Archambault, 1980). The legal framework encompassing Title I requires that "Federal funds made available under this title...be used to supplement and increase...the levels of funds...and in no case, as to supplant such funds from nonfederal sources..." (NIE, 1977a); the pullout structure produces a more easily followed "audit trail" (Shulman, 1983). Simply put, a pullout program enables local and state education personnel to verify compliance with the "supplement not supplant" regulation with ease. The pullout program structure clearly was not motivated by pedagogical concerns, adequate empirical evidence, or learning theory, but rather by the perceptions, or misperceptions, of federal program requirements by local and state education personnel (Vanecko, Ames, and Archambault, 1980). This situation was not improved by "confusion [at the U.S. Office of Education] about the appropriate interpretation of the supplementation provisions..." (NIE, 1977a, p. 39). While several alternatives to pullout structures obviously comply with the regulations, movement away from that traditional program design is not evident.

Curriculum

The pullout program is perhaps the most frequently criticized aspect of Title I services. Kaestle and Smith (1982) note that primarily as a result of this factor, Title I segregation from the classroom is very nearly complete. A result of this separation is the fragmentation of the school experience for Title I students. These students are often required to "deal simultaneously with reading and mathematics instruction from two different textbooks, taught in two different styles..." (p. 400). Johnston, Allington, and Afflerbach (1985) found this fragmentation was quite pervasive in Title I programs with little congruence between classroom instruction and remedial instruction. That is, few remedial students received instruction that supplemented their core classroom reading curriculum, but were taught by classroom and remedial teachers who generally expressed different beliefs about student needs and offered different objectives as targets for instruction. Too often the reading materials represented distinctly different models of the reading process. The result is that remedial students, who often experience "cognitive confusion" (Vernon, 1957), are offered instruction that seems likely to confuse the learner further. Reading strategies that work well in code oriented reading programs often will not work well in meaning oriented reading programs with their lack of strict vocabulary control. The remedial student who receives instruction in a code oriented program in the classroom and a meaning oriented program in the remedial setting is presented two different sets of strategies and skills, neither of which works particularly well with the other program.

The segregation from the classroom is further evident in the fact that half of the reading teachers interviewed were unable to identify even the basal series used in any given remedial student's classroom and more than two-thirds could not identify the specific reader or level of textbook the student was placed in. Further, only one in five classroom teachers could identify the reading material a remedial student from his or her classroom was using in the remedial setting (Johnston, Allington & Afflerbach, 1985). These data, collected in several districts in two states, and those reported by Kimbrough and Hill (1981), suggest that the fragmentation of the educational experience and the segregation of remedial instruction from the classroom program is pervasive.

Although this segregation and fragmentation is, in large part, a result of pullout remedial programs, one can imagine a pullout program that does offer a congruent instructional setting. Therefore, separate curricula in compensatory programs must be related to other factors as well. In particular, two different, but related, factors seem likely candidates. The first, the "modality preference hypothesis," is best represented by the general belief that remedial readers need to be taught differently. This belief stems from the assumption that poor readers receive the same instruction as good readers but fail to attain normal achievement levels, so a different teaching method, or style, is called for. This point of view is well represented in reading and learning disability textbooks, but receives virtually no theoretical or empirical support in the research literature (Allington, 1983; Heibert, 1983; Johnston, et al., 1985; Rohwer, 1980). Despite this, many educators agree that different instruction is appropriate in remedial settings. Even if the lack of theoretical or empirical evidence is discounted, educators should question the rationality of this hypothesis given a half-century of "disappointingly small" (Cooley, 1981) achievement gains produced by programs representing this point of view.

A second factor which may have led to this widespread practice is a basic misunderstanding of the nature of the federal requirement that remedial instruction supplement not supplant the regular reading instruction. Some educators have interpreted this aspect of the regulations to mean that supplementary materials must be used, that it would be a violation of the regulations to use the regular classroom materials for remedial instruction.

I provided forty school administrators who had some responsibility for Title I programs with four brief remedial program scenarios (see the Table) and asked them to identify whether the program would comply with the Supplement not Supplant rule. (Each of the four would, in fact, comply with that regulation, assuming compliance also with "comparability" and "excess cost" provisions.)

Scenarios 2 and 4, in which the reading teacher offers additional instruction using the classroom core curriculum materials, garnered the most incorrect responses with over one-third of the administrators indicating that the Supplement not Supplant rule was being violated. The federal regulations, however, do not refer to the curricular content, but to the fact that the district must be able to demonstrate that the Title I funds provided additional instruction

Scenario	Percent responding "not compliant"
1. A special reading teacher offers remedial instruction *in the regular classroom* after the student's classroom reading period. This additional instruction is in *reading material different* from that used in the regular classroom reading instruction.	25%
2. A special reading teacher offers remedial instruction *in the reading resource room,* away from the regular classroom after the student's classroom reading period. This additional instruction is in the *same reading materials* used in the regular classroom reading instruction.	35%
3. A special reading teacher offers remedial instruction *in the reading resource room,* away from the regular classroom after the student's classroom reading period. This additional instruction is in *reading material different* from that used in the regular classroom reading instruction.	10%
4. A special reading teacher offers remedial instruction *in the regular classroom* after the student's classroom reading period. This additional instruction is in the *same reading materials* used in the regular classroom reading instruction.	37%

over and above that received by the nonrecipient children (Elmore & McLaughlin, 1982). The source of this misinterpretation may lie higher up in the administrative network since the federal program administrators have been inconsistent in their standards for asserting that programs were noncompliant (NIE, 1977a).

Instructional Time

Unfortunately for the remedial reader, the data on this aspect of remedial instruction consistently and clearly indicate additional instructional time usually is not available (Allington, 1980). The most damaging evidence is provided by Lignon and Doss (1982) based on observations of about 1,000 students for whole school days: "Title I instructional services, and probably those of other compensatory programs, are not supplementary (i.e., in addition to) to regular instruction. Instead, instructional time provided by the regular program is supplanted by the instructional time provided by the Title I program. In other words, the quantity of instruction received by a Title I student is not greater than the quantity received by a non-Title I student....Students served by more than one compensatory program during a school year actually receive less instructional time than those served by only one or none" (p. 3).

In the same vein, Vanecko et al. (1980) found that in nine of the thirteen districts they studied students in Title I schools actually received less reading and language arts instruction than students in non-Title I schools (an average of about seven minutes a day less). In eleven of the thirteen districts, Title 1 students received less classroom reading and language arts instruction than non-Title I students. When the amount of Title I instruction was added to the classroom instructional time, the Title I students received about 10 percent more instruction than non-Title I students. Kimbrough and Hill (1981) found that federally funded compensatory education programs tended to replace core classroom instruction, especially in reading. Whenever the remedial program is offered during the regular school day some instruction must be missed, it seems, although about one-third of the schools report that their Title I students miss no instruction during pullout compensatory instruction! The rest report that between 15 and 20 percent of the students miss the classroom instruction in each of the following areas: reading, language arts, social studies, science, or study time (NIE, 1977b). The sad fact is that too often the Title I student does not receive any significant increase in the amount of reading instruction.

Instructional Focus

What does remedial instruction look like? What kind of instruction is offered and how efficiently is it delivered? Only sparse data are reported in the research literature, primarily because few investigators of Title I programs have actually observed remedial instruction, but have relied instead on teacher interviews, questionnaires, and project reports. Quirk et al. (1975) do report on an observational study of 135 compensatory teachers in twenty-one districts. They found that these teachers spent the largest proportion of class time, about one-third, on student management; nearly one-quarter on word recognition activities, with little time devoted to comprehension activities (12 percent) or silent reading (2 percent). Sargent (1981) observed resource room teachers and found that only about one-half of the teacher's time was spent in instructional activities.

Leinhardt (1980) compared transition room reading instruction with regular primary grade reading instruction. The transition rooms were designed for high risk students in Grade One. In this study, some schools had transition rooms while other similar schools in the district did not. The transition rooms had an adult-student ratio three times higher than the regular primary classrooms. While a transition room is different from a reading resource room, the basic objectives were by and large the same, as was the adult-student ratio. In this situation, where the objective was more intensive instruction, the students in the transition rooms actually received two and one-half hours *less* reading instruction per week than did students in regular classes. In addition, they received 50 percent less "test-relevant" instruction and moved at about one-half the pace of their peers in the regular classrooms. Classroom teachers taught and reviewed sight words twice as frequently and had students read materials four times as often as did transition room teachers. In the end, students eligible for the transition room but placed in the regular classroom program instead, had higher reading achievement, even though they had not received any of the "advantages" of the transition room placement. Meyers (1969) reported similar findings. We must question, then, whether compensatory educational programs in general actually provide effective and efficient learning environments.

From audiotaped recordings, I mapped how three different reading teachers spent the time in remedial class sessions. Nearly one-third of the scheduled time was spent in "set up" activities before the beginning of any instructional activity. That is, from the time one previous group was released until the next group began receiving instruction, nearly ten minutes of the thirty minute period passed. During this time the remedial teacher waited for students to arrive, most of whom ultimately did, although in one case the teacher finally traveled to the classroom to get the students who were scheduled. As the children arrived, various noninstructional, usually social, interactions occurred; informal discussions of how the day was going; how a member of the family was; or comments on clothing. The important point is not the exact nature of these activities, but that they had little to do with remedying the reading deficiency that was the reason the students and teachers were there.

Some of the inefficiency observed can be traced directly to the pullout nature of the instructional settings. Arlin (1979) discusses classroom transitions between reading groups or content lessons and notes wide variability in how well different classroom teachers accomplish shifting from one group, or content, to another. He discusses "time drift"—when students are not engaged in academic work but are attending to social concerns, personal movements, and others' movements. Significant amounts of instructional time can be lost on inefficient transitions. Something similar seems to be at work in pullout programs, particularly with the travel time from one location to another. The lack of an explicit signal for the learner that it is time to shift locations leads to a rather inefficient drifting in of remedial clients. Recently (Allington, 1984) I calculated that as much as fifteen minutes per day are lost for instruction in the time that a student 1) stops working and packs up for a resource room, travels there, arrives, greets teacher, gets materials out, gets seated, and, finally, begins to work; plus the time to 2) stop working in resource room, put materials away, say good-bye, travel back to room, get classroom materials out, and finally, begin working again. All this assumes minimal teacher management or coercion. This daily fifteen minute transition time to the pullout program and back results in nearly forty hours per academic year lost for instruction. This forty hours could be used to provide sixteen weeks of thirty minutes a day of instruction—if that transition time were available.

Summary

The most common type of remedial reading program is designed around pullout instruction which is delivered by a special reading teacher. This remedial instruction is typically independent and different from the classroom core reading instruction. In fact, more often than not, neither the classroom teacher nor the reading teacher will know what instruction the other offers. Though generally considered "extra" assistance, the remedial instruction often supplants a significant portion of the classroom reading or language arts instruction, so that the remedial student rarely receives a greater amount of actual reading and language arts instructional time. Contributing to this problem is the loss of time from instruction due to transition activities in each setting. These factors all seem to contribute to the feeling that "after almost a decade of intervention, the Title I program stands primarily as a symbol of national concern for the poor rather than as a viable response to their needs" (Kaestle & Smith, 1982, p. 400).

How Compensatory Instruction Might Be Delivered

Commitment and Leadership

Compensatory instruction for readers who are experiencing difficulty in acquiring reading ability is a good idea. But as Goldenberg (1969) points out, the way good ideas are put into operation do not always ensure that the original objectives will be met. In the case of Title I, it seems that program developers have worried about all the wrong things and have spent very little time in designing programs that focus on what we know about increasing instructional effectiveness. In some instances, this has led to programs that cannot achieve their original objectives—to increase the reading achievement of poor readers.

Leinhardt and Pallay (1982) review a number of studies of special and remedial education and conclude that "the variables which are important for successful student outcomes can occur in most settings...it is the issue of effective practices, not setting, that deserves the attention of educators" (p. 557). I concur, and note that even though millions of dollars have been spent evaluating Title I, the search has been for "overall achievement effects" (Cooley, 1981) rather than for characteristics of effective remedial instruction (Cooley and Leinhardt, 1980). As Light and Smith (1971) noted, we know some programs are successful, some are terribly ineffective, but most make an impact, even if it is "disappointingly small."

The paucity of empirical evidence on characteristics of effective remedial instruction (Wang, 1980) makes offering suggestions on designing more effective programs a somewhat tentative exercise. Though we have relatively few good reports to guide us, the consistency of the characteristics reported provides a reasonable base for prescriptions.

A particularly appealing starting point for reshaping remedial reading programs is to examine the level of commitment the district or school has made to the program. Edmonds (1979) argued that he required "that an effective school bring children of the poor to those minimal masteries of basic skills that now describe minimally successful pupil performance for the children of the middle class" (p. 3). The expenditure of federal funds for Title I is a poor indicator of commitment.

Several examinations of schools which were producing above average reading achievement with disadvantaged students, students whose characteristics would normally suggest a below average achievement level, have without exception argued that strong instructional leadership from the principal or the reading specialist is a critical factor (Edmonds, 1979; Mackenzie, 1983; New York State Office of Performance Review, 1974; Weber, 1971; Wilder, 1978). This leadership was evident in several ways. Both the leader and the instructional staff held high expectations for the effects of their instruction. That is, the staff in these schools felt significantly more of their students would be on grade level, would graduate from high school or would attend college than staff at comparable but low achieving schools.

Another area in which leadership was exhibited was staff development. Inservice training was offered which focused specifically on developing effective learning environments, including training in classroom management and organization. Effective school leaders had achieved consensus among their staff on what the primary objectives were and these goals were clear, attainable, and measurable.

Finally, these schools monitored their performance and used the evaluation data to improve the instructional program. This final characteristic may be of particular interest in relation to compensatory programs since David (1981) found that most local school personnel perceived the required Title I evaluation as "one of the many hoops to go through to receive funds" (p. 28). Her interview study suggests only a few reading teachers or Title I directors view program evaluations as a basis for judging the merits of their program or as a guide for improving that program. She found that when negative aspects of evaluations were cited, local personnel generally either discounted the value of the evaluation or attempted to explain it away. As one of her respondents said, "We're not going to lose any sleep over whether the results show effectiveness" (p. 28). In this case and, unfortunately, too many others, the level of commitment seemingly ends with the expenditure of the federal funds available. As long as some services were provided, the commitment had been met. Whether the services bring about the original goal, improved reading achievement, seemed unimportant.

Improving Local Evaluations

Even in those districts where Title I evaluations are used as evidence of remedial program success the criteria employed are often neatly biased in favor of the program. For instance, the most common method for demonstrating effectiveness is to show Fall to Spring growth on an achievement test. A fairer assessment would result in two changes: 1) measure Fall to Fall achievement patterns; and 2) subtract average learning rate, from student past history, from the Fall to Fall gain. These two adaptations would give a less biased picture of actual improvement. Some would argue that measuring Fall to Fall is unfair since "summer reading loss" would be included. The other side of the coin is that the Fall to Spring assessments do not hold the program accountable for a lack of long term effects. Subtracting average learning rate prior to program intervention is a crude way to get at what additional achievement effects result from the additional instruction. The lack of adequate causal models of achievement hinders full specification of achievement gains attributable to program interventions, but current work in this area is promising (Cooley, 1981). Until these models are developed, however, we can at least subtract the seven month average gain per year that a particular student has achieved before program intervention from the nine month gain after beginning the program. This two month achievement effect, which may be a generous average for a Title I program student, will be a more accurate assessment of program effects than is the common pattern of attributing all nine months growth to the intervention of the program. Thompson and Smith (1982) report no sustained effect for Title I in an analysis of over 2,300 Title I student achievement scores over a two year period. The gain evident in Fall to Spring testing was not evident in Fall to Fall testing. Thus, even the two month gain noted above might be erased if both criteria were employed. In a review of a number of public school systems' Title I evaluations available through the ERIC system, I found no report that used either suggestion. Because of the bias inherent in the common evaluation procedure, I have included few of these reports in this review.

As an alternative method of assessing program effects, Rosenbaum (1980) suggests that since the goal of most remedial, compensatory, and special education programs is "normalization" of achievement or behavior, one could assess a program by determining "its success at returning slower students to regular ability groups" (p. 368). I found no studies or evaluation reports that used this criterion for measuring program effectiveness. However, the high rate of continuing eligibility of Title I students across several years does suggest that few programs would be considered successful were this criterion accepted.

Perhaps the broad goal of "improving reading performance," which seems generally accepted, should be revised to an annual goal of "return at least one-half the students to their regular classroom with no further need for remediation." This goal seems to be implicit in Clay's more successful approach to remedial instruction (1979). In addition, subgoals could specify certain proportions of students, or particular students, to be returned to their classrooms within shorter periods of time than one academic year. This adaptation would require more frequent monitoring of student progress toward a different goal. My prescriptions are very general starting points, but goals are the targets and perhaps our efforts have been aimed at the wrong target for too long.

Program Integration with Core Curriculum

The relationship of the compensatory program to the core curriculum is as important as the level of commitment and leadership to program effectiveness. Various authors have noted the segregation of Title I programs and staff from the core educational services (Cohen, 1982; Johnston, et al., 1985; Kaestle & Smith, 1982; Leinhardt & Pallay, 1982; Lignon & Doss, 1982).

This segregation has several potential negative effects. First, classroom teachers often consider themselves relieved of the responsibility for low achievement in Title I students—that now becomes someone else's problem. This perception may result in the reduced classroom reading instruction reported for many Title I students. As the classroom teacher's feeling of responsibility decreases so does the instructional effort in the classroom.

A second potential effect of the segregation is that little change occurs in core curriculum instruction since weaknesses are supposedly remedied by the remedial instruction. Thus, the "curriculum disability" (Commission on Special Education, 1985; Elkind, 1983; National Coalition of Advocates for Students, 1985) continues with few modifications. Further, segregation reduces communication to only a minimal flow of information between reading specialists and classroom teachers. In point of fact, Cohen (1982) reports that school districts receiving Title I funds had greater numbers of specialized staff members (e.g., reading teachers) but less program coordination than districts which did not receive such funds.

A third effect of the segregation is "interference" with the local core instruction. Interference (Kimbrough & Hill, 1981) is the "conflict between categorical programs and the core local curriculum" (p. 2). Interference is present when the compensatory program causes unintended problems for classroom teachers in providing coherent and coordinated instruction. These problems range from scheduling difficulties to staff conflicts to clashes in instructional methods and philosophies. Glass and Smith (1977) report that the number of pullouts a day negatively correlates with class achievement. Cooley and Leinhardt (1980), however, report that the number of pullouts had no impact on achievement of either those pulled out or those who were not. Suffice it to say that scheduling classroom instruction around pullout schedules is a concern of the classroom teacher. In addition, the lack of communication between the remedial and classroom teacher (Cohen, Intilli, & Robbins, 1978;

Johnston, et al, 1985) seems to lead to interference, at least in terms of student learning. Remedial students who are placed in a meaning oriented basal series (e.g., Scott, Foresman *Reading Systems*) in the classroom and a code oriented program (e.g., SRA, *Distar Reading*) in the remedial setting are going to be confused. The strategies they acquire in each setting will not be particularly useful in the other. In fact, such a contrast could easily result in partial learning or mislearning of important components of either system.

Segregation of the remedial program and staff from the core curriculum does not have to happen, regardless of program structure. While pullout programs may foster segregation and concomitant ill effects, some pullout programs are well coordinated and integrated into the regular school environment. One aspect of the leadership characteristic of effective schools is the development of an integrated whole school instructional effort. While little empirical support can be found for congruent instructional emphasis in classroom or remedial programs, a strong theoretical argument can be made (Johnston, et al., 1985). One is hardpressed to find a learning theory that suggests that uncoordinated and incongruent instruction is more appropriate than coordinated and congruent teaching.

Classroom teachers want better coordination of efforts. In the interviews reported by Johnston, et al. (1985) teachers reported wanting more joint meeting times with the reading teachers. In two surveys of teachers' preference for pullout or in class compensatory instruction, significant numbers of classroom teachers indicated a preference for in class remedial programs (Davis, 1982; Hayes, 1983). Rauhala (1982) describes such a program in which the reading teacher spends from two to eight hours per week in a classroom providing instructional assistance in cooperation with the classroom teacher. On the other hand, Doss and Holley (1982) reported that a similar program was not easily accomplished due primarily to the resistance of classroom teachers who were uncomfortable having another teacher in the room. Perhaps the lesson is that cooperation is not easily implemented, even if mandated. Teachers must adapt to new professional roles, and such adaptation takes time and training.

The leadership of the building principal or reading director is quite powerful on this segregation issue. The Johnston et al. interviews (1985) indicated that three of four remedial programs reflected the bias of the program supervisor. When supervisors thought segregation and different curricula were appropriate, that state of affairs generally existed. When the program director thought that coordination and congruence of instruction were appropriate, that was generally what was found.

Effective instructional leadership is a rather vague description. However, clear, common, and measurable goals; frequent monitoring of progress toward these goals; and a belief in the importance of a coordinated and congruent instructional emphasis are each facets of this trait.

Opportunity to Learn

Beyond effective instructional leadership, another common feature of effective compensatory education programs is a task oriented environment that produces high levels of student engagement in academic work (Cooley & Leinhardt, 1980; Guthrie, Seifert, & Kline, 1978; Kiesling, 1978; Leinhardt & Pallay, 1982; Lignon & Doss, 1982; Mackenzie, 1983; Stallings, 1980). Unfortunately, as Ysseldyke and Algozzine (1982) note, special and remedial education, especially pullout instruction, has received little systematic observational study. However, Leinhardt, Zigmond, and Cooley (1981) report an observational study of the reading instruction offered learning disabled students. They noted wide discrepancies in the amount of time these students spent in reading instruction, but found a strong relationship between amount of time students were engaged in teacher directed silent reading activities and reading growth. Little relationship existed between oral reading or workbook activity time and achievement gain. Stallings (1980) also reports strong correlations between the amount of time spent in teacher directed reading activities and student achievement in secondary school remedial reading classes. Time spent in making assignments and social interactions was negatively correlated with achievement. Cooley and Leinhardt (1980) studied 400 classrooms in an attempt to identify instructional practices that were particularly effective in producing reading achievement in disadvantaged urban children. They identified the "opportunity to learn" as the single most important variable. Expressed another way, children who were taught more learned more. The amount of time allocated for reading instruction was not as important as how effectively that time was used. How skills were taught was not as important as whether they were taught. The most powerful factor was the amount of time students spent actively working on reading tasks, particularly working with teachers in direct instructional settings. Similarly, Lignon and Doss (1982) note that when instructional time increases in classrooms, so does student achievement. Finally, Kiesling (1978) found increased instructional time produced greater gains for lower achievement students than for pupils reading at or above grade level.

The question, of course, is how much time should be allocated for reading instruction for remedial readers? How much time in classroom reading instruction? How much additional remedial instructional time? In a meta-analysis of fifteen studies of programs for poor readers, Guthrie, Seifert, and Kline (1978) provided what clues we have on this latter question. They found that at least fifty hours of additional instruction was needed even when the tutor is a trained specialist and the adult to student ratio is small, no greater than 1:4. Two studies that reported significant remedial program gains had adult-student ratios of 1:1 and 1:3 and provided four to five hours a week of remedial tutoring. Similar in many respects is Clay's report (1979) of a successful early school remedial program. Her program was designed to identify children in grade one who were significantly behind their peers in reading development. These children were provided two individual tutorial sessions of forty minutes in length, twice weekly. About two-thirds of the participants no longer required tutoring after three or four months: Their reading had improved to the point where they could rejoin their classroom instructional program and maintain that pace. Clay suggests that daily individual sessions may be required for some children and would probably be beneficial to all who experience difficulty in acquiring reading skill.

We have only these bits of evidence on how much additional remedial instructional time is needed. However, the question cannot be easily answered in isolation in any event. Other factors, including group size, what is taught, and how effectively it is taught, are important determinants of the outcome one can expect from the allocation of x amount of additional remedial time. In fact, Cooley and Leinhardt (1980) found little relationship in the amount of time allocated for such instruction and ultimate achievement effects.

Of further concern is the classroom reading instruction. The evidence (e.g., Lignon & Doss, 1982) that remedial instruction, when offered, typically results in a decrease in the classroom instructional time suggests that added remedial instruction is not always "added" instruction (Vanecko, Ames, & Archambault, 1980). We have much evidence that the amount of time allocated in the classroom for reading instruction varies widely, even in the same school at the same grade level (for instance, Berliner, 1981, reports a range of 47 to 118 minutes a day). In addition, Hiatt (1979) reports that only 20 percent of the school day was used in "acts of imparting skills and knowledge" in the primary grade classrooms she observed. In reading, the average amount of instruction equalled only 16.3 minutes per day in an instructional setting. The remaining time was spent evaluating, giving procedural directions, inducing cooperation, and managing.

The variability in the amount of classroom reading instruction and in the quality of that instruction makes clear that we can expect no simple answer to the question of how much instructional time is necessary, or optimal, for achieving success. Students who are achieving poorly do, however, benefit from the allocation of additional instructional time (Kiesling, 1978; Guthrie, Martuza, & Seifert, 1979).

Summary

Problems of ineffective leadership, inadequate commitment, program segregations, and supplanted instruction all have worked to undermine compensatory programs. However, it seems more important to attend to how compensatory programs affect the students' opportunity to learn. The available evidence suggests that current compensatory programs are lacking in this area, although this state of affairs may stem from the misguided focus of much of the program evaluation activity. Opportunity to learn has been narrowly defined as allocated time in evaluation studies. While time does need to be allocated for instruction, we must question what goes on during the reading instructional sessions. We need to look at whether students are actively engaged in learning activities, at the relationship of the teaching and learning activities in the classroom and clinic to each other and to the program goals, and at the quality of instruction offered in both settings (Borg, 1980; Brophy & Evertson, 1981; Duffy, 1980). Unfortunately, I could find no studies that investigated compensatory reading instruction in these ways. We have some strong clues from research which looks at effective classroom instruction practices, but we have no adequate empirical base for developing firm prescriptions for a supplementary remedial component.

Nonetheless, let me offer an informed opinion about those factors which most directly affect the success of the compensatory and remedial instruction.

Some Characteristics of Effective Remedial Instruction

Setting

As Leinhardt and Pallay (1982) note, setting is a rather insignificant feature of compensatory instruction. Far more important than setting is what occurs in the setting. I would suggest that any pullout setting can be problematic. Such programs seem to foster segregation of the remedial effort from the mainstream of the school educational effort. As Glass and Smith (1977) argue, "Pupils pulled out of regular classrooms would have to receive remarkably effective compensatory programs to offset the potential risks incurred" (p. 41). Effective and efficient remedial instruction can occur in a pullout program but it is quite difficult to achieve.

On the other hand, Doss and Holley (1982) and Lortie (1976) comment on the practical difficulty of implementing a "floating reading teacher" structure, in which the reading teacher provides instruction to the remedial students in their regular classrooms. Neither classroom teachers nor reading teachers readily adapt to the new demands placed on both parties. A shift to a hybrid model, in which the reading teacher works in both locations some of the time, may facilitate integration of the remedial instruction.

Some (Lignon & Doss, 1982) argue for a complete redesign of remedial education, including the elimination of reading teachers, opting to use the compensatory funding to employ additional classroom teachers, thereby reducing the student-teacher ratio in Title I schools. While some evidence supports the efficacy of such a strategy, ample support exists for the continued need for reading teachers, who have additional training and experience, to facilitate the delivery of more effective and efficient compensatory instruction than classroom teachers can deliver. Reading teachers will be under increasing pressure to justify their positions, particularly to their classroom teacher peers. If the preferences reported by Davis (1982), Doss and Holley (1982), and Hayes (1983) can be generalized to all classroom teachers, reading teachers have substantial reason for concern (Milofsky, 1974). In these reports, classroom teachers indicated no strong commitment to continued remedial reading instruction, at least as offered in their schools. Of further concern is the fact that only half of the compensatory teachers surveyed felt that compensatory reading programs were definitely worth the money expended (Allington, 1980).

Curriculum

There seems adequate theoretical argument for closely tying the remedial curriculum to the classroom core reading curriculum (Bloom, 1976; Johnston, et al., 1985). On the other hand, little theoretical support exists for maintaining the status quo—a distinct and separate remedial curriculum replete with special materials. Little empirical support exists for coordinated remedial instruction, primarily because it seems to occur relatively rarely. Empirical evidence for a separate remedial curriculum consists primarily of two decades of disappointingly small gains from remedial programs organized in this manner.

Adopting the suggestion of coordinated compensatory/classroom instruction requires closer cooperation between the two teachers than has been the case in the past. Moving away from a total reliance on pullout instruction for remedial services is one way to facilitate such coordination. The teacher will have to plan cooperatively more regularly. Another rather simple strategy for achieving more coordination, even with a pullout program, is the "traveling notebook." Basically, both the classroom teacher and the reading teacher jot notes in the notebook on a daily basis. The notebook travels with the compensatory student or a group of students from classroom to reading resource room and back. In their daily notes each teacher simply states what material was completed in each instructional setting, possibly noting special problems as well. For instance, the classroom teacher could note that the remedial students silently read a particular story and answered several questions. In addition, the success, or lack of it, in the question answering could be noted. The reading teacher could then choose to work on free recall of the story structure through retelling or work on identifying cause-effect relationships in text (supposing, of course, that had been the source of problems). The reading teacher would sketch the content of instruction offered in the remedial setting and send the notebook back to the classroom teacher. This strategy will not eliminate the need for meetings, but it does facilitate the information flow about the instruction offered, and the instructional needs of the remedial students, and helps to generate cooperation among the teachers.

Instruction

Now imagine a hybrid in class/pullout program with a coordinated instructional effort in which the reading teacher supports and extends the instruction offered on the core reading curriculum by the classroom teacher. Given this, what would we want the remedial instruction to look like?

First, the remedial instruction needs to be achievement focused. An emphasis on developing self-concept or improved attitudes about school does not produce achievement gains that are as impressive as instruction focused clearly on improving reading abilities.

Second, the instruction should involve as much direct teaching as can be packed into the time available. Durkin (1978-1979) and Duffy and McIntyre (1982), among others, have reported that classroom teachers offer little explicit teaching of either comprehension or word analysis skills and strategies during classroom reading instruction. This obviously is a most pertinent role for the reading teacher. Direct teaching seems primarily to involve explanation and modeling of the skills and strategies necessary to develop reading proficiency (Duffy & Roehler, 1982; Rosenshine, 1979).

Third, remedial instruction should be strategy oriented. Basically, this involves offering instruction in utilization strategies and monitoring strategies. Many remedial students seem to have acquired skills knowledge (Allington & Ohnmacht, 1979), but have not developed effective and efficient strategies for using such skills. Brown and Palincsar (1982) and Johnston (1984) offer examples of such strategy based teaching. Relatedly, Johnston (1984) and Wang (1983) discuss the importance of developing remedial students' sense of personal responsibility for learning, something remedial students often have not developed. Routines for developing self-management are available and should be integrated into remedial efforts.

Fourth, remedial instruction should be efficient. By efficient I simply mean that instruction should begin on schedule and maintain a smooth activity flow so that students do not spend time waiting for directions or task checks or instruction. A guiding question here is, "How much more can be accomplished?"

Fifth, remedial instruction must be of appropriate difficulty as well as appropriate content. Much evidence suggests that students need wide experience reading at a near error free level (Beck, 1981; Gambrell, Wilson, & Gantt, 1981; Jorgenson, 1977). When error rates rise, students become increasingly distractible and are less likely to remain engaged in their academic work.

Finally, I could suggest that remedial teachers consider assigning homework on a daily basis. As Thomas, Kemmerer, & Monk (1979) note, we need to consider out of school time for learning and practice as well as available in school time. If remedial students are to overcome their deficits the instructional effort should attempt to take advantage of every opportunity to effect achievement. Daily out of school reading assignments is one such strategy that is too seldom used.

Time

Given what we know of the importance of available time for learning, one might question why anyone ever supposed that remedial efforts could be simply squeezed into the fixed length school day and succeed. Simply, remedial students most typically have no additional time for learning or instruction when remedial programs operate during the school day. Remedial instruction must necessarily supplant some other instruction time if scheduled during the school day, reports to the contrary notwithstanding (Archambault & St. Pierre, 1980).

As a general rule, remedial instruction time should not come from student classroom reading or language arts time. Unfortunately, something else will be missed and, whatever the choice, the remedial student will not receive instruction in the full core curriculum.

The matter of amount of time allocated for remedial instruction has no clear answer. As noted before, this is primarily because other variables, such as content of instruction, are more directly related to achievement. However, the time allocated for remediation must be ample enough to allow for effective instructional delivery. The time allocated is also tied to several other program variables such as student-teacher ratio and instructional quality.

Students

We have some evidence to suggest that low student-teacher ratios (1:1 to 1:4) produce better achievement in remedial settings (Clay, 1979; Guthrie, et al., 1978). One factor integral to this finding may be that when teachers, including reading teachers, instruct in groups they cannot easily attend to individual needs, even in planning (Shavelson & Stern, 1981). Clay (1979) argues that a 1:1 ratio must be maintained in order to focus attention on each individual learner's instructional confusions and instructional needs. While this 1:1 ratio may seem an unlikely luxury to many reading teachers, twice weekly thirty minute tutorial sessions would allow nearly thirty students to be served, assuming a five and a half hour instructional day. This figure is near the average student load of remedial reading teachers. If students are returned to the classroom with no further need for remediation during the school year, as in Clay's study (1979), additional students could receive tutoring.

Identification of students who need remediation should be rather straightforward. When remedial services are limited by resource limitations or regulation, the matter may become somewhat less so. Ideally, identification would involve a combination of formal assessment data and teacher referral plus observation of the potential students during their classroom reading instruction. Probably the most neglected population is those students identified as learning disabled. Birman (1981) reports that Title I eligible learning disabled students rarely received Title I services. She argues this is because many state and local education agencies enforce policies based on a misinterpretation of the federal regulations for either or both Title I and PL94-142. She did find some schools in which nearly all learning disabled students who were eligible for Title I were receiving those services. In those few instances the availability of Title I remedial instruction was considered essential to successful mainstreaming efforts.

All economically disadvantaged students, including those identified as handicapped under PL94-142, are entitled to Title I remedial services (Breglio, Hinckley, & Beal, 1978). Likewise, if a reading disability exists in a handicapped student, eligibility for remedial services should not be denied simply because of identification as a handicapped learner.

Evaluation

Most often evaluation of remedial programs have been poorly done and rarely used by remedial program staff (David, 1981). Rather than continue in this manner evaluations need to be improved in three ways.

First, if a measure of the general program effect is desired, pre and posttesting should be a Fall to Fall or Spring to Spring comparison. Beyond looking for an overall achievement effect, the evaluation should also focus on the number of students released from the remedial program and returned to the regular classroom with no further need of remedial assistance.

Second, the progress of individual students needs ongoing monitoring (Edmonds, 1979). This monitoring should encompass regular classroom performance as well as performance in remedial instruction. Monitoring of this type should be informal, in the sense that student performance on daily tasks is the focus, rather than performance on standardized achievement tests (Clay, 1979). Accurate

Allington

records of content taught and mastered are necessary features for demonstrating the effectiveness and efficiency of remedial instruction (Airasian & Madaus, 1983).

Finally, evaluation should examine whether the remedial treatment is increasing the amount of curricular content mastered. Remedial students are so classified because they have not maintained a standard learning pace. In other words, they have a record of past learning that indicates a reduced learning rate. However, the pacing of instruction, the rate at which new skills and strategies are presented, is a critical factor in learning rate (Barr, 1982). This is not to suggest that the pace of instruction should be increased willy-nilly but rather that the pacing of instruction deserves evaluation. When instruction is coordinated between the classroom and reading teacher, then pacing of instruction becomes a part of the cooperative planning.

A Final Option

Given that remedial programs are designed to provide additional instruction and that finding additional time during the school day is literally impossible, more consideration should be given to more widespread use of after school and summer remedial efforts, either of which allows for true increases in the amount of instructional time (Stanford Research Institute, 1977). Another advantage is the potential of summer programs for alleviating the summer reading loss so often reported for remedial students. If additional instructional time is necessary for students to advance through the core reading curriculum, then after school and summer reading instructional programs need serious consideration.

Summary

Identifying characteristics of effective remedial instruction requires some effort since few empirical reports have focused on this aspect of schooling. Critics of remedial programs abound, a situation not unrelated to the lack of available evidence supporting current practices. Compensatory education programs, particularly in Title I, have remained static for too long with too little systematic investigation by those most directly involved, members of the reading profession. Unfortunately, not only is empirical support for the traditional remedial effort somewhat less than compelling, but also other educators, particularly classroom teachers, have a moderate to low level of support for continuation of such programs as currently organized. All of us involved in compensatory reading programs must evaluate our efforts and the outcomes we achieve. Compensatory reading programs can be improved; it is time to initiate the changes indicated.

References

Airasian, Peter W., and Madaus, George F. Linking testing and instruction: Policy issues. *Journal of Educational Measurement*, 1983, *20*, 103-118.

Allington, Richard L. Teaching reading in compensatory classes: A descriptive summary. *Reading Teacher*, 1980, *34*, 178-183.

Allington, Richard L. The reading instruction provided readers of differing abilities. *Elementary School Journal*, 1983, *83*, 548-559.

Allington, Richard L. So what is the problem? Whose problem is it? *Topics in Learning and Learning Disabilities*, 1984, *3*, 91-99.

Allington, Richard L, and Onhmacht, Fred. *Task performance as a function of age and reading achievement level*. Paper presented at the National Reading Conference, San Antonio, 1979.

Archambault, Francis X., and St. Pierre, Robert G. The effect of federal policy on services delivered through ESEA Title I. *Educational Evaluation and Policy Analysis*, 1980, *2*, 33-46.

Arlin, Marshall. Teacher transitions can disrupt time flow in classrooms. *American Educational Research Journal*, 1979, *16*, 42-56.

Barr, Rebecca. Classroom reading instruction from a sociological perspective. *Journal of Reading Behavior*, 1982, *14*, 316-329.

Beck, Isabel L. Reading problems and instructional practices. In G.E. Mackinnon and T.G. Wallace (Eds.), *Reading research: Advances in theory and practice*, Volume 2. New York: Academic Press, 1981.

Berliner, David C. Academic learning time and reading achievement. In J. Guthrie (Ed.), *Comprehension and teaching: Research reviews*. Newark, DE: International Reading Association, 1981.

Birman, Beatrice F. Problems of overlap between Title I and PL 94-142: Implications for the federal role in education. *Educational Evaluation and Policy Analysis*, 1981, *3*, 5-19.

Bloom, Benjamin S. *Human characteristics and school learning*. New York: McGraw-Hill, 1976.

Borg, Walter R. Time and school learning. In C. Denham and Ann Lieberman (Ed.), *Time to learn*. Washington, DC: National Institute of Education, 1980.

Breglio, V.J., Hinckley, R.H., and Beal, R.S. *Students' economic and educational status and selection for compensatory education*. Technical Report No. 2. Santa Monica, CA: System Development Corporation, 1978.

Brophy, Jere E., and Evertson, Carolyn M. *Student characteristics and teaching*. New York: Longman, 1981.

Brown, Ann L., and Palincsar, Annemarie Sullivan. Inducing strategic learning from texts by means of informal, self-control training. *Topics in Learning and Learning Disabilities*, 1982, *2*, 1-17.

Clay, Marie M. *The early detection of reading difficulties: A diagnostic survey with recovery procedures*, second edition. Exeter, NH: Heinemann, 1979.

Cohen, David K. Policy and organization: The impact of state and federal educational policy on school governance. *Harvard Educational Review*, 1982, *52*, 474-499.

Cohen, Elizabeth, Intili, Jo-Ann K., and Robbins, Susan H. Teachers and reading specialists: Cooperation or isolation? *Reading Teacher*, 1978, *32*, 281-287.

Commission on Special Education. *Special education: A call for quality*. New York: Commission on Special Education, 1985.

Cooley, William W. Effectiveness in compensatory education. *Educational Leadership*, 1981, *38*, 298-301.

Cooley, William W., and Leinhardt, Gaea. The instructional dimensions study. *Educational Evaluation and Policy Analysis*, 1980, *2*, 7-25.

David, Jane L. Local uses of Title I evaluations. *Educational Evaluation and Policy Analysis*, 1981, *3*, 27-39.

Davis, Marie A. *A survey of teacher attitudes towards in class versus pullout compensatory reading programs*. Unpublished master's thesis, Kean College of New Jersey, 1982.

Doss, David A., and Holley, Freda. *A cause for national pause: Title I schoolwide projects*. Paper presented at the American Educational Research Association, New York, 1982.

Duffy, Gerald G. *Teacher effectiveness research: Implications for the reading profession*. Occasional paper No. 45, Institute for Research on Teaching, Michigan State University, 1980.

Duffy, Gerald G., and McIntyre, Lonnie D. A naturalist study of instructional assistance in primary grade reading. *Elementary School Journal*, 1982, *83*, 15-23.

Duffy, Gerald G., and Roehler, Laura. The illusion of instruction. *Reading Research Quarterly*, 1982, *17*, 438-445.

Durkin, Dolores. What classroom observations reveal about reading comprehension instruction. *Reading Research Quarterly*, 1978-1979, *14*, 481-533.

Edmonds, Ronald. *A discussion of the literature and issues related to effective schooling*. St. Louis: CEMREL, 1979.

Elkind, David. The curriculum-disabled child. *Topics in Learning and Learning Disabilities*, 1983, *3*, 71-78.

Elmore, Richard F., and McLaughlin, Milbrey W. Strategic choice in federal education policy: The compliance-assistance trade-off. In A. Lieberman and M.W. McLaughlin (Ed.), *Policy making in education*. Eighty-first Yearbook of the National Society for the Study of Education. Chicago: University of Chicago, 1982.

Gambrell, Linda B., Wilson, Robert M., and Gantt, Walter N. Classroom observations of task-attending behavior of good and poor readers. *Journal of Educational Research*, 1981, *74*, 400-404.

Glass, Gene V., and Smith, N.L. *Pull out in compensatory education*. Washington, DC: Department of Health, Education and Welfare, 1977.

Goldenberg, Ira. Reading groups and some aspects of teacher behavior. In F. Kaplan and S.B. Sarason (Eds.), *The psychoeducational clinic: Papers and research studies*. Community Mental Health Monograph No. 4, Department of Mental Health, Commonwealth of Massachusetts, 1969.

Guthrie, John T., Martuza, Victor, and Seifert, Mary. Impacts of instructional time in reading. In L.B. Resnick and P.A. Weaver (Eds.), *Theory and practice of early reading*, Vol. 3. Hillsdale, NJ: Erlbaum, 1979.

Guthrie, John T., Seifert, Mary, and Kline, Lloyd W. Clues from research on programs for poor readers. In S. Jay Samuels (Ed.), *What research has to say about reading instruction*. Newark, DE: International Reading Association, 1978.

Hayes, Mary V. *A survey of teacher attitudes toward in class versus pullout compensatory reading programs*. Unpublished master's thesis, Kean College of New Jersey, 1983.

Hiatt, Diana Buell. Time allocation in classrooms: Is instruction being shortchanged? *Phi Delta Kappan*, 1979, 289-290.

Hiebert, Elfrieda H. An examination of ability groupings for reading instruction. *Reading Research Quarterly,* 1983, *18,* 231-255.

Johnston, Peter H. Instruction and student independence. *Elementary School Journal,* 1984, *84.*

Johnston, Peter H., Allington, Richard L., and Afflerbach, Peter. Curriculum congruence in classroom and clinic. *Elementary School Journal,* 1985, *85,* 465-478.

Jorgenson, Gerald W. Relationship of classroom behavior to the accuracy of the match between material difficulty and student ability. *Journal of Educational Psychology,* 1977, *69,* 24-32.

Kaestle, Carl F., and Smith, Marshall S. The historical context of the federal role in education. *Harvard Educational Review,* 1982, *52,* 383-408.

Kiesling, Herbert. Productivity of instructional time by mode of instruction for students at varying levels of reading skill. *Reading Research Quarterly,* 1978, *13,* 554-582.

Kimbrough, J., and Hill, P.T. *The aggregate effects of federal education programs.* Santa Monica, CA: Rand, 1981.

Kirst, Michael, and Jung, Richard. *The utility of a longitudinal approach in assessing implementation: A thirteen year view of Title 1,* ESEA. Research Report #80-B18, Institute for Research on Educational Finance and Governance, Stanford University, 1980.

Leinhardt, Gaea. Transition rooms: Promoting maturation or reducing education? *Journal of Educational Psychology,* 1980, *72,* 55-61.

Leinhardt, Gaea, and Pallay, Allan. Restrictive educational settings: Exile or haven? *Reviews of Educational Research,* 1982, *52,* 557-578.

Leinhardt, Gaea, Zigmond, Naomi, and Cooley, William. Reading instruction and its effects. *American Educational Research Journal,* 1981, *18,* 343-361.

Levin, H. A decade of policy development in improving education training for low income populations. In R. Haveman (Ed.),*A decade of federal antipoverty policy: Achievements, failures, and lessons.* New York: Academic Press, 1977.

Light, Richard J., and Smith, P.V. Accumulating evidence: Procedures for resolving contradictions among different research studies. *Harvard Educational Review,* 1971, *41,* 429-471.

Lignon, G.D., and Doss, David A. *Some lessons we have learned from 6500 hours of classroom observations.* Pub. No. 81.56, Office of Research and Evaluation, Austin Independent School District, Austin, TX, 1982.

Lortie, D.C. Discussion of "Integration of the handicapped child into regular schools" by E. Martin. *Minnesota Education,* 1976, *2,* 16-20.

Mackenzie, Donald E. Research for school improvement: An appraisal of some recent trends. *Educational Researcher,* 1983, *12,* 5-17.

McLaughlin, Milbrey W. *Evaluation and reform: The elementary and secondary education act of 1965.* Cambridge, MA: Ballinger, 1975.

Meyers, Albert E. The reading readiness program in New Haven schools. In F. Kaplan and S.B. Sarason (Eds.), *The psychoeducational clinic: Papers and research studies.* Community Mental Health Monograph No. 4, Department of Mental Health, Commonwealth of Massachusetts, 1969.

Milofsky, Carl D. Why special education isn't special. *Harvard Educational Review,* 1974, *44,* 437-458.

National Coalition of Advocates for Students. *Barriers to excellence: Our children at risk.* Boston, MA: National Coalition of Advocates for Students, 1985.

National Institute of Education. *Compensatory education services.* Washington, DC: U.S. Department of Health, Education and Welfare, 1977a.

National Institute of Education. *Administration of compensatory education.* Washington, DC: U.S. Department of Health, Education and Welfare, 1977b.

New York State Office of Education Performance Review. *School factors influencing reading achievement: A performance review.* Albany, NY: 1974. (ED 089 211)

Quirk, Thomas J., Trisman, Donald A., Nalin, K., and Weinberg, S. Classroom behavior of teachers during compensatory reading instruction. *Journal of Educational Research,* 1975, *68,* 185-192.

Rauhala, Ritva A.I. Remedial teacher as cooperator—Finland. *Reading Teacher,* 1982, *35,* 412-417.

Rohwer, William D. How the smart get smarter. *Quarterly Newsletter of the Laboratory of Comparative Human Cognition,* 1980, *2,* 35-39.

Rosenbaum, James E. Social implications of educational grouping. In D.C. Berliner (Ed.), *Review of educational research,* Vol. 8. Washington, DC: American Educational Research Association, 1980.

Rosenshine, Barak V. Content, time, and direct instruction. In P.L. Peterson and H.J. Walberg (Eds.), *Research as teaching: Concepts, findings, and implications.* Berkeley, CA: McCutchan, 1979.

Sargent, L.R. Resource teacher time utilizations: An observational study. *Exceptional Children,* 1981, *47,* 420-425.

Shavelson, Richard J., and Stern, Paula. Research on teachers' pedagogical thoughts, judgments, decisions, and behaviors. *Review of Educational Research,* 1981, *51,* 455-498.

Shulman, Lee S. Autonomy and obligation: The remote control of teaching. In L.S. Shulman and G. Sykes (Eds.), *Handbook of teaching and policy.* New York: Longman, 1983.

Stallings, Jane. Allocated academic learning time revisited, or beyond time on task. *Educational Researcher,* 1980, *9,* 11-16.

Stanford Research Institute. *Research on the effectiveness of compensatory education programs: A reanalysis of data.* Final Report, Menlo Park, CA, 1977.

Stonehill, Robert M., and Groves, Curtis L. U.S. Department of Education policies and ESEA Title I evaluation utility: Changes in attitudes, changes in platitudes. *Educational Evaluation and Policy Analysis,* 1983, *5,* 65-73.

Thomas, J. Alan, Kemmerer, Frances, and Monk, David H. *Equity and efficiency in educational finance: The classroom perspective.* Paper presented at the National Conference on Efficiency and Equity in Educational Finance, Urbana, May 1979.

Thompson, Pat A., and Smith, Elizabeth P. *Title I achievement sustained effects across two years.* Paper presented at the American Educational Research Association, New York, 1982.

Vanecko, James J., Ames, Nancy L., with Archambault, Francis X. *Who benefits from federal education dollars?* Cambridge, MA: ABT Books, 1980.

Vernon, M.D. *Backwardness in reading.* New York: Cambridge University Press, 1957.

Wang, Ming-mei. *Evaluating the effectiveness of compensatory education.* Paper presented at the annual meeting of the American Educational Research Association, Boston, 1980.

Wang, Margaret C. Development and consequences of students' sense of personal control. In J.M. Levine and M.C. Wang (Eds.), *Teacher and student perceptions: Implications for learning.* Hillsdale, NJ: Erlbaum, 1983.

Weber, George. *Innercity children can be taught to read: Four successful schools.* Washington, DC: Council for Basic Education, 1971.

Wilder, Gita. Five exemplary reading programs. In John T. Guthrie (Ed.), *Cognition, curriculum, and comprehension.* Newark, DE: International Reading Association, 1977.

Ysseldyke, James E., and Algozzine, Bob. *Critical issues in special and remedial education.* Boston: Houghton Mifflin, 1982.

Part Six
Commentary

N o research monograph would be complete without a critical look at itself relative to the goals that inspired it.

In this last section of the book, Barr offers a critical summary and analysis of the work presented in previous chapters. Further, she suggests important areas where research on effective teaching might direct its attention in coming years.

13

Rebecca Barr

What We Know and What We Need to Learn about Reading Instruction

T he chapters in this volume collectively portray a search for knowledge about reading instruction. It is useful to put this search into broader historical perspective and to examine how our questions about reading instruction and our ways of answering them have evolved. As described by Rupley, Wise, and Logan in the first chapter, researchers in the field of reading were deeply engaged in the study of instruction during the 1960s. The well known Cooperative Reading Studies of primary grade reading instruction were conducted during this period. Because of the equivocal results and emerging developments in psychology, concern with reading instruction diminished and gave way to intensive study of the cognitive processes of reading during the 1970s. The study of instruction has only recently become the focus of renewed interest among reading researchers.

Concurrently, and in contrast, the 1970s was a decade of considerable activity for instructional researchers, mainly from outside the field of reading. Instead of being discouraged by research findings indicating that instruction has little differential influence on learning (Coleman, et al., 1966; Bond & Dykstra, 1967), these researchers believed that the negative results arose from the limited extent to which instruction was actually observed in the prior investigations. The first chapter summarizes the nature of the research undertaken by this group of researchers during the 1970s which has become known as the "process-product" or the teaching effectiveness literature.

During this period, a great deal of evidence about how classroom instruction actually works was accumulated, and a large portion of it concerns instruction in basic skill areas such as reading and mathematics. Reading researchers are fortunate to have this body of work from which to learn. The teaching effectiveness approach represents a vast improvement over the research on reading methods undertaken in the 1960s. In particular, knowledge about instructional practices is based on observational evidence rather than teacher reports or other less direct measures.

This volume is unique in that it contains not only summaries of the research on teaching effectiveness, but also descriptions of how this knowledge has become incorporated into practice through school interventions during the past few years. Further, it includes a selection of alternative approaches to the study and improvement of teaching. This chapter considers what this body of knowledge teaches us about classroom reading instruction, about doing instructional research, and about changing existing programs.

This critical evaluation will focus first on those reports describing process-product research and related intervention and then on the "new" directions in research in effective reading. The process-product research and intervention studies cluster into two main groups. The first, exemplified by Brophy's report (Chapter 3) and the intervention studies of Griffin and Barnes (Chapter 7) and Condon and Kapel (Chapter 5), focuses mainly on *teaching behaviors*. The second, represented by the Stallings report (Chapter 4) and the description of the Cupertino project (Chapter 6), primarily concerns the *use of time* during instruction.

Reports on new directions in research in effective reading instruction cluster into three main groups. The first, focusing on recent investigation of teacher decision making as reviewed by Duffy and Ball (Chapter 8), represents a direct outgrowth from earlier teaching effectiveness research. The second, represented by the intervention projects of Roehler and Duffy (Chapter 9) and of Calfee and Henry (Chapter 10) arise from outside the teaching effectiveness tradition and are directly based on knowledge about reading and the teaching of reading. The third, represented by the Hunter model (Chapter 11), also arises from other traditions including basic learning theory and practical knowledge.

Each of these clusters of research is examined in order to evaluate the nature of the knowledge that is used to inform practice and to consider what conditions maximize the effectiveness of intervention efforts. Following this analysis, in the final section of the chapter, we return to the central question: What can reading researchers and practitioners learn from these studies of instruction and intervention?

Process-Product Research and School Intervention

Teaching Behaviors

Nature of Knowledge. We find in the process-product tradition a characteristic way of developing knowledge about effective instruction. On the basis of plausibility and demonstrated association with learning in past studies, teaching behaviors are selected for further study. In the first grade reading group study reported by Brophy, forty-eight teaching behaviors were selected and organized around twenty-two principles believed to promote effective teaching in small group settings. These principles pertained to such aspects of group management as getting and maintaining student attention, introducing lessons and new materials, calling on individuals, and dealing with individual learning rates. The authors refer to this list as an instructional model; however, interconnections among teaching activities are not specified. Similarly, Griffin and Barnes in their attempts to change teacher practice selected 115 teaching behaviors and classified them around ten principles pertaining to instruction and management.

Both investigations examine whether teaching practice could be changed: in the case of Brophy, through direct intervention with teachers with prescriptive materials; in the case of Griffin and Barnes, through indirect contact via supervisory support. Both provided evidence showing that some of the target behaviors investigated were more common among the experimental than the control teachers. Although both also predicted that the selected teaching behaviors would be associated with higher learning, only Brophy provides evidence on this important issue. Interventions to change teaching behaviors should be defended on the basis that learning is enhanced or that some other desirable outcome occurs.

This work makes a noticeable conceptual advance over earlier process-product research, which selected and classified teaching process variables arbitrarily, in that teaching activities are related conceptually to salient instructional issues such as control of groups, consideration of individual learning rates, and the provision of incentives. But even with this conceptual advance, the investigators consider seriatim the relationship between some aspect of teacher behavior and achievement and depend on numerous tests of significance to determine what is important. There are several reasons why this way of proceeding yields ambiguous knowledge about classroom practice.

First, and most obvious, when many tests of significance are made, some occur simply on the basis of chance and it is difficult to know which are spurious and which reliable. Replication of studies may provide a means for assessing the stability of results, but replications frequently produce inconsistent and conflicting results for similar variables.

Second, when teaching behaviors are examined one at a time, it is impossible to know how much of the variance in learning has actually been accounted for. For example, in the Brophy report we learn that certain teaching behaviors account for as much as 29 percent of the variance in learning. Do the other teaching behaviors studied account for additional variance or is about 30 percent the most that is accounted for by teaching behaviors? If nearly 70 percent of the variance in learning outcomes is unaccounted for, then it is important to consider and investigate conditions other than teaching behaviors.

The Brophy research is interesting because it does include other plausible conditions beyond those subsumed by the twenty-two principles that make up the model, such as time use, curriculum content, and reading method emphasis. Some of these conditions account for as much as 24 percent of the variance in learning, but we cannot determine from the report whether this variance is the same as that accounted for by teaching behaviors or whether it is unique. Most process-product reports fail to provide the multiple regression results which would enable researchers and practitioners to assess the joint contribution of conditions considered to enhance learning.

Beyond these more technical problems, other problems of interpretation have serious implications for how process-product knowledge may be used to improve teaching. In particular, two major problems should be considered. First, correlational evidence does not demonstrate that selected teaching behaviors actually cause gains in achievement. Second, treating one variable at a time decontextualizes knowledge so that it is impossible to reconstruct the situations in which the behaviors may in fact be effective. Because of the importance of these problems, we will consider them in some detail.

In an intervention study, such as the one conducted by Brophy and associates, many teaching behaviors are the focus of intervention and some of the targeted behaviors are increased as a consequence of the intervention treatment. However, the correlational analyses that are then used to link these behaviors with learning do not represent an experimental test of their causal influence on learning. When many behaviors are changed at the same time, it is possible that only one is responsible for the learning gains and that the others are associated, but noneffective, conditions. It is also possible that none of the conditions is responsible for the gain but rather that some more general influence in the order of a Hawthorne Effect is responsible for the changes observed in teaching behaviors and is directly responsible for the achievement gains.

In the Brophy report slightly more than half of the teaching behaviors are significantly associated with reading achievement. But not knowing the nature of the relationship between these conditions and learning makes interpretation difficult. For example, does minimizing pupil choral responses and call outs lead to higher achievement directly or does their absence permit the occurrence of other more productive activities, such as overviews and pupil practice?

When teaching behaviors are treated one at a time in relation to learning, it is often forgotten that certain behaviors are part of a larger package. The fractionalization of the teaching process leads to the decontextualization of variables. But most teaching behaviors may be effective depending on the context in which they occur. To provide a lesson overview before reading a story may be an effective strategy; to provide one half way through the story may be disruptive and may indicate that the teacher has noted the problems. Similarly, choral response may be effective in the context of certain instructional materials, but not others. We cannot assess the effectiveness of certain practices unless we know how they were combined with other conditions and when they occurred during instruction.

To make sense of the evidence, process-product researchers have assumed that the set of variables which are significantly associated with learning go together. But the set of principles used during the two intervention studies were abstractions, perhaps representing no teacher at all. Assume for a moment that two ways of managing reading instruction lead to high achievement and that some of the procedures used with one approach are incompatible with those forming the other. A research methodology that abstracts behaviors from their context may end up with a set of behaviors representing no existing strategy; indeed, the approach may be impossible to implement in its totality.

Intervention into Practice. We can also learn something about the intervention process itself. Brophy and colleagues provide knowledge to teachers in the form of a manual that describes "good" teaching procedures. The manual also includes a series of vignettes which show how to put the principles into practice. Similarly, Griffin and Barnes provided their supervisors with videotapes showing how to apply certain "effective" practices in instructional situations. We do not know from the report, however, the extent to which the supervisors actually used the tapes with their teachers. In any case, any learning gains which resulted may have been a function of procedures that concretely recontextualized the variables. That is, useful knowledge about teaching may not be conveyed in the form of abstract principles.

In such form, principles not only fail to specify the immediate context in which they are effective, but also the broader context defined by the subject matter and instructional goals and the age of the students. The "Direct Teaching Model" applied in Jefferson county in fact arises from a collection of findings across many studies. Yet the majority of studies showing the effectiveness of direct instructional methods have come from studies involving primary age students instructed in reading and mathematics. For such groups, direct instructional methods do indeed seem to enhance the learning of basic skills. The evidence does not show, however, that direct instruction is more effective than other approaches in developing reasoning and interpretive strategies. Most important, we should not generalize these findings to other curricular areas and objectives and to older students until a sufficient number of studies show positive results.

Effective Time

Nature of Knowledge. The Stallings research arises from the same process-product tradition and the evidence collected pertains to instructional and social activities not unlike those documented in the previously discussed research. But the way in which the evidence is organized and the variables reported constitute a different perspective on how to view classroom instruction. Unlike evidence based on the number of times a certain behavior is observed, Stallings characterizes different sorts of teacher and student activities in terms of their temporal duration. Teachers differ in how much of a class period they spend on managerial versus instructional activities. The instructional activities are characterized in terms of what the teacher and students do: silent reading, seatwork, oral reading, and interactive discussion.

Exactly how a teacher gets students to work or how instructional interaction is managed is not the issue. Within this approach, teachers have some latitude in selecting among alternative ways to increase the duration of certain types of activities and to decrease those of others. The focus is on the goal, the duration of certain activities, and there is some flexibility in the means.

Activities as the target of change seem to bear decontextualization better than specific teaching behaviors. That is, from a Stallings profile of a teacher's use of time, we can more easily imagine how instruction may have transpired than from a list of teaching behaviors and their frequency of occurrence.

Based on a study of twenty two high school reading classes that differed widely in reading achievement, Stallings found that time spent in management and in having students work independently was associated with lower reading achievement, while having students actively engage in interactive instruction was associated with higher achievement. Some of the more effective ways of using time accounted for as much as 35 percent of the variance in learning. But again, as in the Brophy investigation, from this consideration of variables one at a time, we do not know what the joint contribution of conditions might be. And as a consequence, we cannot know from the report whether there is a little or a lot of unexplained variance in learning.

The Stallings research demonstrates how other conditions may influence the nature of the relation between a selected instructional condition and learning. In particular, Stallings shows how a finding may hold for certain students but not others by undertaking further analyses of subgroups distinguished on the basis of initial reading achievement and gain. She finds that effective practices differ from group to group. Most dramatically, oral reading proves to be most effective for classes scoring low on the pretest, from the first to the fifth or sixth grade level, but not beyond. Accordingly, oral reading may be effective but only for certain groups of students. By contrast, in the Brophy study, important information about how instruction influences the learning of students of low and high reading proficiency may have been masked by the data organization procedures. Observation was made of each teacher instructing the low and high groups in each class and teaching behaviors were averaged over groups for teachers. Thus, from this sort of analysis, we cannot identify practices that may be contextually specific, that is, differentially effective with able learners as opposed to those encountering some difficulty learning to read.

The Stallings work, similar to the Brophy study and other process-product research, is atheoretical. Although certain central conditions are selected for study, how these conditions interact with each other to facilitate learning is not formulated. Because of this lack of theory, it is sometimes difficult to make sense of contradictory findings. For example, Stallings reports that oral reading is an effective way for students to use time to improve their reading achievement. By contrast, Leinhardt, Zigmond, and Cooley (1981) report that oral reading is not associated with general reading achievement gains, but silent reading is. How can we make sense of this? We can't unless we know more about the other conditions of instruction. For example, oral reading may be effective for Stallings' students because of the relative difficulty of the reading selections. They may be so difficult in fact that students may be unable to read silently with comprehension; consequently, they fail to do much reading. Oral reading overtly controls their participation, and the teacher may explain difficult concepts.

By contrast, in the Leinhardt research, silent reading may be an effective predictor of reading gain because it reflects choice on the part of students to read during part of their relatively unsupervised time. On the other hand, those children who do not read much independently may be those who find reading to be hard and distasteful. Accordingly, the relationship between silent reading achievement may be artificial in nature; that is, choice to read silently may reflect other conditions such as getting pleasure from reading and well developed skill which supports silent reading, and these underlying conditions, rather than their manifestation in classroom silent reading, may lead to reading gains. To get reluctant readers to do more reading may not necessarily result in achievement similar to those who choose to do silent reading.

Intervention into Practice. Although Stallings' report pertains only to the first phase of an intervention project and is descriptive in focus, it exemplifies a useful model for other intervention projects. Intervention begins with documentation of existing teacher practice. That is, based on observational evidence, a profile showing how each teacher uses instructional time is developed. Then through inservice experiences, teachers learn strategies for more effective management and instruction. They then select alternative teaching strategies that appear to be applicable within their setting and experiment with their use. Finally, each teacher's instruction is observed

observed in order to develop another profile of time use, and this profile is compared with the preintervention profile in order to identify areas of more effective time use.

Contrast this intervention approach with that reported by Brophy. First, in the Brophy research, no preassessment data were collected for individual teachers. Accordingly, we do not know how many of the target behaviors teachers evidenced at the beginning of the study. More important, such evidence thus could not serve as the basis for setting individual teacher goals. Knowledge about effective practices was presented in written rather than in oral interactive form and the same set of principles was given to all of the experimental teachers. Specific goals for change established through dialogue were not part of the intervention. Finally, posttest observation did not provide information concerning the changes made by individual teachers but rather general evidence on the teaching behaviors of the experimental and control groups and their association with learning. In fairness to Brophy and colleagues, note that their investigation was not primarily one of intervention but one of research. Nevertheless, the comparison of the two approaches leads to the conclusion that basic classroom research and good intervention strategies are not incompatible. That is, the Stallings approach yields not only information that is relevant to the instruction of individual teachers, but also general information on change and correlation.

The Cupertino intervention is similar to the Stallings approach in that teacher behavior is studied at the beginning of the study, followed by the identification of target growth areas and monthly inservice instruction, and finally, individual assessment of areas of change. Nevertheless, the areas of behavior targeted for change were not limited to those of time use. In addition to trying to spend less time on management and discipline and more on teaching, teachers were encouraged to use a variety of activities during reading and math lessons, to increase student to teacher interaction and the participation of more students, to increase monitoring strategies, and to ask more probing and inferential as opposed to literal questions. Although the authors state that the teacher effectiveness literature was used in generating these objectives, the research does not show that *all* of these behaviors are associated with achievement gains.

New Directions in Research in Effective Reading

Teacher Decisions

Nature of Knowledge. An alternative way of approaching the question of the nature of knowledge that is useful in informing teaching is to examine what decisions teachers actually make and the information they bring to bear on these decisions. As described by Duffy and Ball, most researchers who undertake this type of research begin with a conception of teacher decision making as conforming to a rationalist model. But as the review notes, the evidence calls into question the view of teachers as active and extensive instructional decision makers.

As noted in the chapter, reading educators have long believed that the hallmark of an effective reading teacher lies in appropriate decision making with respect to matters of reading content, the selection of appropriate strategies, and interpretation of content. Yet, evidence now exists that runs counter to the presuppositions of reading educators. One contribution to this research literature may be to force reconsideration of generally accepted beliefs. Nevertheless, Duffy and Ball's response to this evidence is not to accept the conclusion that the role of decision making during instruction is limited, but rather to conclude that finding no evidence of decision making is an insufficient basis for deciding that it cannot occur. They suggest that we do not find relevant evidence because our research procedures lack conceptual and methodological sophistication. While this may be so, I prefer to follow another strategy and to assume that the evidence collected to date does accurately represent at least some aspects of the phenomenon of teaching. The questions that follow are: What does the evidence reveal about the sort of knowledge that does inform practice? What are the implications of the evidence for instructional intervention?

The picture that emerges is that of teacher preoccupation with the flow of activities and procedural matters during interactive instruction. Teachers do not weigh alternative courses of action during the rapid give and take of instruction; they rely on routine strategies to reduce the complexity of the situation. They do note when a planned activity is not going well, but rarely do they abandon a plan.

While the absence of contemplative decision making during interactive teaching is not too surprising, the fact that the evidence reveals only limited areas of planning before instruction is unexpected. Also unanticipated, the decision making that does occur does not correspond to the models developed by teacher educators. For example, teachers rarely identify an objective for instruction and then develop appropriate materials and activities for achieving that objective. Rather, teachers usually begin with the materials and then develop appropriate activities. They may never fully explicate the objectives that are achieved through the activities. This truncated form of planning apparently occurs because the materials used in most classes are determined before the school year and must be used. Although most experienced teachers have accumulated a stock of supplementary materials, these often constitute a small proportion of the materials actually used during instruction. Further, although teachers have the opportunity to select among alternative activities to be used with the materials, the evidence suggests that they feel compelled to follow the activities recommended in the basal manuals.

Intervention into Practice. Several implications may be drawn from this description. First, the form of the knowledge provided to teachers about instruction should not be in the form of principles to guide alternative courses of action, but rather in the form of routines that represent effective responses to selected situations. Second, the focus of the process-product research on classroom organization and management is responsive to the central concerns of teachers during interactive instruction. Nevertheless, development of knowledge in the form of decontextualized principles may be less effective than in the form of integrated teaching routines for managing such activities as transitions, seatwork, work check, and small group lessons.

With respect to the decisions that teachers make before instruction, a major implication can be drawn. Given the constraints that exist in teaching, a body of knowledge that may be of use to teachers is one which would enable them to judge the appropriateness of the basal materials and the effectiveness of the activities recommended in the basal manuals. Such knowledge would provide a basis for making decisions in planning instruction. Further, this type of intervention strategy assumes the teacher will use the basal materials, but perhaps more effectively after an evaluation. One consequence of such evaluation might be the elimination of nonproductive activity, thereby making time available to more appropriate reading and language arts activities.

Knowledge of Reading

Nature of Knowledge. The intervention approaches described by Calfee and Henry and by Roehler and Duffy do not derive from the process-product research, but are based on traditional knowledge about reading instruction and recent new knowledge about reading processes. As was mentioned in the initial section of this chapter, during the 1970s most reading researchers directed their attention to the cognitive processes involved in reading and reading acquisition. It is mainly on this research that the Calfee/Henry and the Roehler/Duffy interventions are based. However, whereas Calfee and Henry describe a comprehensive schoolwide intervention into reading instruction, Roehler and Duffy examine the consequences of intervention that focuses on a single teacher strategy.

Both projects depart sharply from the process-product research in their concern for the content of instruction and how that content may be effectively conveyed. Whereas the process-product research attempts to develop knowledge about instruction that is "content free" and thereby presumably applicable to any content area, this research is concerned with teaching strategies that are specific to the curricular area of reading and to specific objectives in reading such as developing phonics concepts, story comprehension, and the use of context clues.

The knowledge that is conveyed to teachers in the Calfee and Henry intervention is of three main sorts: 1) a theoretical formulation of the elements and themes in reading instruction, 2) procedures for critically evaluating the curricular materials in reading and language arts, and 3) scripts or generalized reading lessons for the achievement of central reading objectives and procedures for the creation of microscripts. Calfee and Henry claim simply that the approach is based on what has been learned recently about the nature of thinking, how the mind works, and the conditions that enhance learning. But the formulation of elements and themes in reading instruction does not derive directly from the cognitive literature, nor do procedures for evaluating curricular materials and developing scripts. For example, while the methods and concepts developed in the area of text analysis provide a useful starting point for the consideration of the appropriateness of instructional materials, they do not actually constitute procedures that teachers may immediately apply. Thus, using this knowledge developed in cognitive psychology, Calfee and Henry have evolved procedures that may be useful to teachers. Some of the procedures, such as generic lesson types, have been used in reading education for some time, for example, the directed reading and thinking activity (Stauffer, 1970) and SQ3R (Robinson, 1961).

The Calfee/Henry approach provides potential solutions for some of the problems raised in recent studies of teacher decision making. First, the fact that many teachers appear to follow recommendations of the basal manual in a noncritical fashion may be altered by the sort of theoretical and practical knowledge provided by the workshops described. That is, if teachers are provided with a theoretical framework concerning the nature of reading components, criteria for evaluating basal lessons (knowledge of effective teaching routines, the goal of having a single teaching objective, and the inclusion of group problem solving), and social support for critical evaluation of proposed activities, they may assume greater responsibility for instruction.

Second, the development of scripts as a means of modifying instructional behavior is consistent with the finding that teachers typically follow routine forms of behavior during the active give and take of instruction. Calfee and his associates have packaged knowledge about effective instructional procedures in a form that teachers can easily use.

Roehler and Duffy are also concerned with teaching strategies. In their chapter, they focus on the use of context clues to infer word meaning, and examine how effectively two teachers explain this strategy to their students. The criteria used to assess teaching effectiveness is the extent to which students became aware of what they had learned and when and how they would use context clues to derive word meaning.

The two teachers studied were part of a larger investigation of teacher instructional explanation (Duffy, et al., 1984). Although this report does not contain a description of the specific knowledge conveyed to the teachers during the training, we can infer that the general teaching model involved four main components: 1) initial teacher explanation about the reading strategy, 2) teacher modeling of the strategy, 3) practice trials in which students use the strategy, and 4) transfer trials in which students use the strategy with real text.

The focus of the contrastive case study is not to examine how well the experimental teachers implemented the prescribed teaching strategy, but to explore how two teachers who effectively provided explicit teacher explanation differed in the precise form of their explanation and guidance. Because certain students of one teacher were more metacognitively aware of the nature of the strategy and its use than were students of the other teacher, it was presumed that differences between the two teachers might account for this relative effectiveness. Certain differences were noted. For example, in the initial explanation, the first teacher described situations in which the strategy would be useful, whereas the second teacher described the nature of context rather than its use. Similarly, during practice trials, the first teacher gradually shifted responsibility to students whereas the second teacher did so abruptly.

The study generates new knowledge about what may be effective teaching strategies. Further, the knowledge that is generated is contextualized in form. That is, not only is it related directly to a certain reading objective, but also it is organized within a general teaching model. Nevertheless, some caution should be exercised in accepting the validity of these findings. To have examined the approaches of a larger number of teachers may have revealed alternative and equally effective strategies. However, if the same activities were shown by other effective teachers, this would increase the confidence that we might have in the results. Further, before teachers should be encouraged to use such teaching strategies, further investigation is needed to determine whether students who are metacognitively aware of a strategy are also effective in using the strategy and if the strategy enhances reading achievement.

Intervention into Practice. It is instructive to compare the Calfee/Henry intervention with that conducted by Stallings. In both projects, teachers are viewed as agents in their own development. Whereas in the Stallings project teachers participate in setting objectives for change, in the Calfee work teachers select lessons for application of the concepts being learned. Both involve school systems as the unit for intervention, require participation of school leaders as well as teachers, and foster the development of peer observation and support.

But the differences between the two approaches, aside from substantive focus, are also of interest. While Stallings begins the intervention with observation in order to establish existing practice, Calfee and Henry assume that instruction consists mainly of rote tasks from a piecemeal curriculum. In the Stallings model, areas for change are determined on the basis of problem areas identified within each teacher's existing approach. By contrast, the Calfee/ Henry and the Roehler/Duffy projects assumed that the same solution is appropriate for all teachers and that the teaching procedures recommended should replace rather than build upon those currently in use.

In any case, more systematic evidence that specifies the impact of these interventions is needed. For example, with respect to instruction, does the intervention result in a greater amount of the desired forms of class interaction than was previously the case and in what ways does the script implementation alter the nature of the discussion that occurs? With respect to children's learning, do the new procedures help children think and read better and be more articulate and better at explaining what they know than old procedures? Finally, with respect to teacher development, does the intervention help teachers become more aware of their goals and those of others? While some of these questions were answered partially, none was addressed fully; the claims made concerning the effectiveness of the intervention approaches must be supported with systematic evidence.

Learning Theory

Nature of Knowledge. Just as the findings from the teacher decision making literature run counter to the presuppositions of reading educators, they are also at odds with the perspective offered by the Hunter model which is based on a view of teachers as active instructional decision makers and instructional planners. The model may be viewed as consisting of two major components. The first concerns teaching: the selection of objectives at the proper level of difficulty, teaching to an objective, and monitoring the progress of learners. The second concerns the proper use of eight principles of learning: mental set, closure, covert behavior, overt behavior, motivation, reinforcement, retention, and transfer. Whereas aspects of the second component had their origin in the behavioristic studies of learning conducted before the ascension of cognitive psychology, these early learning principles are not interpreted in a strict sense, but rather have been modified to be more applicable to classroom learning.

The first component draws from a wide set of instructional techniques and procedures including task analysis and Bloom's taxonomy. The general model of a lesson is one that has long been used among teacher educators: explanation, questions, activities (guided practice, independent activities), and response to the learner. The reader will note the similarity of this to the one followed by Roehler and Duffy. Learning principles are incorporated into aspects of this basic model in order to enhance its effectiveness. Further, teachers are trained to use the procedures through a similar instructional model that involves theory and demonstration, guided practice, feedback, and classroom application.

Thus, although many of the principles that are incorporated in the model have their roots in learning theory, these principles have been modified and others incorporated to enhance the teacher's ability to select appropriate objectives and to follow effective teaching and monitoring procedures. The nature of the knowledge that is conveyed through the Hunter model is eclectic in origin and based on practical experience. Weisberg, in her interpretation of the Hunter model, frames the model in terms easily understood by reading professionals, those of the directed reading activity. In fact, the two approaches have much in common because they both evolved from practical experience.

Intervention and Practice. The Hunter intervention approach is not unlike that described by Calfee and Henry in that teachers participate in a series of lectures and demonstrations to convey basic knowledge and procedures, guided practice and feedback, and classroom application of the knowledge being learned. Unlike the Stallings approach which builds a limited intervention onto what the teacher already does, the Hunter model imposes a new way of viewing instruction.

Because new ways of doing things may be modified or not incorporated at all, it is important to supplement evidence on achievement results with actual descriptions of teacher practice in order to specify areas in which the intervention is successful and those in which it is ineffective. The teacher decision making literature suggests that aspects of classroom instruction preclude the type of individual learner consideration that is assumed by the Hunter model; thus, it is important to document the ways that teachers are able to change their activities in response to the intervention.

Summary and Future Directions

This review of the studies of instruction and intervention provides the basis for taking stock and asking what we have learned. On the basis of these conclusions, directions for further investigation can be established.

Nature of Knowledge

Establishing what we know about instruction occurs in two ways in this volume. The one that has received the most scrutiny in this chapter consists of the reports of basic research on instruction and intervention. But no less important to building a knowledge base about reading instruction are reviews of the research literature that provide an overview of the types of research and an integration of findings. In particular, the reviews by Rupley and associates (Chapter 1) and by Allington (Chapter 12) provide a comprehensive sense of two important bodies of research. Whereas Rupley and his colleagues develop a useful frame of reference for subsequent reports of research and intervention, Allington provides a much needed summary of research on remedial instruction. In the 1970s various government programs provided funding to insure the acquisition of basic reading skill. Allington not only summarizes the findings from evaluation reports and other basic research but provides insightful commentary which should make us wiser about how we provide reading support in future years.

As previously discussed, the process-product research has provided evidence concerning the importance of how instructional time is used and the usefulness of good teacher management and support to keep students involved in academic work. But beyond this, we can also learn from this research what not to do. To examine a multitude of variables that have been abstracted from context is not the most productive way to proceed. Research of the future needs to examine teaching behaviors as they occur within a more general teaching context. For example, the case study of Roehler and Duffy exemplifies a research approach that examines teaching activities that occur within a general model of teaching.

But beyond the problem of decontextualized knowledge, the examination of one variable at a time, as is characteristic of the process-product research, does not come to terms with the interconnection among instructional conditions. The research of the 1970s was preoccupied with linking aspects of instruction to learning. As a consequence, the problem of how various aspects of instruction go together was addressed by only a limited number of researchers. For example, in thinking about the teaching process, it is useful to distinguish the activities of teachers from the ways in which students may spend their time and then to propose that certain teaching activities directly influence student time use and that time use in turn influences student learning. This way of distinguishing among types of instructional conditions and formulating their interconnections provides a useful way to avoid becoming lost in a maze of univariate findings. Such theoretical formulations have been proposed by Fisher and associates (1978) and by Leinhardt, Zigmond, and Cooley (1981). In addition, theoretical work has been undertaken that looks at instruction in the context of school organization. This work (Barr & Dreeben, 1983) explores how teachers' instruction is limited and influenced by such conditions as instructional materials, class composition, and time schedules.

The basic knowledge provided by the process-product research is limited in still another respect: The approach does not consider the content of instruction. The basic knowledge introduced in the Calfee-Henry intervention suggests that knowledge about reading materials and instruction complements the approaches based on a process-product research with their concern for instructional management and time use. Instructional research conducted within the field of reading (see, for example, Beck, Omanson, & McKeown, 1982; and Palincsar & Brown, 1983) provides experimental tests of teaching strategies and analyses of instructional materials that should further develop our knowledge about teaching strategies. Nevertheless, knowledge developed under experimental control requires further testing in actual classrooms using observational methodologies developed not only by process-product but also by ethnographic and sociolinguistic researchers (see Bloome & Green, 1984, for a review of the latter work; see Barr, 1984, for further discussion of why such further testing is needed).

Intervention into Practice

From this body of research, we learn not only what sort of knowledge is needed to inform instructional practice, but also how one might proceed to introduce this knowledge to teachers. The successful interventions, as well as those that failed, provide the basis for speculating about the conditions that facilitate implementation.

The interventions reported differed in the extent to which teachers participated in designing the changes versus having the changes imposed on them. The Jefferson County project represents the extreme of an imposed plan with little teacher participation; the Calfee and Hunter models reflect some degree of teacher participation in that teachers selected from the formal selections aspects to implement within their classes; the Stallings and Cupertino interventions represent the approach most responsive to teacher practice. In the latter, the existing practices of teachers were observed and then on the basis of this evidence and the knowledge presented in workshops, teachers were encouraged to set goals for change. Subsequent discussion and observation supported the implementation of these objectives. The history of educational intervention is not a glorious one; as soon as forces that support the use of a particular innovation are no longer operating within a system, teachers revert to their original practices (Stephens, 1967). Certain conditions would logically seem to maximize the stability of change. In particular, the extent to which teachers participate directly in change and set their own goals should directly affect the extent to which they retain new practices after formal intervention ends.

Several of the interventions exemplified a schoolwide approach. That is, principals and supervisors as well as teachers participated in the intervention effort. In some, teachers supported each other during the period of experimenting with new strategies. The support of the larger school community for the implemented changes should lead to increased stability. In this respect, recent school organizational studies indicate that intervention must not be directed only to the practices of teachers but to those of school and district officials as well (Dreeben & Barr, 1983; Moore, et al., 1981).

Finally, it is not fair to impose practices on teachers during intervention unless two things have been demonstrated. First, it is necessary to show that the approach as proposed can be incorporated by teachers. Given the teacher decision making literature which suggests that some very real conditions limit what teachers can accomplish, it is important to document the effects of intervention efforts. As noted in the discussion of the Hunter model, if a baseball team is losing badly, it is not helpful to examine the scores. It *is* useful to watch the team as it plays. The Stallings intervention approach represents direct application of this principle. Beyond this, to test whether an intervention is effective, it is important to look at what teachers do with their classes following intervention. That is, the observational techniques that have been developed during the 1970s should be employed to assess the consequences of interventions. However, to determine whether the anticipated changes have occurred, the nature of practice before intervention must be documented. Thus, the Stallings intervention model provides the basis not only for individualizing intervention to match the needs of particular teachers, but also for assessing whether the intervention approach leads to the changes desired.

Second, although the score of a baseball team may not be diagnostically useful, it does help to establish whether a team is playing well or losing badly. The score on how well students are learning is also important to intervention efforts. Unless it can be shown that a particular intervention approach enhances student learning or other important outcomes, there is no basis for asking teachers to modify the teaching strategies they have developed over a number of years.

Summary

Considerable progress has been made in instructional research during the 1970s, not only in the process-product research but in other research approaches as well. Substantively, we have identified some of the important components of the instructional process and we are beginning to think about their interconnections. As the discussion here indicates, basic research on instructional processes and intervention efforts are complementary and when undertaken in tandem should provide sound knowledge for improving reading instruction.

References

Barr, R. *Instructional research on reading.* Paper presented at the third annual University of Wisconsin Reading Symposium on Factors Related to Reading Performance, Milwaukee, 1984.

Barr, R. and Dreeben, R. *How schools work.* Chicago: University of Chicago Press, 1983.

Beck, I.L., Omanson, R.C., and McKeown, M.G. An instructional redesign of reading lessons: Effects on comprehension. *Reading Research Quarterly,* 1982, *17,*, 462-481.

Bloome, D., and Green, J. Directions in the sociolinguistic study of reading. In P.D. Pearson (Ed.), *Handbook of research in reading.* New York: Longman, 1984.

Bond, G.L. and Dykstra, R. The cooperative research program in first grade reading instruction. *Reading Research Quarterly,* 1967, *2,* 5-142.

Coleman, J.S., Campbell, E.Q., Hobson, C.J., McPartland, J., Mood, A.J., Weinfeld, F.D., and York, R.L. *Equality of educational opportunity.* Washington, DC: U.S. Government Printing Office, 1966.

Dreeben, R., and Barr, R. Educational policy and the working of schools. In L.S. Shulman and G. Sykes (Eds.), *Handbook of teaching and policy.* New York: Longman, 1983.

Duffy, G., Roehler, L., Vavrus, L., Book, C., Meloth, M., Putnam, J., and Wesselman, R. *A study of the relationship between direct teacher explanation of reading strategies and student awareness and achievement outcomes.* Paper presented at the annual meeting of the American Educational Research Association, New Orleans, 1984.

Fisher, C.W., Filby, N.N., Marliave, R., Cahen, L.S., Dishaw, M.M., Moore, J.E., and Berliner, D.C. *Beginning teacher evaluation study.* Technical Report, V-1. San Francisco: Far West Laboratory, 1978.

Leinhardt, G., Zigmond, N., and Cooley, W. Reading instruction and its effects. *American Educational Research Journal,* 1981, *18,* 343-361.

Moore, D.R., Hyde, A.A., Blair, K.A., and Weitzman, S.M. *Student classification and the right to read.* Chicago: Designs for Change, 1981.

Palincsar, A.S., and Brown, A.L. *Reciprocal teaching of comprehension monitoring activities.* Technical Report No. 269. Champaign: University of Illinois, Center for the Study of Reading, 1983.

Robinson, F.P. *Effective study,* revised edition. New York: Harper and Row, 1961.

Stauffer, R.G. *The language experience approach to the teaching of reading.* New York: Harper and Row, 1970.

Stephens, J.M. *The process of schooling.* New York: Holt, Rinehart and Winston, 1967.

IRA Teacher Effectiveness in Reading Committee

Contributors

Richard L. Allington
State University of New York
Albany, New York

Deborah L. Ball
Michigan State University
East Lansing, Michigan

Susan Barnes
Texas Education Agency
Austin, Texas

Rebecca Barr
National College of Education
Evanston, Illinois

Jennifer Reese Better
Cupertino Union School District
Cupertino, California

Jere Brophy
Michigan State University
East Lansing, Michigan

Robert Calfee
Stanford University
Stanford, California

Mark W.F. Condon
University of Louisville
Louisville, Kentucky

Gerald G. Duffy
Michigan State University
East Lansing, Michigan

Gary A. Griffin
University of Illinois
Chicago, Illinois

Martha Rapp Haggard
Sonoma State University
Rohnert Park, California

Marcia K. Henry
Stanford University
Stanford, California

James V. Hoffman
The University of Texas
Austin, Texas

Marilyn B. Kapel
Our Lady of Holy Cross College
New Orleans, Louisiana

John W. Logan
Texas Tech University
Lubbock, Texas

Laura R. Roehler
Michigan State University
East Lansing, Michigan

William H. Rupley
Texas A&M University
College Station, Texas

Jane A. Stallings
George Peabody College for Teachers
Nashville, Tennessee

Renée Weisberg
Beaver College
Glenside, Pennsylvania

Beth S. Wise
McNeese State University
Lake Charles, Louisiana